Scholars Without Walls

Scholars Without Walls:

A History of the Minnesota Independent Scholars' Forum 1983-2018

by Lucy Brusic, Evelyn Klein, and Mike Woolsey

Minnesota Independent Scholars' Forum
PO Box 80235, Lake Street Station
Minneapolis, MN 55408-8235
www.mnindependentscholars.org

Scholars Without Walls:
The History of the Minnesota Independent Scholars' Forum (1983–2018)

Copyright 2019 Minnesota Independent Scholars' Forum. All Rights Reserved.

Unless otherwise specified all the works quoted in this publication have been written by the persons cited as authors and permission to quote has been secured. Copyrights revert to the authors after the book is published.

No part of this publication may be reproduced, stored in a retrieval system, or transmitted in any form or by any means, electronic, mechanical, photocopying, recording or otherwise, without the permission of the Minnesota Independent Scholars' Forum.

Book designed by Kim Morehead

ISBN 978-1-63489-164-6
Library of Congress Control Number 2018955375

Wise Ink Creative Publishing
Printed in the United States of America.

CLEAN
WATER
LAND &
LEGACY
AMENDMENT

This publication was made possible in part by the people of Minnesota through a grant funded by an appropriation to the Minnesota Historical Society from the Arts & Cultural Heritage Fund. Any views, findings, opinions, conclusions, or recommendations expressed in this publication are those of the authors and do not necessarily represent those of the State of Minnesota, the Minnesota Historical Society, or the Historical Resources Advisory Committee.

MISF has remained of interest to me for so long, I don't recall how or when I joined. It was good that I did, else I would have missed a lot of what is good in life. Truth is what binds us all.

—George Anderson, MISF president 1999–2001

Once education becomes more student-oriented, rather than teacher-oriented, then I hope the floodgates open and organizations like ours can take a more active role. . . . We could do more to further this if we had lots and lots of money.

—Curt Hillstrom, MISF president 2008–2012

One hardly needs to argue that many of the greatest advances in human thought and civilization have come from self-educated scholars, operating on their own or in small, informal groups of their peers.

—Mike Woolsey, MISF president 2012–2016

Acknowledgments

The following people graciously gave permission to quote their writing: Tom Abeles, George Anderson, Bob Brusic, Marilyn Chiat, Cheryl Dickson, Gus Fenton, Rhoda Gilman, Kim Heikkila, Curt Hillstrom, David Juncker, Evelyn Klein, Bill McTeer, Steve Miller, Dale Schwie, Peter Shea, Susan Smith, Robert Thimmesh, Lee Wenzel, David Wiggins, Morgan Grayce Willow, and Mike Woolsey.

In addition,

Rich Anderson gave permission to reprint material by Ginny Hanson.

Louise Jones gave permission to reprint the article by Roger Jones.

David Naftalin gave permission to reprint material by Arthur Naftalin.

Kate Shamblott gave permission to reprint material by Rhoda Lewin.

Eric Watkins gave permission to reprint material by Helen Watkins.

Charles and Christopher Whiting gave permission to reprint material by Shirley Whiting.

The articles were initially printed in our journals with the understanding that the authors retained the copyright. In all cases the copyright on material quoted in this book reverts to the original authors after the publication of this book.

Table of Contents

Preface by David Grabitske 2

Introduction 5

Part 1: The Past: The Story of the Scholars
    Chapter 1: Before the Beginning 10
    Chapter 2: The Early Years (1983-1988) 28
    Chapter 3: A Model Emerges (1989–1995) 48
    Chapter 4: Growing Pains (1996–2000) 75
    Chapter 5: The New Millennium (2001–2004) 95
    Chapter 6: New Journal, New Initiatives (2005–2011) 115
    Chapter 7: MISF Comes of Age (2012–2016) 140

Part 2: The Present: What MISF Does Today
    Chapter 8: Study and Discussion Groups 154
    Chapter 9: Grants and Fiscal Agency 168
    Chapter 10: Meetings 196
    Chapter 11: The Journal: Good Writing by Thoughtful People . . . 211
        A. Science
        B. Political and Economic Philosophy
        C. Writing about History

Part 3: The Future of MISF
    Chapter 12: What is the Future of Independent Scholarship? . . . 259

Appendices

Essays in Chronological Order 265
Presidents of the Scholars 268
Bibliography 270
Books by MISF Scholars 272
Index 276
About the Editors 291

Preface

Minnesota voters adopted the Land, Clean Water, and Legacy Amendment in November, 2008, which has transformed many things in the state, not the least of which is history work. Indeed, "Legacy" funding, as it is known, makes this work possible.

The early days of Legacy funding found me as the titular Grants Manager, a temporary appointment spanning better than five years. During that time I took very seriously the charge to make the funding available to all who performed history work. One area over which I worried greatly was finding a legal way to fund scholars. Through the aegis of friend and neighbor Barbara W. Sommer, I had the very good fortune in 2013 to be introduced to the Minnesota Independent Scholars' Forum (MISF). Though successful with grants from the start, Mike Woolsey, David Megarry, Lucy Brusic, and others shared with me that they felt uncomfortable promoting history scholars when the organization represented the breadth of scholarship in Minnesota. As we discussed their concerns, I noted that everything has a history, and I asked about the history of MISF. That was the genesis of the work before you now.

The purpose of this work is to show how both thought and an organization of thinkers changed. It reminds me of how historians in the early twentieth century transformed their profession by democratizing inclusion through activating and unleashing underutilized resources. The same is true for MISF—from para-academics to an urgent and complementary activity.

History is the story of change. MISF President David Juncker reflected in 1997, "Change, no matter how necessary, seems to take a bit of time to accomplish" (see chapter 4). That was certainly true of MISF and independent scholars over time. For the first decade of the shrinking job market, beginning in the 1970s, independent scholars saw themselves as scholars-in-waiting for a market that was presumed to re-expand. By the mid-1980s, when re-expansion did not materialize, independence as a new profession awakened in these scholars. That awakening by the 1990s also meant discussing their profession in positive terms, further democratizing access and expression, and encouraging the proper use of scholarly powers. Democratizing inclusion meant that by the mid-2000s MISF ceased to define itself internally, but sought external descriptions recognizable by the general public. Therefore, understanding the trajectory of the organization shows a strong foundation to the present.

History is the record of what is possible. This book returns again and again to the relationship between scholars and affiliations, definitions, expectations, etc.—to the very nature of qualifications for scholarship, expected treatment of scholars, and the value of independent, experimental production of scholarship. Several times the narrative explores what the future might hold for scholars. These "yesterday's tomorrows" shed light on how the history of scholarship could change in the future.

Most importantly, the book reminds us to seek the skills "to inquire in revolutionary ways after unheard-of knowledge" (chapter 4). Therefore, history is the repository of solutions for a brighter future. Future members of MISF need to return to this book, not to find reasons that a future won't work, but to search out ways to arrive in a workable future.

The book properly limits itself to what is often an invisible discussion. Namely, MISF has explored its identity. As the identity unfolded over the years, the discussion became more nuanced, rich, and expressive. This limitation should prove useful to students of organizational behavior.

In sum, MISF activated independent scholars by raising their profile; reimagining their complementary, middle-ground purpose between academia and the general public; and representing their collective voice in broader discussions among groups of peers.

Saying I am pleased by this publication is an understatement. The careful work in these pages is an invaluable contribution to Minnesota history and the history of Minnesota scholarship. MISF has transformed itself and achieved a fuller meaning of scholarship for the state as it leads a nation of independent scholars.

> David Grabitske
> Site Manager, Texas Historical Commission,
> Landmark Inn State Historic Site
> Castroville, TX
> January 2018

Introduction

The title of this book comes from Mary Treacy, a longtime member of the Scholars, who writes a blog called "Poking Around with Mary." She highlights various aspects of life in the Twin Cities. On August 22, 2010, she wrote:

Scholars Without Walls

The walls of academia, that is . . . Though I was present at the birth of the Minnesota Independent Scholars' Forum over two decades ago, I've never really poked around the details of independent scholarship, its various permutations and connections . . . What I did know is that, in the early 1980s, an assemblage of disenfranchised researchers, educators, and lifelong learners, working with the Minnesota Humanities Commission, joined forces to address the critical needs of serious scholars working on their own and without the perks of academic life. To some extent their inspiration came from an emerging national recognition of independent scholarship, manifest in one way by publication of the widely read *The Independent Scholars' Handbook* by Ron Gross (Ten Speed Press: Berkeley, 1982, 1993).

After much deliberation (as becomes a gathering of independents), these folks agreed that independent scholars experienced specific needs—for access to library resources; for recognition of writing, speaking, and other scholarly pursuits; for foundation and government funding; and above all, for opportunities to share information and ideas with colleagues.

Many of the barriers, the group concluded, were remediable. Thus, they created the Minnesota Independent Scholars' Forum, now a 501(c)(3) nonprofit. Though time and technology have alleviated some of the problems, e.g. access to library resources, others persist. Time constraints and a dearth of venues that support sharing information top the list.

Today the MISF works to anticipate, address, and meet the changing needs of scholars working on their own. At the same time, the scholars enrich the community by sharing their research and insights with the community at large. Membership is open to learners of all stripes—no degree requirements. The current MISF membership sports a lively mix of active learners in a host of settings—homemakers, part-time students, attorneys, librarians, and government, museum, and corporate employees. MISF provides a structure that offers common space and opportunity for independent learners—physicists, historians, literary scholars and creative writers, musicians and artists, even lurkers like me...[1]

Mary Treacy's words are a fitting introduction to the subject of this book. It remains for the editor of this book to fill in the details.

The Forum, for the most part, has been a group of people who have something to say and are only too happy to say it in print. The organization has published a journal for more than twenty-five years; it has also generated a large number of paper records. As I read this material, it occurred to me that the parallel stories of the history of the Forum and the emergence of independent scholarship as a phenomenon in its own right could be told in large part through the writings of MISF members—both past and present.

---

[1] http://www.tcdailyplanet.net/scholars-without-walls

Thus, the format of the book is a narrative history connecting essays by various members. In reading the Scholars' records, it was very apparent, at the beginning of the organization, that independent scholars and scholarship were fighting for a place at the institutional table. Gradually, however, the Forum has become a standalone group with its own ethos, expectations, and pleasures. This shift is very apparent in the nature and tone of the essays in the issues of the journal.

In order to give a full flavor of the discourse, I have quoted the essays at full length in almost all cases except two. Ellipses mark my excisions.

The longer I worked on this book, the clearer it became to me that emphasizing the emergence of independent scholarship would mean that I was going to leave out a lot of interesting scholarly writing. I have tried to address this problem in the closing chapters, where I have quoted varied writing that has appeared in the journal. Among a wealth of good essays, there was much to choose from and selection was difficult. As I moved toward the end of the book, I tended to favor authors whom I had not previously quoted.

This project has involved the work and cooperation of a lot of people. Books like this one need the steadying hand of someone who is not the writer. I thank Mike Woolsey and Evelyn Klein for their cooperation and advice. Evelyn Klein particularly contributed publishing advice based on her experience as book editor, artist, and author. Mike Woolsey wrote the chapter on grants, secured the grants for the publication of this book, and located a publisher.

Other members of the Scholars have been variously helpful. Dave Megarry interviewed David Wiggins and David Juncker. Mary Treacy gave me good background about the early days of the scholars and how to contact people. The late Rhoda Gilman spent an afternoon with me to tell me about the early organization. Rhoda was also helpful in tracking down people who were no longer on the membership rolls. My brother, Bill McTeer, offered sage advice at various points. Barbara Sommer, who is well known in Minnesota Historical Society circles, also advised.

David Grabitske, while he was project administrator for Legacy grants, set the project in motion by encouraging us to try to publish a history. Cheryl Dickson gave us permission to use her very important speech and helped me find a couple of other pieces of information as well.

The members of the current MISF board have been helpful throughout the process. Those who have not previously been named are Curt Hillstrom, Emily Pollack, Gus Fenton, Joe Amato, and the president Steve Miller. Shirley Whiting, who died while this book was in progress, also helped with her support.

Likewise, the staff of Wise Ink, especially the production coordinator (and proofreader), Graham Warnken, and the cofounder, Dara Beevas, have been both helpful and patient in achieving the finished quality of this book.

I thank my husband, Bob, and my son, Adam, who put up with the various pushes and pulls that book writing asks of families.

Various people have read and reread parts of this book in the hope of eliminating errors. If, in spite of all our collective diligence, errors still remain, I accept the responsiblity for them.

                                          Lucy Brusic
                                          St. Paul, MN
                                          May 20, 2018

PART 1
The Past: The Story of the Scholars

NOTE: For the purposes of this narrative, the terms MISF, the Scholars, the Forum, and the Minnesota Independent Scholars' Forum are used interchangeably. They all refer to the organization in a collective sense.

CHAPTER 1

Before the Beginning

The point of this book is to show that the raison d'être of independent scholarship has moved from trying to be a parallel academy to being a free-standing movement with its own rationale. By the end of the narrative it should be apparent that independent scholarship has come into its own.

Setting the Stage

"Colleges and universities did not anticipate the 'me decade' and zero population growth, and continued to encourage and produce the doctoral degree at [an] accelerated rate even after the need had abated. As a result, the U.S. has thousands of individuals who have trained for careers in teaching and scholarship for whom no jobs exist." (1982 Proposal submitted by the Minnesota Independent Scholars' Forum and the Minnesota Humanities Commission to the Northwest Area Foundation[1])

"The history of independent scholars has three turning points. Around 1970, the curve for Ph.D. production, going up, crossed the curve for numbers of full-time faculty positions, going down. Around 1980, Ronald Gross helped start local groups and discipline-based national groups of independent scholars.

Now, as a new decade approaches, the 'Ph.D. cabdriver' should be laid to rest, and the independent scholar, with or without a Ph.D., should be recognized as a legitimate social type." (Jim Bennett[2] article, "Independent Scholars: An Interim Report," of which these are the first two sentences, in Vol. 1, no. 2 of *The Forum*, 1989)

"In various definitions, independent scholars are those unaffiliated with an academic, or with any institution, or whose work duties do not include research and scholarship. Typically, they are Ph.D.'s in the humanities, often women, who are unable to find scholarly employment ('independent,' a wit says, is a euphemism for 'unemployed'), [and] pursue scholarly interests on their own." ("Independent Scholars: A Neglected Breed" by Harold Orlans,[3] in *Society*, November/December 2002, p. 12)

The Beginnings

The independent scholar movement grew out of a surplus of Ph.D. candidates in the late 1970s. Students had stayed in school—males because they did not want to be drafted for Vietnam and women because the social movements of the 1960s had inspired them to believe that they could find a place in previously male-dominated fields such as college teaching. Most of these students finished their degrees with anticipation of employment in college teaching jobs, with the expected perks and privileges.

In 1973, however, the draft ended and college enrollments dropped. In addition, the national birth rate dropped and the pupil-teacher ratio in public schools rose. The demand for new college teachers dropped correspondingly, creating a surplus of new Ph.D.'s. These trends were particularly pronounced in the humanities, such as English and History.[4] Although many men with Ph.D.'s were eventually able to find employment, often by moving to another part of the country, women did not always have such flexibility. Nor was the college teaching profession particularly welcoming to an invasion of women in previously male fields.

National research into the phenomenon of "advanced learning by adults without academic affiliation" began with funding from the Exxon Education Foundation in 1977. The purpose of this initial funding was to identify the emerging "learning society." Ronald Gross (b.1935 and associate director of the presidentially appointed national commission of Educational Technology) and his wife Beatrice (b. 1935 and a freelance writer) identified the specific demographic problem of "no room in academe" and were awarded a grant from the College Board for the investigation of persons "not absorbed" by academe. The Grosses carried out this research between 1980 and 1982.[5]

The research work by the Grosses culminated in early November (3–5) 1982, at the Spring Hill Conference Center in Wayzata, MN. This invitational conference drew 50 participants from both coasts "as far south as Los Angeles and Virginia and as far north as Montana."[6] This conference is usually considered to be the founding meeting of Independent Scholarship. A number of Minnesotans (many associated with Humanities Councils) attended. Martha Butt, Cynthia Buckingham, Marsha Davis, Cheryl Dickson, Jean and John Ervin, Sarah Evans, Michael Kathman, Timothy Glines, Patricia Loose, Eldred Smith, James Smith, John Taylor, John Wallace, Steven Weiland, and Stanley Williams all listed Minnesota addresses.

The conference was documented in *Independent Scholarship: Promise, Problems, and Prospects*[7] and concluded with recommendations to academe to support independent scholars; recommendations to humanities councils to do the same; recommendations to independent scholars to "vigorously and aggressively" pursue organization of themselves for support; recommendations to learned societies to seek out independent scholars; and recommendations to libraries and publishers to assist scholars, and so on. Under miscellaneous remarks, the conference report recommended that "[t]here should be an underground scholars' manual, a brown-paper wrapped book, with suggestions on "how to beat the system."[8]

It is tempting to say that what has become MISF, the Minnesota Independent Scholars' Forum, emerged from this meeting, but, in fact, there were at least two meetings of independent scholars in Minnesota before the Spring Hill conference. As reported by Cheryl Dickson, then the head of the Minnesota Humanities Commission (see next page), a meeting of independent scholars took place at the Minnesota Humanities Commission on May 19, 1982, to discuss ways in which "scholars who do not have the advantages of affiliation with a major institution can work together to address common problems."[9] These problems were identified as "[l]ack of recognition, [d]ifficulty in obtaining access to university libraries, lack of cooperation from academic institutions, inability to interest publishers in their work, and small but insurmountable budget problems."[10] Forty-five people attended. Six months later, October 16, 1982, 65 people attended a formal organizational meeting of the Minneapolis Scholars' Forum at the Minneapolis Library. A draft of bylaws was presented and various ways to help unaffiliated scholars were discussed.[11]

Then, November 6, 1982 (the day after the Spring Hill Conference), the Forum was formally organized in a meeting at the Minneapolis Public Library. John Butt[12] was the chair of the steering committee, with Deborah Leuchovius[13] as vice president. A set of bylaws was drafted. Six study groups were established: Late Eighteenth Century; Twentieth Century German Literature; Historiography; Discussion of the Consequences of Pragmatism; Discussion of Physics as Metaphor; and Children's Literature.[14]

The key player throughout this period of formation was Cheryl Dickson, the head of the Minnesota Humanities Commission. She invited people to the first meeting in May. It is also Dickson's remembrance that she developed the Spring Hill Conference with the assistance of John Taylor, president of the Northwest Area Foundation (NWAF).[15] Founded in 1934, NWAF's mission for its first 50 years was as a traditional grant-awarding agency, giving grants in categories ranging from the arts to medical research. The MISF grant was awarded under these auspices. (In 1997, the NWAF shifted its focus to concentrate on poverty reduction in the area it serves—that is, the states once served by the Great Northern Railroad.)

It was certainly because of friendship and communication between Taylor and Dickson that Taylor offered funds from NWAF for the "Recognition and Encouragement of Independent Scholarship." The initial NWAF grant of $60,000—spread over five years—permitted MISF to offer publishing subsidies, underwrite visiting professorships, and award $3,000 to a scholar of the year. All of these were emoluments that might have been available in some form to scholars regularly employed in academe, but which were conspicuously and painfully absent from the lives of scholars working outside the university.

The following two essays set the stage, narratively and financially, for the beginning of MISF. The speech, although dating from 2003, is the best single account of the ethos from which MISF and similar organizations emerged and of the beginning of the Scholars. While the preceding paragraphs give a feeling for the politics surrounding the beginning of the Minnesota Independent Scholars' Forum, the following essay conveys the urgency of the period of the early 1980s. We are grateful that Cheryl Dickson was able to recall so many details about this event. This speech, here quoted in its entirety, was written and delivered in 2003 for the 20th anniversary of the founding of the Scholars. Dickson explains her connection in this speech. She also expands on the worries and concerns she still had in 2003 about the future of scholarship and higher learning in general.

A Scholar Writes

Somebody Had to Do It: The Beginnings of MISF
Cheryl Dickson, former director of the Minnesota Humanities Commission, 2003

Thank you for inviting me to be with you to celebrate your accomplishment. Twenty years is a good long time, and I am so pleased to see how long and how far you have come since the idea for the Independent Scholars' Forum first landed . . . Because I was director of the Humanities Commission, my talk will center on the concern for humanities scholars—more specifically, those with Ph.D.'s in the humanities. But more about that later.

I want to remind you of conditions for the humanities in the Sixties, when the National Endowment for the Humanities (the NEH) was founded by Congress, and the early Seventies, when the NEH began what they called the state programs. Under pressure from Congress, the NEH somewhat reluctantly began the programs in the states, beginning in 1971. The Congress was aware of the state arts boards and wanted parallel, or similar, organizations for the humanities. NEH conducted startups in eight states in 1971, Minnesota being one of them. In the fall of 1971, the Minnesota group, four men from the Twin Cities who were picked by the NEH, named the organization, formulated guides for grants, received their first operating grant of $100,000, and hired an executive director. In January of 1972, they opened an office and began accepting applications for grants for public humanities projects.

Humanities in the 1970s
Please remember that in the early Seventies, there were few nice catalogs for museum exhibits, even fewer with essays by

scholars. There were identifying, but not contextual, labels on the walls at exhibits; there were no after-play discussions led by scholars; there were few public lecture/discussion programs in public venues; and humanities scholars were never on the radio or on television. The state humanities agencies welcomed all of these ideas and supported them with grant dollars.

I joined the Minnesota Humanities Commission in April of 1975 as an intern. I was completing a B.A. in Humanities at Metropolitan State University, and the internship was beyond my imagining. The Commission was still inventing itself as it went along. Questions continually arose: Could anyone "do" the humanities on the radio? Could anyone do justice to the humanities in less than fifty minutes? Could a slide "presentation" be a humanities program? and so on. Such questions seem downright silly now, but at that time, the humanities were so firmly imbedded in the academy and held so closely by the priesthood that wrestling them away became one of the biggest battles.

My consciousness was raised, and my conscience pricked, at the second meeting of the Humanities Commission board of directors I attended. The board was discussing grant applications, and the definition of "humanities scholar" was a hot issue. Could someone be a "humanities scholar" and not hold a faculty position? Could someone be a "humanities scholar" and not be a full-time member of a college faculty? "Definitely not!" said one board member. "I hold two full-time positions myself." I knew then that if that logic and those ethics prevailed, I would have a short tenure at the Humanities Commission. It was also clear to me that an intern had no standing; if I wanted to change things, I would have to be in a different position.

I worked on and off for MHC for a year and a half until the fall of 1976, when I accepted a full-time job. The following fall, the director was offered a job at the National Endowment for the Humanities and I moved into the director's position.

At the time, I took the job with MHC with my Metropolitan State University BA. The National Endowment for the Humanities was even more obsessed with credentials than the board of the Minnesota Humanities Commission. I remember the outcry over Barbara Tuchman, author of *A Distant Mirror* and *The Guns of August*. She was termed a popularizer, a very dirty word at the time . . . my first hire at MHC was a newly minted Ph.D. who, I believed, would stave off the NEH's criticism of me. It worked.

I remember the mid- and late-Seventies as a time of real excitement for the Humanities Commission. There was a large group of scholars in the state in Scandinavian studies, so MHC funded endless conferences, videos, and movies on Danes, Finns, Swedes, and Norwegians. Because of an NEH rule that conferences funded by the state councils had to be for the public, and because the conference stars had to be humanities scholars, and because no one had yet figured out a way to connect the two, I sat through many conferences in the company of bewildered immigrants and first-generation Americans as they listened to esoteric papers on obscure Scandinavian writers. While the audience, including me, couldn't understand a fraction of the proceedings, we were all proud that the conferences were taking place.

The arrival of Women's Studies scholars on the scene provided the partner MHC needed for a long and happy marriage. The Humanities Commission had money for public programs and the Women's Studies scholars needed audiences. Furthermore, women's history was "hot," interesting to the public, and fit naturally into the kinds of programs MHC was founded to fund.

Meanwhile, my colleague and I were working to get the board to accept barely employed, or unemployed scholars. In nearly every meeting, we found ways to counter . . . arguments of "who is a humanities scholar and who isn't." We figured out pretty early that some of our best public teachers did not have the security of a faculty position. This is not to say that no full-time faculty joined our cause of bringing the humanities to the public. But we found many unemployed, under-employed, or other-employed scholars who were eager to teach in public settings and were good at the work.

No Work for Ph.D.'s

My interest was not only professional. By 1981, I had married my present husband, who was working on his Ph.D. in Philosophy at the University of Minnesota. He had a number of part-time teaching jobs, but was unable to find a tenure track position and had gone to work outside the academy. When my oldest son was about to graduate from the University of Minnesota, summa in English, I did not encourage him to go on to graduate school in English. There were no jobs.

At this time, when I advertised a position at the Humanities Commission, I got 300 to 350 applications, many of them from Ph.D.'s in the humanities who were looking for something, anything, related to the field. One morning when I arrived at the office, there was a man sitting on the floor by the door waiting for me. He had a Ph.D. in the humanities and was looking for work.

Clearly someone had to do something, and I had the position and the resources to do it. I talked about the problem with John

Wallace, who taught philosophy at the University of Minnesota. John wanted to do what he could, so he and I hosted a meeting at the University that introduced Human Resource directors of large companies to University humanities scholars to talk about employment for humanities Ph.D.'s. It was a disaster. The humanities scholars were badly behaved, and the business people were doubtful and uneasy. The latter sneered at the idea of anyone who had earned a Ph.D. in the humanities working for a corporation.

Professor Wallace and I had a number of discussions regarding the moral position of the people in charge of graduate programs. If there were no jobs, how could graduate programs continue "to encourage students to invest their time and money in a Ph.D.?" The *Chronicle of Higher Education* reported that a survey of graduate students in the humanities revealed that they knew there were few or no academic positions awaiting them, but some 85 percent thought that they, nevertheless, would get a job. I don't know what kind of discouragement it would take to counter that confidence, hopefulness, or denial, but at least they were not being deceived and lured into the programs by false promises.

Although our business/humanities meeting was not what we had hoped, I still believed that there might be a way to encourage some corporations to hire humanities Ph.D.'s because they said they wanted people who could think critically, write, and speak. I called an acquaintance who had risen very high at General Mills and asked him if he ever employed humanities Ph.D.'s. He said, "No, they are too selfish." Selfish, did I hear him correctly? "Yes," he said. "They do what they have to do here as quickly as possible so they can get on with their own work. Working here is just a way to get money so they can do what they really want to do."

These, and a few other failed attempts and revelations, made me realize that people would still pursue doctoral degrees and that corporate Minnesota was not going to be much help, so I turned to the foundation world.

First Meeting

On May 12, 1982, we sent out an invitation for the first meeting of independent scholars. The meeting was held May 19th at the Humanities Commission's office to "discuss the possibility of establishing an institute for independent scholars in Minnesota. . . . The institute would encourage scholarly work in the humanities by providing some of the services that unaffiliated scholars need most, including some administrative support, access to libraries and special collections, opportunities for colloquia and study groups, and information regarding opportunities for participants in conferences, symposia, and public programs."

Forty-five people showed up, which was more than capacity for the room. I was pleased and dismayed, hoping, I think, that my concern was mine alone and that there would be no interest.

At that first meeting, I said that if people wanted to found an organization, MHC offered some support, such as a mail drop, an affiliation on the letterhead, photocopying, and clerical help. We did not have computers, so the offer was for use of our secretary and typewriters. There was interest, and the Forum's true birth was that evening.

Although we had no national organization, we decided to hold a national conference in the fall of 1982. Harry Day of Springhill Conference Center in Wayzata and John Taylor, President of the Northwest Area Foundation, agreed to host and fund the conference. The conference, which took place November 3 -5, attracted the top people in the country. This list included Ronald Gross, director of the Independent Scholarship Project, funded by a Foundation for Improvement of Post-secondary Education (FIPSE) grant; Steven Weiland of the Federation of State Humanities Councils; John Bennett of the American Council on Education; Malcolm Scully of the *Chronicle of Higher Education*; Catherine Rolzinski of FIPSE; Richard Schlatter of the American Council of Learned Societies; and independent scholars representing their organizations in New York, Denver, Wisconsin, and Berkeley.

The group participated in sessions on "Independent Scholarship and the Public Interest," "Needs and Current Responses" and "Identifying New Ways to Meet Needs." The conferees concluded that independent scholars are important to national life and they should be encouraged and supported. John Taylor of NWAF called me after the conference and offered funds for independent scholars to the Humanities Commission. The grant, for $12,000 a year for five years, was broken down into the following categories: $3,000 a year for the Independent Scholar of the Year, $7,000 for a publication subsidy for a book, and $2,000 for small grants for projects by independent scholars. The Humanities Commission (MHC) named an Advisory Council to make the awards and grants. Before the five years elapsed, Mr. Taylor left the Foundation, and his successor was not interested in renewing the grant. I believe that grant of $60,000 was the first substantive grant ever awarded to a state humanities council, and it was of critical importance to the independent scholar movement.

Meanwhile, the Minnesota Independent Scholars' Forum was begun. I am happy to see it continues to this day, and, I understand, is still receiving grants from MHC. And both MHC and the Forum, I am happy to say, have expanded the definition of "scholar" to "one who does scholarly work."

The Future

I want to talk about the future, because I see change coming faster than it ever has. This past summer, Governor Ventura appointed me, among others, to the board of trustees of the MN State Colleges and Universities (MnSCU). MnSCU has 35 four-year, community, technical, and comprehensive colleges on 55 campuses in 46 MN communities. The system serves 230,000 individuals a year in college courses, certification courses, apprenticeships, and re-certifications. The system has a huge inventory of buildings and grounds—more than 22,000,000 square feet of roofs, for one thing. Maintaining the physical plants is getting more and more expensive. The first thing I hear from legislators when they learn I am on the board is that "MnSCU must close some of its campuses." That sounds just fine until you ask which one, and then it is always "not the one in my district." I know the legislature will be looking for solutions to the budget shortfall, and I have some inkling of where they might go if they cannot close campuses.

In these first months, I have visited a number of the MnSCU campuses, and what I have learned is that the students in these institutions are not 18- to 22-year-olds who can go to another place and live in a dormitory for four years. They are mostly grown-ups with spouses, children, jobs, and aging parents. They are place-bound and they need postsecondary education.

Every college I have visited demonstrated their fastest-growing area is online education. I have been astonished to see that biology teachers have figured out ways to create virtual lab courses and to hear humanities teachers talk about the richness of their online offerings. Many faculty members resist online teaching, of course, but those who embrace it are excited about the results.

Colleges tell us that many students go online at 10:00 PM on Fridays and work off and on all weekend. These students expect someone to be on the other end of the line all weekend, too, and that does not fit the image of the work week many academics want for themselves.

It appears to me that there is a real opening soon for people outside the academy who want to teach. I expect that sometime in the next few years, the MnSCU system will have an online office to "vet" courses that community faculty want to teach. I imagine that, in the beginning, degrees will be very important.

If we try to look twenty or thirty years into the future, it can look very bright or very dark for scholars and scholarship. In the worst case, if money remains scarce, eventually some campuses will have to be closed and there will be hiring freezes. I envision very small departments whose members spend their time vetting online courses proposed by people who are not employed by the colleges. If your goal is to save money—and for some the only goal is to save money—then it makes sense to shrink physical plants and full-time, tenured faculties, and pay online teachers for piecework. They would not need offices or classrooms, and they would not get benefits. Education could be delivered anywhere at any time.

Let's spin this even further. Imagine a legislative session when MnSCU is asking for more money to develop more online courses. Imagine a legislator saying, "Why should we spend money to develop courses? Why don't we just buy our courses from the best places—MIT, Harvard, and places like that? That way, everyone gets the best and there is no second- or third-rate institution or degree."

Thinking such thoughts makes me worried about the future of scholarship. In my worst moments, I imagine a new dark age when a few of you will have to keep the lamps of learning and scholarship alive.

In another scenario, I can imagine that courses will be put on the web, vetted and certified or not, and millions of people around the world will teach millions of others. The opportunities to teach and learn will be unbounded, and most people will have the opportunity to educate themselves, at home. I can imagine girls and women who are not allowed out of their homes still able to learn—at home. I can imagine people who are disabled given a new freedom to learn. I can imagine a new flowering of learning and scholarship.

We may have to go through a dark period to get to the light, but we know how to do that—we *have* done that. We know that learning and scholarship will always lead to the light.

What followed in 1982 was a grant request to the Northwest Area Foundation for the Recognition and Encouragement of Independent Scholarship by the Minnesota Humanities Commission. The request was for $60,000 to be spread over five years. Foundation funding was awarded in 1984 and continued over the next five years. From this grant, the Minnesota Independent Scholars took its beginning. The closing paragraphs of the grant request, probably written by a committee of concerned educators and scholars, are quoted below.

A Scholar Writes

Grant Request Submitted in 1982 to the Northwest Area Foundation for the Recognition and Encouragement of Independent Scholarship (excerpt)

... The Commission will administer the funds with the cooperation and assistance of the Minnesota Independent Scholars' Forum, affiliated scholars, and current and former Minnesota Humanities Commission members.

It is our hope that through this project the Commission can encourage scholarship, build a partnership between affiliated and independent scholars in the state, turn the spotlight on good independent scholarship, and encourage the study of the liberal arts by demonstrating that an academic position is not the only place for those who do so.

As for every human endeavor, independent scholars need to know that someone knows what they are doing, that someone appreciates what they are doing, and that they are not alone. And we can all agree that a country in which historians staff legislative committees, literary scholars work as journalists, philosophers serve as hospital administrators, and anthropologists double as business executives might be a better one.

An effort by the NWAF and the MHC would also serve as a model for other state humanities councils. Since the Commission began working and organizing independent scholars in Minnesota, other state councils (Alaska, Arkansas, Wisconsin, and Washington, D.C.) have expressed an interest in exploring options and opportunities for unaffiliated scholars in their own states. The National Federation of State Humanities

Councils, headquartered in Minneapolis, has also taken a lively interest in the project. The Federation's publication (*Federation Reports*) would be a logical vehicle for a lengthy treatment of this unique public-private partnership.

We are requesting funds for a period of five years. This five-year span is an important component of our plan. In order to get the full effect of the publicity generated by the project, the project must become annual and take advantage of the cumulative effect. Furthermore, the MHC has a rotating board; while this year's members are totally committed to this project, the subsequent members may not be so interested. This would make annual renewal unnecessarily risky. The Commission's current staff and Director are also dedicated to the idea but cannot ensure the attitudes of future staff. If the plan were locked into place, so to speak, with a five-year commitment from the NWAF, we could all be assured of its continuation.

Notes for Chapter 1

1 A proposal submitted to Northwest Area Foundation for the Recognition and Encouragement of Independent Scholarship by the Humanities Commission, 1982. Typewritten manuscript, p. 1.

2 Proposal submitted to Northwest Area Foundation for the Recognition and Encouragement of Independent Scholarship by the Humanities Commission, 1982. Typewritten manuscript, p. 1. Articles by Bennett appeared in the first two issues of the *Forum*, in the Spring and Summer of 1989.

3 Harold Orlans (1921-2007) was a scholar and a writer. He established the Capital Area chapter of the Association of Independent Scholars.

4 <onlinelibrary.wiley.com/store/10.1002/j.2333-8504>1978. These trends are also documented in "Humanities Graduate Education and the Undergraduate Curriculum: Concert or Conflict" by Ernest Frerichs in the *American Council of Learned Scientists*. Occasional paper No. 10. 1989.

5 The Grosses' work is documented in *Independent Scholarship: Promise, Problems and Prospects* published by the College Entrance Examination Board in 1983 and available on the web at <gross spring hill.pdf>.

6 Ibid, p. 39.

7 Ibid.

8 Gross, *Independent Scholar's Handbook*, p. 52.

9 *Humanities Scholars Newsletter* (HSN) 1, no.1, October 1982. This monthly newsletter published by the Humanities Commission under the editorship of Peter Shea is a resource for understanding the multitude of extramural humanities events that emerged in this time period. Shea regularly published news about the Scholars' Forum.

10 Proposal submitted to NWAF, 1982, p.4.

11 HSN 1, no. 2, November 1982.

12 John Butt was teaching religion at Macalester College.

13 Deborah Leuchovius, M.A. in Art History, was an instructor at Winona State University.

14 HSN 1, no. 3, December 1982.

15 See speech by Cheryl Dickson at MISF annual meeting, November 2003, following.

CHAPTER 2

The Early Years (1983–1988)

It is clear that the first plan for MISF was that it would parallel the academy by supplying academic awards and study groups, subsidies for publishing books and visiting professorships, and various funds that might be made available for "child-care, mileage, air fare . . . and other mundane requirements that are no less pressing because they are modest and ordinary."[16] It is worth noting that the group did not have computers and that the need for babysitting money (i.e. time off) was oriented toward women.

The best source for information about the early years of the Scholars is the *Humanities Scholars Newsletter*, published by Peter Shea as an outreach of the Minnesota Humanities Council. Shea ran as much information about the Scholars as he could glean or was fed to him by MISF. (Scholars were subsidized subscribers.)

A HISTORY OF THE MINNESOTA INDEPENDENT SCHOLARS' FORUM

HUMANITIES SCHOLARS NEWSLETTER

Volume 1, Number 1 — October 1982

CALENDAR

This calendar is mostly limited to Metro area events; we have concentrated on those not usually listed in other public calendars. Conferences are discussed in a separate section. We have tried to make this calendar accurate; however, if you must sacrifice greatly to attend an event, please double-check time and place.

Friday, October 1 and Saturday, October 2 — Conference: 'A Question of Balance: Evolving Responsibilities in an Information Society'
Tuesday, October 5 — 6-9:30 pm
'Minnesota's China Connection: Labor' — a program on industrial modernization in the People's Republic of China
Minneapolis Area Vocational Technical Institute, 1415 Hennepin Av S. For information, call the Midwest China Center, 641-3233.
Tuesday, October 5 and Wednesday, October 6 — Nobel Conference: Darwin's Legacy
Wednesday, October 6 — 7:30 pm
Minnesota Museum of Art lecture, for the series 'The 1930's: Society and the Artist' — Helen Harrison, art critic and writer for The New York Times: 'A Decade in Turmoil'
Weyerhaeuser Auditorium, Landmark Center, St Paul. $4 charge.
Thursday, October 7 — 7:30 pm
First Unitarian Society Salkin Memorial Lecture: William A Williams, American historian: 'The Real Crisis of Democracy'
First Unitarian Society, 900 Mount Curve Av, Mpls; free.
Thursday, October 7 — 7:30 pm
U of M Gallery exhibition lecture for 'The Divided Heart: Scandinavian Immigrant Artists, 1850-1950'; Mary Swenson, curator, lectures on the exhibition. 45 Nicholson Hall, U of M East Bank
Friday, October 8 through Sunday, October 10 — Conference: 'Orthodox Americans: Awaiting the Third Millenium'
Friday, October 8 — 10:50 am
Carleton Literature and Society Series lecture — Fredric Jameson, Marxist literary critic, 'The Culture of Post-Modernism: Schizophrenia and Utopia'
Carleton Concert Hall, Northfield.
Tuesday, October 12 — 12:30 pm
Hamline Second Tuesday Luncheon lecture — Walter Blue, professor of modern languages at Hamline: 'Cameroon Revisited'
Manor House Lounge, Hamline University, Hewitt Av and Snelling Av N; $4.
Tuesday, October 12 — 3:30 pm
Minnesota Center for Advanced Studies in Language, Style, and Literary Theory lecture — Siegfried Schmidt, professor of German literature at Muenster, West Germany: 'Empirical Study of Literature'
110 Lind Hall, U of M East Bank, Mpls; free.
Tuesday, October 12 — 7:30-9:30 pm
Austria Series slide/lecture — William E Wright, Director of the Center for Austrian Studies: 'The History and Architecture of Vienna'
Volkshaus, 301 Summit Av, St Paul. Series costs $25; for information, call 373-9743.
Tuesday, October 12 — 8-10 pm
Beginning of Minnesota Science Museum lecture series: 'Challenges: Minnesota Looks to the 21st Century'. This lecture: 'Work and Daily Life' with six speakers representing a variety of perspectives
East Building Auditorium, Science Museum of Minnesota, 10th and Wabasha, St Paul; cost is $5 for series of six. For more information, call 221-9459.
Calendar continued on page 3

Dear reader,
This is the first issue of THE HUMANITIES SCHOLARS' NEWSLETTER, a publication about humanities events, and about opportunities to work in the humanities as teacher, writer, or research scholar. The NEWSLETTER is sponsored by the Minnesota Scholars Forum, an eclectic group of unaffiliated scholars, with funding for the initial issue from the Minnesota Humanities Commission. It is intended to serve two audiences – those with a general interest in humanities events and activities in the metropolitan area, and those with specific scholarly and professional needs. We publish a selective but comprehensive calendar of lectures, presentations, and conferences in the humanities as well as information on library resources, places to publish, grants and fellowships, and possible sponsors for classes and lectures.
The need for this kind of publication is clear. While many newspapers and magazines publish events calendars, none attempts to gather and present information on metro area lectures and conferences in any systematic or comprehensive way. We found in our research that, even within colleges and universities, there is seldom a central gathering place for such information. Further, much information on resources needed for serious, sustained study in the humanities outside of traditional academic institutions is widely scattered and difficult to locate. A publication with a mandate to gather these kinds of information can be of service to a variety of people interested in the humanities.
I invite you to read our newsletter and to take its measure, as a resource and as a companion. If anything seems out of place to you, or if you see evidence of oversights, please let me know. If you wish to subscribe, please fill out the form in this issue and send it to me. We will contact you with more specific subscription information.

Cordially,

Peter Shea

This prototype NEWSLETTER was produced with research and editorial assistance from Sylvia Quast. R. W. Scholes consulted on the design.

This is the first edition of the *Humanities Scholars Newsletter*, which appeared in 1982. The editor, Peter Shea, attempted to list all of the humanities events that were occurring in the Twin Cities. HSN appeared more or less monthly.

As mentioned in the previous chapter, the Minnesota Independent Scholars' Forum (which was at first the MN Forum for Independent Scholarship) takes its starting date as October 16, 1982. On that date, 65 members met at the Minneapolis Public Library to discuss a draft of proposed bylaws, organize study groups, and talk about ways to help each other and other unaffiliated scholars. Then, three weeks later, on November 6th, immediately following the Spring Hill Conference (see preceding chapter), a formal organizing meeting for the Minnesota group took place. The group approved the bylaws and elected officers with John Butt as the president and Deborah Leuchovius as vice president.[17]

Scholars went into action. One of the complaints of independent scholars in the early 1980s was that academic libraries were closed to them or only available upon payment of a fee and that academic librarians were "unhelpful."[18] Thus it was a small, but significant, victory when, in March of 1983, Shea could report that "[t]he Historical Society and the Hill Manuscript Library had invited the Scholars to use their facilities" and that "Steven Blake was negotiating with the University of Minnesota on behalf of the Forum."[19] In the following month's issue, it was reported that Blake had secured access at the University of Minnesota for MISF members. An interesting side note, which is confirmed in Dickson's remarks about the preservation of academic privilege,[20] is that the University at first required scholars to renew their privileges every three months. Eventually, when the University came to the realization that independent scholars paid their fines and renewed their books, paid-up members of the Scholars were granted renewable cards that gave them "undergraduate" privileges.[21]

The Minnesota Independent Scholars' Forum (formerly the MN Forum for Independent Scholarship) was formally incorporated[22] a year later in November, 1983. The bylaws that had been adopted in 1982 were revised.[23] Rhoda Lewin was elected president of the newly incorporated organization. Lewin, a journalist and oral historian with degrees in journalism and American Studies, was elected for a one-year term. The fiscal year ran from November 1 to October 31. At this time, the Forum began to publish a one-page bimonthly update, "News and Views," which was inserted in the *Humanities Scholars Newsletter* (HSN).

Narrative continues on page 33.

SCHOLARS WITHOUT WALLS

news & views from MINNESOTA INDEPENDENT SCHOLARS' FORUM

May 1984

News & Views from Minnesota Independent Scholars' Forum is mailed with every other issue of Peter Shea's monthly *Humanities Scholars Newsletter*, which circulates statewide to more than 250 college department heads and other subscribers (including Forum members). The Forum insert includes updates on study groups, Forum news, and a "Points of View" section for abstracts, essays, or reviews by Forum members. Sandra Sandell (377-8849) coordinates this probject, with assistance from Patricia Kulisheck (822-7607). Both welcome submissions from Forum members. This month we introduce a new feature for members and prospective members of the Minnesota Independent Scholars' Forum—a letter from the president—which will provide additional news and views.

"1884 REVISITED"

The Minnesota Independent Scholars' Forum joins with two other local groups in presenting "1884 Revisited: An Informal Portrait of Another Era—Readings and Reflections on Life a Century Ago," on Thursday, May 10, at the Earle Brown Center, University of Minnesota, St. Paul Campus. The evening, meant as a whimsical contrast to the attention 1984 is receiving, provides an opportunity for members of the Forum, Minnesota Women in Higher Education, and Sing Heavenly Muse!—the sponsoring organizations—to become acquainted with one another. The schedule begins with a social hour at 6:00 p.m., followed by dinner at 6:30. The program runs from 7:15 to 8:30. Payment for reservations ($7.00 per person) should be sent to Minnesota Women in Higher Education, P.O. Box 13171, Minneapolis, MN 55414. For questions or directions call Ann Pflaum at 376-1420.

A presenter for each of the groups will give a brief talk on how people thought about themselves and the future in 1884. Carolyn Shrewsbury, professor of political science at Mankato State University, will speak for MWHE, and Judith Roode, artist at the Minneapolis College of Art and Design, for Sing Heavenly Muse! For the Forum, Jim Casebolt will present "The Case of the Sick Theologian: Medicine Meets Religion in 1884." The audience is invited to bring brief readings or "reminiscences" (less than two minutes) about art, science, literature, politics, or religion in 1884.

Sing Heavenly Muse! is an organization of women in the arts. Minnesota Women in Higher Education is a multi-disciplinary group of teachers, administrators, students, and graduate students interested in the welfare of higher education. The groups proposed a joint meeting to Forum President Rhoda Lewin after reading her letter to the editor repudiating C. Peter Magrath's denigration of scholarship outside academia.

JANE CURRY TO ACCEPT AWARD

Forum member Jane Curry, 1984 Independent Scholar of the Year, will present her award lecture—"River Rats and Mother Wits: The Many Voices of an Independent Scholar"—at 7:30 p.m., Thursday May 17, in the Hamline University Theater, St. Paul. A reception, sponsored by the Forum, will follow the lecture, which is free and open to the public. Curry will receive a cash prize of $3,000, the first awarded under a five-year incentive program for Minnesota's independent scholars funded by the Northwest Area Foundation through the Minnesota Humanities Commission.

The competition is open to full-time state residents who hold an advanced academic degree, engage in research or writing, and have no current full-time academic affiliation. The award, based on the winner's published works, is being given to Curry for two books published in 1982—*The River's in My Blood: Riverboat Pilots Tell Their Stories* and *Marietta Holley: Samantha Rastles the Women Question*. In addition to writing, Curry tours the country as the down-to-earth Samantha Allen, Holley's turn-of-the-century fictional vehicle for promotion women's rights through humor.

Curry says she is thrilled by this recognition of scholars who work on their own yet want the respect of their peers. After five years of effort, she is pleased to see all her patience rewarded. Quitting her job as an assistant professor and striking out on her own was a big risk, she admits, and might have turned out badly. Instead, the past year has been "incredible", with the award, publication of the books, increased bookings of her show, and another tour as cruise director on the *Delta Queen*, a Mississippi riverboat. Curry hopes to make the lecture fun but substantial, a celebration for all independent scholars.

Because the award is the first of its kind in the country, Curry hopes that it will bolster the national independent scholars movement and serve as a model for other states. It is significant that a major foundation has seen the need to support independent scholarship. Funding is important, Curry points out, especially to someone like her who works free-lance. Also a boon is the fund provided by the Northwest Area Foundation to facilitate publication. Many university presses request a subsidy, Curry notes, and her Samantha could have used one.

In light of C. Peter Magrath's now notorious comments (see the letter from the president), Curry hopes that independent scholars. In fact, the money and publicity involved are more recognition than one might get at an institution. She also believes that her award is proof that an interest in public pedagogy exists and that the Foundation recognizes efforts like her one-woman show as valid contributions. She points out that in tenure reviews faculty members often receive no credit for nontraditional contributions such as performing in plays.

News and Views was a bi-monthly update inserted into the *Humanities Scholars' Newsletter* with particular information for Scholars.

Shortly after she was elected, Lewin responded to some remarks from Peter McGrath, the president of the University of Minnesota, in which McGrath suggested that a glut of Ph.D.'s who did not have teaching jobs was a "myth," and that when teaching positions opened up in the 1990s those who had been working at other jobs in the interim would be out of touch with scholarly discourse and research.[24]

Lewin responded, "By the 1990s, college presidents may be surprised to find that the humanities scholars now being forced out of academe by the shortage of teaching positions may have taken their more intellectually adventurous colleagues with them by showing them that a stimulating life of the mind and scholarly prestige exist outside academe." She cited Dorothy Walker, of the Newberry Library, and Leo Miller, a Milton scholar, as examples of scholars working outside of academe. Barbara Tuchman and Rachel Carson are likewise often cited as independent scholars of this period.

Scholar of the Year Awards

In May of 1984, MISF gave its first Scholar of the Year Award to Jane Curry. Curry, who held a Ph.D. in American Studies, had gone freelance after teaching for several years. Curry had published two books on Mississippi River history and had developed a humorous lecture on women's rights. The Scholar of the Year award carried a $3,000 stipend; Curry pointed out that "the money and the publicity were more recognition than one might get at an institution."[25]

In 1984, the Forum published a membership directory, with 81 members. It listed, among other things, the topics on which members could speak and advertised their availability as speakers. There were seven active study groups at this time. In addition, some members were trying to set up an adjunct group in Duluth with a "bed and breakfast" network included. Three thousand copies of an MISF brochure had been printed.

Jim Casebolt, a Ph.D. in ethics/religion and technology, became the second president of the Scholars in 1985. At the time of his election, there were eight potential study groups, including Politics and Aesthetics, Social Change, and Gender Roles and Culture. In June, 1985, MISF awarded its second Scholar of the Year Award to Helen McCann White for *Down to Earth History*. White was a writer and journalist who worked for the Minnesota Historical Society archives.

Sandra Sandell succeeded Casebolt as president in November of 1985. Sandell held a degree in English literature, and was the executive director of the Minnesota Association for Non-Smokers. Doug Birk, an archeologist and one of the founders of the Institute for Minnesota Archeology, was the third Scholar of the Year; his talk was entitled "Shadows in the Wilderness: The Archeology of the Early French Presence in Minnesota." At this time, there were six study groups.

In October/November, 1986, Board member Susan Margot Smith wrote an article called "Does the Forum Have a Future?" for "News and Views" (in HSN).[26] In this two-page "open letter" to Forum members, Smith wondered how the Forum might find a place in the "intellectual-social" architecture of the future. She placed the identity problems of the Forum in the spectrum of the identity problems of the whole educational establishment, which included reports of low student achievement, poor faculty performance, and the general patchwork quality of higher education. According to Smith, educational institutions were being called upon to focus and streamline their efforts—all in the name of efficiency.

Smith located the scholars of the Forum somewhere outside the customary educational spectrum: people who did not work well in "professional systems" or who were doing work that was outside of the system. Recognizing that the Forum was "below the radar," Smith suggested that the Forum make itself more visible, both within and without the academy. She saw this increased visibility as a three-year task. In the first and second years, the Forum should initiate and promote monthly meetings (as opposed to the three or four times a year that had been customary).

Frequent and well-publicized meetings should bring in new members so that when the third year came, the increased membership could run workshops and study groups and provide small grants. Ominously, Smith concluded that if all this effort did not produce more funding by the end of the third year, the board should "recommend . . . dissolution before the beginning of the fourth year."

Later in this same year, 1986 (whether from weakness or strength it is impossible to say), the Scholars opted to stop supporting Peter Shea's *Humanities Scholars Newsletter* (which had changed its name to *Affinities*). This decision means that we know slightly less about the overall humanities scene in the Twin Cities from this point forward. On the other hand, MISF made the production of the one-page "News and Views from the Minnesota Independent Scholars' Forum" more frequent and extensive. Thus, we have a fairly good record of what happened to MISF in 1987.

For one thing, we have a response by Curt Hillstrom to Susan Smith's "Does the Forum Have a Future?" Smith's question was the subject of the November 1986 member meeting. Member Curt Hillstrom responded to Smith's article in the following way. It is worth noting that Hillstrom is proposing a more democratic organization than had heretofore been envisioned. Hillstrom, a philosopher, has been a member of the Scholars since 1986 and has served as treasurer and president. His vision of the Scholars, presented in the seven points at the end of his response, is pretty much what the Minnesota Independent Scholars' Forum has become.

A Scholar Writes

The Role of the Independent Scholars' Forum
Curt Hillstrom, 1986 [27]

The discussion on the role of the Minnesota Independent Scholars' Forum is one well worth having. For the first time,

I am viewing the Forum as more than just an access to the University of Minnesota libraries. It is also gratifying to hear the members seeking a way of pursuing our objectives in a manner which fits us, and not trying to be a sort of quasi-university of our own. It is, however, very tempting to keep playing "bash the system," and, as a former graduate student who quit in disgust, I often find myself engaging in this quite satisfying game. It is time now, I think, to take a closer look at some of the paradigms we object to, why we object to them, and ways we can use this knowledge to structure the Scholars' Forum to our own liking.

Social Categorization

When one begins to examine the problems with the values, assumptions, and points of view of the educational establishment, it becomes clear that these just reflect the values, assumptions, and points of view of our society in general. Educational institutions are the way they are because that is the way we want them to be. So perhaps the place to start is to look at our way of viewing social life as a variety of specialized categories. If one wants religion, one goes to a church or synagogue or similar organization; if one wants to engage in business, one goes to the business community; if one wants an education, one goes to school. Careers are determined by choosing one of these or other areas and filling one of the well-defined roles within each. I do not wish to discredit the value of specialized function or social institutions, but I do want to point out that the clear delineations we make between these categories are artificial. Religion does not belong just in church. We live our religions, good or bad, every day. Business is not just conducted in the business community. We frequently need to examine finances to make decisions and trade-offs on a variety of important things regarding our lives. And school is not the only place to be educated. We can learn and teach every day.

But lives are actually a complex melding of all these functions. To think of them as separate aspects of our lives may be useful, but is also artificial and, at times, misleading.

Academic Membership

Schools are well-defined institutions. Either you are a part of one or you aren't. To get into one, as a teacher or as a student, you need to demonstrate your qualifications through academic credentials, recommendations, and test scores. Exit is equally distinctive, if more varied, through graduating, flunking, dropping out, retiring, quitting, or being fired or laid off. At any rate, you belong if you are in and you don't belong if you are out. The sense of belongingness is strengthened through logos, mascots, sports teams, the concept of an alma mater, the fact that the campus has a particular physical location, and the idea of school as an employer. For most, particularly students and particularly at well-regarded schools, the organization becomes a part of their identity. And the privileges and prestige of membership are considerable. Those without similar membership have less social prestige and are not considered to be "educated" or in the process of becoming so. Meaningful educational experiences in other spheres are not taken seriously as formal education and are thus without prestige. Nor is there any attempt at systematization or social provisions for individual enhancement in nonacademic learning situations. One is simply not considered educated in our society without proper documents. While credentials are certainly important for certain types of social functioning, to discount learning and education outside the traditional method is shortsighted and socially damaging.

Academic Discipline

Once one has become a part of an educational institution, one has the proper label appended, teacher and student being the most important labels. With each of these roles there are certain expectations with regard to what the person should or should not be doing. Teachers make lesson plans, teach, evaluate, research, and publish. They set good public examples and do not get caught in compromising situations. Students study, learn, take tests, write papers, and do not go partying the night before a big test. Individuals can thus easily be judged as good or bad teachers or students, and significant rewards and punishments are used to enforce and enhance this role-driven system.

This all falls under the rubric of academic discipline. It involves controlling a person's action in order to accomplish some specific goals. It is also sometimes called self-discipline, because one is supposed to do these things without a supervisor standing and looking over one's shoulder. But as long as there are punishments involved which are external to the individual, such as a bad grade or removal from membership in the school, it cannot be considered truly self-discipline. Self-discipline must be totally voluntary. If one allows the effects of external rewards and punishments and socially applied labels to control one's actions, then the role will determine what the individual does, meaning he or she will be living according to the values and expectations of others. If one, instead, acts according to one's own values and perspectives on the needs of society, then one's role is defined by the actions of the individual. It is one of action determining role, rather than role determining action.

Academic Standards

The primary judgments made in a school are academic, based mostly on one's ability to demonstrate knowledge through test-taking or publishing scholarly papers. These judgments are made by reference to academic standards which are often loosely stated and are external to the individuals being judged. The system operates like a series of screens, sifting people from one level to a finer one below, with those who pass through all the screens being given appointment as professors in the most prestigious universities. The ones who fail to pass through a screen are, at best, told they have reached their station in life or, at worst, rejected as inferior material. The system is an uncaring one, in spite of having caring people as a part of it. It regards people as having somewhat fixed abilities, and ignores the fact that, from my observations at least, most people who fail do so for reasons other than academic inadequacy. With its clear sets of academic objectives and rewards, the system can claim distinctive winners and losers. But not everyone shares, nor should they share, these same objectives and standards. When each person determines one's own objectives, one's own standards, then it can become possible for each of us to become winners. This does not mean the traditional academic standards are wrong or should be ignored. Academic standards are a necessity. My complaint is that the system is standards-oriented rather than people-oriented, and it manages to leave most citizens operating well below their potential.

Teacher/Student Dichotomy

The two most important roles in schools are teachers and students. Teachers teach the students and students learn from the teachers. And while teachers admit they can learn much by teaching a class and students often help each other, each thinks of him- or herself either as a teacher or as a student, but not both. This sharp dichotomy is unnecessary and misleading, if not downright destructive. As for me, I can learn from anyone who knows something I don't. I am also very glad to share what I know with others, and I delight in exploring new horizons with anyone. We are all learners; we are all teachers.

The Forum

The Minnesota Independent Scholars' Forum is an educational organization. We are individually working to learn and to share that learning with others. I feel we should do this with the recognition that it is only a part, albeit an important part, of our lives, and that we do it as an organization, without corporate identity campaigns, recognizing that each of us is responsible ultimately for our own education; that we have unique needs and goals and outlooks which must be respected; and that we are all traveling together toward deeper understanding. This means the Scholars' Forum should be a loosely structured, voluntary organization, almost like a brokerage, connecting people with others who are knowledgeable and searching, and to other sources of information. It should be non-elitist, open to anyone with serious interest in learning and sharing knowledge, with no tilt toward academic credentials for their own sake. It must use persuasion rather than coercion to encourage scholarly behavior. And, above all, it must be people-oriented, supporting each in reaching his or her own legitimate goals, bestowing neither punishment nor reward (such as scholar of the year), but recognizing that the pursuit of the goal should be sufficient reward in itself.

In order to accomplish these goals, I would suggest the following, more specific, recommendations for the Forum to undertake:

1. Produce a periodical publication which is more than just a newsletter, containing serious articles and debates of interest to members.

2. Maintain and publish a list of schools, libraries, museums, and other institutions and sources of information which may be of use to the independent scholar.

3. Publish a reference of members with their areas of interest and expertise listed.

4. Ask a commitment of each member to help other members without expecting remuneration.

5. Broaden the role of the discussion groups; we can begin by calling them special interest groups.

6. Encourage members to give public lectures or seminars in their areas of expertise, provided there is sufficient interest.

7. Look for ways the Forum could operate as a support group to give encouragement when encouragement is needed.

I hope that this discussion will help lead to a stronger, more effective organization for those who prefer operating outside the traditional educational establishments.

How Applying for 501(c)(3) Status Affected the Scholars

In 1984–85 and again in 1985–86, MISF published a directory listing resumes of MISF members. In 1986, it mailed this directory to deans and colleges throughout the state in the hope that scholars would be offered visiting professorships or speaking engagements. Then, in 1987, under the leadership of Sandra Sandell,[28] MISF began the application for 501(c)(3) status. At that time, the IRS ruled that MISF could not spend money on a self-promoting activity such as the directory and still call itself a nonprofit organization. The ruling came down that publishing a directory would make MISF a business or professional organization. Although the Humanities Commission printed an abbreviated membership directory in 1986, the Scholars have not printed a directory since 1985. (As will be seen, the IRS granted 501(c)(3) status to MISF in 1990 retroactive to 1983.) The ruling by the IRS and the Scholars' willingness to abide by it changed the shape and scope of the organization from a placement organization to a self-supporting club.[29]

Independent Scholarship Continues

In 1987, Jeffrey Hess became the fourth Independent Scholar of the Year. Hess was a historical consultant with a specialty in documentary research and artifact evaluation. His talk was titled "History for Hire." It took place at the Minneapolis Institute of Art in October, 1987, and was attended by many members of the Humanities Commission.

Narrative continues on page 44.

"History for Hire"
a public lecture presented by
Jeffrey A. Hess
1987 Minnesota Independent Scholar of the Year

and sponsored by the

Minnesota Independent Scholars' Forum

Wednesday, October 7   8:00 p.m.

Minneapolis Institute of Arts Auditorium

This invitation for the Jeffrey Hess lecture in 1987 is the first time MISF used the Bernardo Bellinzone woodcut as its logo.

Also in 1987, a progress report by MISF for the Humanities Commission cited a significant increase in the hiring of independent scholars as adjunct professors in local institutions such as the University of Minnesota, Saint Olaf College, and the University of Minnesota at Duluth. Independent scholars were awarded a stipend by the MISF grant. (Local institutions provided faculty privileges but not all matched the stipend, which was $2000.) The report also noted with pride that it had given a 1986 subsidy grant for the publication of Hjalmar Peterson of Minnesota: *The Politics of Provincial Independence* by Steven Keillor (Minnesota Historical Society Press, 1987).[30]

Considerable attention was still focused on obtaining library access for scholars. In May 1984, Metronet (a seven-county library network) hosted a workshop, "Resourcefulness," to help scholars access library resources in the Twin Cities.[31] This workshop was not especially successful; Mary Treacy,[32] a prime mover in Metronet, reported in 1988:

In June, 1986 a group of academic and public librarians met with representatives of the Minnesota Independent Scholars' Forum. At that time, we agreed that the workshop had not been the best forum for presenting information and for establishing communication between independent scholars and the "institutionalized" library community. We agreed at that time to produce instead the resource kit about area libraries which was then distributed to independent scholars through the Forum... I will be meeting... to discuss future possibilities—programs presented by libraries for MISF, the service of independent scholars on appropriate advisory committees, ways in which the information about Minnesota information resources, especially new technologies, can be delivered to scholars throughout the state.[33]

In May 1988, the Scholars recognized their fifth (and final) Scholar of the Year; Marilyn Chiat, who spoke on "Independence and the Scholar: A

Conflict of Terms?" Chiat, an architectural historian, held a Ph.D. in Art History. Chiat's talk took place at Temple Israel where the reception was planned and funded by the Temple Sisterhood. This lecture was effectively the last event of the initial funding for the Minnesota Independent Scholars' Forum. Due to changes in the leadership of the Northwest Area Foundation, the funding was not renewed at the end of the granting term.

Notes for Chapter 2

16 Proposal submitted to Northwest Area Foundation (NWAF), 1982, p.6.

17 HSN 1, nos. 1-3, 1982.

18 See *Independent Scholarship: Promise, Problems, and Prospects* by Ronald and Beatrice Gross, 1983. Passim, but especially page 60 and following. <gross spring hill.pdf>.

19 HSN 1, no. 6 March 1983.

20 Grant proposal to NWAF, p. 5, and Gross, *Independent Scholarship: Promise . . .*, p.47-60.

21 HSN 3, no. 5, January 1985. MISF was by now publishing a bi-monthly page, called News & Views from MISF, folded into the back of *HSN*.

22 HSN 1, no. 6, March 1983, says that the Scholars' Forum met February 5, 1983, approved revised bylaws and discussed a variety of topics.

23 I have not been able to locate a copy of these early bylaws. However, the statement of the purpose of the Scholars has stayed basically the same through all the versions of the bylaws up to the most recent (2015): "The Minnesota Independent Scholars' Forum is a non-profit organization formed to encourage and promote independent scholarship both outside and within formal institutions of higher education. To accomplish its purpose, the Forum supports research, writing, and publication of independent scholars; fosters scholarly discussion; educates the public about the role and value of independent scholars and their scholarship; and engages in other educational and charitable services to meet its goals."

24 *Star Tribune*, February 18, 1984, p. 13A, "Scholarship thrives outside the academic portal" quotes Lewin and cites McGrath.

25 News and Views from MISF, May 1984.

26 News and Views, HSN, October/November 1986.

27 This paper was included as part of the newsletter to members for January 1987. To the best of the editor's knowledge it does not otherwise appear in print.

28 Sandra Sandell, Ph.D. in English, was an instructor in the Department of Independent Study at the University of Minnesota.

29 Members' Newsletter, March 1987. The 1984 directory listed resumes for 17 men and 25 women, although the membership roster had almost equal numbers for women (41) and men (42).

30 Progress Report on Independent Scholars Project for the NWAF Grant, July

1987.

31 News and Views, Summer 1986.

32 She was then Mary Treacy Birmingham.

33 Letter from Mary Treacy Birmingham to Deborah Leuchovius, August 25, 1988.

CHAPTER 3

A Model Emerges (1988–1995)

Susan Margot Smith, whose academic work was in History and American Studies, became the president of the Scholars in 1988. Describing this first presidency, David Wiggins, in an interview with David Megarry in July 2015, said that "Susan Smith was doing all the work: newsletter, finances, and organization—with full board approval. It was a fledgling organization. It had a working board, although the board was not doing much."

Smith agreed with Hillstrom (see chapter 2) that publishing a journal/newsletter was an important step toward making the Scholars better known.

A History of the Minnesota Independent Scholars' Forum

The Forum

The Newsletter of the Minnesota Independent Scholars' Forum

Vol. 1, No. 1 — Spring 1989

Independent Scholarship Enters a New Era

Contemporary independent scholarship, that of the last ten years or so, has been consistently associated with the academic crises that beset higher education in the seventies and early eighties. Until recently, so-called "independent" scholars have been identified as "the lost generation" of academics, refugees from a shrinking market and a dwindling student population.

The consequences were professional isolation on the fringes of the academic world, and the development of a caste system in which part-time instructors and one-year appointees roamed the academic terrain trying to make their rootlessness seem like opportunity rather than a visible sign of intellectual limitation.

Toward the end of 1985, another view of independent scholarship began to take shape in the face of the term "focus" which had come to connote elitism and economy in intellectual matters. In the new view independent scholars began to think of themselves not as outsiders looking in but as a completely different professional genre. One that might have a distinctive intellectual contribution to make.

Simultaneously, long-standing ways of knowing were being challenged; while independent scholars were struggling to define themselves, the definitions of scholarship in general were shifting. In 1981, cultural historian William Irwin Thompson was pointing out that "forms of knowledge change as society changes" and further, "As fiction and music are coming close to reorganizing knowledge, scholarship is becoming closer to art. Our culture is changing, and so the genres of literature and history are changing as well" (*The Time Falling Bodies Take to Light*). Several years later, he wrote "the Scientific Method is canonized into a sanctified procedure

New Era *Continued Page 2*

Changing The Patterns: The Boise Peace Quilt Project

Joint Soviet-American Peace Quilt

Boise Quilters

A history and interpretation of the Boise Peace Quilt Project will be offered by Forum President, Susan Smith, on Saturday, April 22nd, at 9:30 a.m. in Guild Hall, Plymouth Congregational Church, 1900 Nicollet Ave. So., Mpls. Titled "Changing the Patterns", the program will feature the award-winning documentary film, "A Stitch for Time".

The Boise Peace Quilters have made twenty quilts since they first came together in 1981 to work for peace by "stitching the world together". Their quilts have been given in friendship to the people of the Soviet Union and Japan, to honor peacemakers such as Frank Church, Sister Marjorie Tuite, and Norman Cousins, and to carry messages of peace to places like Greenham, England and Nicaragua.

This project has also given us the means to look at the American patchwork quilt not only as a design tradition, but as a long active agent for social change. Smith will make comments about the contemporary significance of that fact, and discussion will follow the film.

The first issue of the *Forum*, the Scholars' newsletter, was published in the spring of 1989. It was edited by Susan Milnor and included ads and photographs. The original intention was to publish quarterly.

Accordingly, in the spring of 1989, MISF began to publish a quarterly newsletter/journal, the *Forum*. The first issue had eight pages, and included ads and photographs. The first editor was Susan Milnor, who listed her interests as sculpture and photography. The journal featured articles by Susan Smith, reports of past meetings, announcements of upcoming meetings, and a page of reports on study groups. Only two study groups were active (Eighteenth Century and Science and Humanities); six were inactive but still carried on the rolls. A page of this issue was devoted to a membership application form, and a list of services supplied by the Scholars (public programs, study groups, access to the University of Minnesota libraries, and a quarterly newsletter). Job opportunities, a balance sheet, and list of contributors filled the rest of this initial publication.

In the first editorial of the first journal, Susan Smith (who sustained MISF through this entire early period) articulated her vision of what the Scholars could be. Having said, in November of 1986, that the Forum needed to work on several fronts at once, she now tried to define independent scholarship in a new and more approachable way.[34]

A Scholar Writes

Independent Scholarship Enters a New Era
Susan Margot Smith, 1989

Contemporary independent scholarship, that of the last ten years or so, has been consistently associated with the academic crises that beset higher education in the Seventies and early Eighties. Until recently, so-called "independent" scholars have been identified as "the lost generation" of academics, refugees from a shrinking market and a dwindling student population.

The consequences were professional isolation on the fringes of the academic world, and the development of a caste system in which part-time instructors and one-year appointees roamed the academic terrain, trying to make their rootlessness seem like opportunity rather than a visible sign of intellectual limitation.

Toward the end of 1985, another view of independent scholarship began to take shape in the face of the term "focus" which had come to connote elitism and economy in intellectual matters. In the new view, independent scholars began to think of themselves not as outsiders looking in, but as a completely different professional genre. One that might have a distinctive intellectual contribution to make.

Simultaneously, longstanding ways of knowing were being challenged; while independent scholars were struggling to define themselves, the definitions of scholarship in general were shifting. In 1981, cultural historian William Irwin Thompson was pointing out that "forms of knowledge change as society changes," and further, "As fiction and music are coming close to reorganizing knowledge, scholarship is becoming closer to art. Our culture is changing, and so the genres of literature and history are changing as well" (*The Time Falling Bodies Take to Light*). Several years later, he wrote, "The Scientific Method is canonized into a sanctified procedure that has very little to do with the actual way individual human scientists make discoveries and invent new theories," (*Gaia, A Way of Knowing: The Cultural Implications of the New Biology*, 1987). He is not alone when he speaks in this different voice.

Given all this radical questioning of how things are, these frontal assaults on academic disciplines and methodologies, what is the independent scholar to do? The answer is simple. Rejoin the academic conversation, on an equal footing. And do not waste precious energy at this particular moment in defining independent scholarship when all the definitions of traditional scholarship are in the process of being evaluated.

This is a time for inclusiveness within our own ranks, a time for the best that we can offer by way of imagination, the reformulation of old patterns and canons, and new insights. It may well be that this is an era of transformation, and too much self-definition is premature. Above all else, it is a time for questions!

The *Forum* Continues

Susan Milnor produced two more issues of the *Forum* in its first year, 1989. The second and third issues of the *Forum* included articles by the guru of independent scholarship, James Bennett, and by Roger Sween, who was a Library Cooperation Specialist for the State of Minnesota. Bennett went to some length to discuss the contributions and survival skills used by independents;[35] Sween discussed ways in which independents could use libraries and how libraries and librarians could be helpful to them.[36] Both early issues of the *Forum* included reports on study groups and calls for volunteers to help with the newsletter. There was also a suggestion that scholars who were having trouble affording individual subscriptions to academic journals might pool resources and share subscriptions.

Susan Margot Smith was still the president of the Scholars in 1990, but there was a new *Forum* editor, Merryalice Jones. Smith's editorial in the Winter 1990 issue of the *Forum* continued to build on her vision of what the Scholars were becoming. "Our challenge as an organization for independent scholars is to support this work with structures that do not inhibit or define it. . . . High on our list of priorities are material support for individuals [and] improved procedures for communicating with each other and the public . . ."[37]

Technology Revolution

A harbinger of the coming change in communication technology—the personal computer—is this article by David Wiggins. Wiggins, a historical specialist with very wide-ranging interests—from evolutionary theory to experimental archaeology—wrote the lead article in the Winter 1990 edition of the *Forum*. It is the first signal of the growing revolution in communication technology. Wiggins was already using computers in a sophisticated fashion. In this article, he comments on the changes he believed computers would bring to the world of independent scholarship.

A Scholar Writes

Independent Scholarship and the Revolution in Information Technology
David Wiggins, 1990

Scholarship didn't begin with the technology of the book and it will not end with the technology of the computer. But, just as the book forever changed what scholars do, so too the computer is redefining scholarship in ways that we are just beginning to imagine. As independent scholars, the implications of this major revolution in information technology are both heartening and frightening.

First, let me clarify my position about computers. I'm not [among the] enthusiasts who believe that machines will soon think so much better than humans that we can turn the business of thought over to our supercomputers and sit back and wait for the truth to print out. I'm also not one of those who insist that everyone must use a computer or lose my respect. The dictum "publish or perish" would have excluded Socrates and many others; just as today, the dictum "compute or be condemned" would exclude some of our best minds.

The computer is only a tool—but what a tool! At every stage of the business of scholarship, the computer (and the related technology of modems, storage devices, etc.) is changing what we can do. The computer can help us find the work of scholars around the world and deliver it to our offices at the push of a button. It allows us to write a draft of a lengthy work, send it electronically (via modem) to another scholar for comment, make any suggested changes, and then submit it to a publisher, all without ever having to print a hard copy. (Sure beats the typewriter and the Xerox machine method.) The computer can also help us manipulate large and complex collections of information. [. . .]

I think that independent scholarship is not only going to become easier with the developing technology (a heartening prospect), [but] it is going to become the prevailing way to learn. In a world of ideas where people are regularly redefining what is considered important, learning will be ongoing—it can't possibly be confined to a period of formal education leading to a career or job. Nor will teachers any longer be the sole experts in a particular body of knowledge. Rather, the division between teachers and students will, of necessity, break down when teachers can no longer master whole subject areas and their students will work with them in a common exploration of subject matter. At some point, the job of the schools will have to change from teaching truths to developing students' attitudes and skills for independent learning.

At the college and university level, computers and the revolution in information technology are transforming the old academic order, in part because much of that order has been closely tied to the technology of the printed word. Writers of scholarly books, articles, or Ph.D. theses have had to conform to the orthodox interpretations that precede their works. The processes of peer review for publication and other standards of form [sic] have ensured that any new interpretations will follow in a linear way from the old. The related institutions of tenure for faculty and degrees for students have helped perpetuate those ideas that passed the filter of publication.

Today, new electronic paths open to scholars are far less encumbered by filters for academic orthodoxy. Instead, there are other barriers that don't necessarily have anything to do with content of information or the qualifications of scholars (a disheartening aspect). For example, people who don't have the machines to get into this game or the money to pay for online research services are left out. Also, there are some who may attempt to restrict access to information for reasons of "national security" or corporate profit and have the power to keep whole subject areas out of the hands of independent researchers. These can be serious obstacles, but on the whole, I believe the new technology is opening rather than restricting areas of scholarship. Most important, the power of computers to assemble and interconnect the vast amounts of information being generated by specialists makes it possible for us as scholars to begin to tackle the interdisciplinary connections and to articulate the fundamental principles that underlie complex subjects. This is not a reductionist approach that seeks to tease out the fine detail of the world's complexity, although that work will continue, but rather one calling for grand syntheses and open debate about basic philosophical issues—the kind of work that is well-suited to the talents of the independent scholars I know.[38]

Computers Arrive

The Scholars followed the technological trend with a program in January, 1990: "Computer Tools for Independent Scholars." Three presenters, Claire McInerney, John Wickre, and David Shupe, demonstrated how they used computers for research with such technology as Hypercard and XYwrite. Shupe went so far as to present "his vision of a future in which books can be published on demand and conceptual structures regularly reconfigured . . . [which] would have seemed unbelievable had we not just seen a glimpse of the future in the first two presentations."[39] This program was described "as a vision of the future" and invoked a lengthy and lively discussion, so much so "that time had to be called."[40]

Active Study Groups

As might be expected from this sort of response, a new study group, "Communications and Information Technology Group," was established in the spring of 1990. It joined five study groups active at that time: Chaos, 18th/19th Century, Science and Humanities, Patterns in Women's Spirituality, and Diversity. While the study groups met on their own schedules, general public programs were scheduled about once a month with subjects such as "Culture Under Canvas," "Witnesses to the Holocaust," and a "Chaos Festival."

Susan Smith, still president of MISF, summarized the Scholars' progress in her editorial in the spring of 1990:

> I think we are ready, as a distinctive intellectual genre and structure, to establish new working relationships with traditional education organizations . . . the Board has taken some first steps in that direction with encouraging results. With Roger Sween's help, 130 libraries have been sent a first mailing to introduce them to the Minnesota Independent Scholars' Forum and to the concept of independent scholarship. [. . .]
>
> It is hardly original to argue that an organization needs a steady source of income *and* a broad base of support . . . I believe "steady income" is more likely with a broad financial base, so it is the latter that concerns me here.
>
> Breadth . . . involves . . . membership . . . grants . . . and gifts.[41]

Smith also appointed a committee to build membership and raise funds and asked the treasurer to create an operating budget.

MISF Achieves 501(c) (3) Status

In June of 1990, MISF was granted 501(c)(3) status, retroactive to 1983. Smith and Wiggins wrote a letter to all MISF members and supporters, pointing out that henceforth contributions to the organization would be tax deductible and thanking those who had faithfully contributed even when contributions were not deductible. At this time, MISF had over 100 members; its most attractive membership perk was library borrowing privileges at the University of Minnesota.

David Wiggins was elected president of the Scholars in 1991. In the first issue of his tenure (Spring 1991) as president, Wiggins supplied a spirited take on the significance of the Scholars. Wiggins can be said to be struggling to figure out exactly what the role of the Forum will be, but is a little more confident than some of his predecessors had been of its place in the history of intellectual endeavors. [42]

A SCHOLAR WRITES

MESSAGE FROM THE PRESIDENT
DAVID WIGGINS, 1991

[...] All members who would like to get involved in helping any of these committees with their work should feel free to contact me or the committee chairs. We are still running entirely on the labors of volunteers, and the fact that we can get so many people with consuming interests of their own to take the time to help the Forum is to me the best evidence that what we are doing as an organization is important.

But what are we doing? Who are we? These are questions that are always good to keep in mind, but particularly appropriate at the juncture of a change in leadership. To take a focused look at our mission and how our specific activities relate to that mission, the board of directors scheduled a special meeting at the home of Jill Waterhouse[43] in the middle of January.

There, over [a] potluck and surrounded by Jill's artwork, we discussed who we are and where we go from here. "The vision thing" has been with us for a while, and the debate over who is an independent scholar and what constitutes independent scholarship has been with us since we were founded. The discussion went beyond abstractions to talk about some of the specifics of what we mean to our members and how we fit in with our community.

What I took away from the meeting was a sense that we serve both the community of independent scholars and the larger community in which we live. The Forum has long recognized the value of assisting independent scholars with access to information, networking, and ways to share their understanding with the general public. Some belong simply for the library lending privilege, some for the discussion groups, and some because of our public programs. For many, we serve a role simply by validating independent scholarship as a legitimate activity and being an independent scholar as a legitimate identity.

The term "independent scholar" scares a lot of people away from joining us because they think of themselves as either not a scholar ("I don't have a Ph.D.") or not independent ("I work for an educational institution"). I even tossed around the idea that we should try to change our name into something like the "Minnesota Interacting Scholars' Forum" or the "Lifelong Learners Forum," but the name is less important than our actions.

Our members' activities are not merely a pale imitation of what takes place inside academic institutions. Scholarly independence does not automatically imply opposition to the academy, or unemployment. We are by no means just some sort of ad-hoc, unemployed post-doc club, as I think we are sometimes seen by those who don't know us. Rather, the highly diverse backgrounds and activities of our members are the organization's special strength. I would not want to diminish that diversity by too narrow a definition of independent scholarship.

To me, living one's beliefs requires both learning and teaching. While I strongly believe in rewarding scholars for their labors, the formal systems for education have often gotten in the way of both learning and teaching. I hope to build on our strength by encouraging as much intellectual exchange between our members as possible, and by identifying and recruiting promising new members to join us.

In our successful effort to win not-for-profit status as a 501(c)(3) organization, we have been doing a great deal of programming for the general public over the past few years. We plan to continue with such programs. I also intend to work with the board to identify how best to connect with the many other organizations with which we share some common goals and objectives. Our cosponsorship of programs with the Science Museum of Minnesota and with Women Historians of the Midwest are only two examples of this sort of cooperation.

Independent scholars are also being recognized as role models demonstrating an active approach to information that others would do well to emulate. At a recent Metronet symposium on "Information Literacy," the fate of our democracy was said to rest on the cultivation in the citizenry of an active approach to information and a pattern of life-long learning that includes informed community discussion of ideas and issues. The *Utne Reader*'s latest issue trumpeted the rebirth of the "salon" as a path to reviving the discussion of ideas in the community. I am beginning to suspect that our Forum was just a little ahead of its time and that we can look forward to considerable growth in the years ahead. Someday we may well get to the size that will allow us to have our own office and hire staff to support the Forum's programs and to undertake new programs. I would like to work in that direction, but growing to that stage puts quite a burden on everyone volunteering their efforts, including me. I ask for your assistance, patience, and understanding as we manage to do what we can to make our dreams for the Forum come true.

Wiggins Writes a Five-Year Plan

In July 1991, Wiggins further elaborated his ideas in a five-year plan which called for increasing the membership and seeking grants to support an administrative assistant. He also hoped to reestablish the "Independent Scholar of the Year" award, provide fiscal agency and mentors for scholars, and eventually rent office space and hire support staff.[44]

During Wiggins's tenure as president, the Scholars sponsored several timely programs, including several on the Gulf War, which caused Wiggins to wonder whether the IRS might possibly restrict MISF's tax-exempt status for discussing political issues. There were also programs on Women's History and Ethnic Adaptation.[45] It is worth stating that many of these programs were sponsored in conjunction with other organizations, such as Women Historians of the Midwest, Macalester College, and the Minnesota Historical Society. Five study groups were active during this time: Science and Humanities, Intercultural Diversity, Chaos & Complexity, Patterns in Women & Spirituality, and 18th &19th Century Study.

In his Winter 1992 editorial, Wiggins, writing on Super Bowl Sunday, reflected that one in seven persons worldwide would tune into TV that day. At the same time, the unique voices of a much smaller number of scholars would be condemned to obscurity. He continued:

> [I]ndependent scholars need to do two things to better connect their ideas to others. First, we need to value what it is that we know, credit the idea that we can communicate with others, and believe that it might do the world some good for us to do so. Secondly, to avoid frustration about ignorance, we need to cherish the value of the traffic in ideas that takes place off of the main "information highways" (or streams if we want to avoid mixing metaphors). The small press, the cable television show, the art exhibition, the computer bulletin board, the discussion group, and the simple dialogue with another person are small, but nonetheless valuable, ways to communicate with the world outside of our studies.[46]

In the same issue, Ginny Hansen gave her reflections on what the Scholars meant to her. Hansen, an editor, medical writer, and poet, had been a member of the Scholars since the first days of the organization. She served on numerous committees, and was especially helpful in arranging programs. This piece, which reflects the enthusiasm of a longtime, faithful member, gives an accurate picture of what the organization was doing in 1992—and what, to a large extent, it still does. It is worth noting that Hansen points out that MISF was not particularly good about having regular meetings, but that the organization did seem to be able to get newsletters out once in a while.[47]

A Scholar Writes

A Charter Member Reflects on Benefits
Ginny Hansen, 1992

My first benefits from the Minnesota Forum were the suggestions that one should pursue knowledge—even contribute to it or examine what it is—independently of faculty agendas and institutional priorities, and that there can be forums for collegial exchange "outside of walls." It is easy, once past a plotted course of study, to feel that only those "in departments" advance one's field of study. In my field (English), such folks teach necessary courses, over and over, and research whatever topic gets sanctioned or funded by somebody—rarely can they explore what simply fires their curiosity.

These revolutionary thoughts were nurtured by MISF programs. Scholars of the Year validated a new vision not only in their addresses but by example—performance scholarship! and community-based history, architecture, politics, even archeology (I had not known Minnesota had either archeologists or sites!). Presenters told about ancient philosophers who were women; questioned the tenets of physics (holy cow!); showed how dance could embody a national approach to government; [and] told how to connect with 300 small publishers, 130 libraries, book fairs, readings, and groups that regularly sponsor lectures. Rarely were the topics "in my field," but that didn't prevent their approaches and even much of the subject matter from striking sparks in my own mind and work.

Attending a Study Group

Somewhere along in here I was privileged to attend a study group. In the latter, I found a changing mix of people in various fields, interested in a topic that might not be discussed in institutions but is much mulled over in private—in this case, the interplay of the sciences and the humanities. This group continues to modulate through ranks of people representing not only diverse formal trainings but deep private thinking in directions I would never have discovered alone. Discussion varies as each book attracts or fails to interest individuals, but constants have included (1) new vistas of bibliography previously unknown to me (with recommendations sometimes by the authors themselves); (2) feedback on how my reception of that book compares to its reception by readers in other fields; (3) discussion that often never gets to the book but explores the questions it suggests. This Sciences/Humanities study group once had an all-day retreat and still never got through all the tangential topics to explore.

Sciences/Humanities so stimulated my thinking that I thought I'd just sit in on another group as it formed, even though I knew zilch about the topic, and it wasn't pertinent to anything I'd ever done—"just go and listen," I thought; learn about chaos theory. I'm still in the Chaos group, too, regularly counting my blessings as I not only see computer screens full of new worlds of mathematical art and hear Nobel laureates and other pioneers in person, but also converse with people who have become local experts called on by our Science Museum. Even I have published on this subject I intended to "audit."

Hansen Joins the MISF Board
I next joined the MISF Board and became [even more] active. There has been much hard-won progress in bylaws, 501(c)(3) registration, bulk-mailing and networking rosters, library privileges and interfaces, and cosponsorship with many other groups to whom we are now a presence. Through it all, our newsletter has become quarterly and attracts hard work from editors, designers, and fundraisers. (I would love to see

it become a full journal with original articles, but for now it would be great to get more submissions from members.) Our programs have sometimes managed to be monthly and are always fascinating and unique. (Where would Minnesota be if no one presented these unique facets?) I learned that we are one of eight such organizations in the United States (the largest, most active, most diverse—arts, sciences, and social sciences—and most accessible; the only group between Yale and L.A.!)—and that a national organization publishes a newsletter out of Berkeley. I learned that we have a dynamic and unique perspective on the definition of independent scholarship, one that differs from that of a published study on "independent scholars"; the latter would acknowledge few of our members and little of our broader implications for study itself.

But our work has just begun. We have a copy machine and a scanner; we borrow a phone and an address; but we have no space for members to use equipment, meet, or study. Cosponsors, grants, and friends have donated for our programs, our early awards, and our newsletters, but we have not yet mounted concerted financing efforts and are just beginning to explore possibilities for assisting members to get research funds, exchange information (both in person and in print and online), and present their findings (so far, mostly in public programs.) Needs range from the simple (copy paper, volunteers to phone about upcoming programs scheduled) to the complex (fundraising, office and meeting spaces) and we need your input.

Call a board member—regularly.

Why the Scholars?

As a longtime editor of the *Forum*, the author of this book is inclined to add a personal reflection in this place. Hansen's article (quoted above) was intended to be the first in a series on "the meaning of MISF." Although the series did not run for long, it did inspire a second article.

This second article of the series on the meaning of the Scholars was "Building the Noosphere" by Curt Hillstrom.[48] As previously stated, Hillstrom has been a member of the Scholars since 1986, when he wrote "The Role of the Independent Scholars' Forum" (see chapter 2). Here is another take on what it means to be a scholar.

A Scholar Writes

Building the Noosphere
Curt Hillstrom, 1992

I didn't quit my job to be a scholar. I quit for other reasons. I had been working as a systems analyst, designing a database for a small distillery in Kentucky. Every day I would go to work and face [company and distillery] management that would serve Tom Peters, guru of excellence in business, as [a] good bad [example]. Eventually, the distillery's entire data-processing department management was replaced, and the company I worked for had their contract terminated. But I was already gone by then. My story here, however, is not to tell about my leaving, but to explain why I never went back to work in the traditional sense.

Deciding to return to the very basics, I spent time trying to decide what I really wanted to do. I had majored in philosophy in college, but being a philosopher was not a practical consideration. What I really wanted was to understand just what sort of universe we inhabit and how we ought to live our lives. But isn't that what a philosopher does? I gave in. After all, why should I give up what's most important to me to spend what I believed was my only lifetime helping distillers keep track of their data? So philosopher it was. But what does a philosopher do? I could spend thousands of dollars and go back to school for several years, possibly getting a Ph.D., in order to be qualified for a questionable job market. And what about my wife and kids?

The solution wasn't easy. Being a house-husband requires a cooperative wife who is just as delighted to go to work outside the home as she is to stay home. In making these decisions and accepting the considerable constraints of two kids, the care of a house, attendance at PTA and committee meetings, [and unsureness as to] how to go about this, my career path has seemed to meander. I have had my successes: Sunday school classes that worked, meetings in which I clarified terms and concepts that created solutions, and my own philosophical epiphanies. Unfortunately, failures have been at least as frequent; half-finished projects clutter my desk.

Then one day, shortly after we returned to Minnesota, I ran across a MISF brochure. I wish that I could say that the Forum has transformed my life, enriched my knowledge, and led to planes of discernment I had never imagined before. And it could do that, someday. But what I found, when I joined the Forum, was an organization still learning to walk. We can take too long responding to people [and] occasionally lose track of members, and our publicity can consist of some posters put up a few days before an event. Still, I belong. I belong because the Forum's mission is consistent with my own: to learn and to teach. And the Forum is learning to walk: fundamental things are going on that will enable us to better support those who choose to be independent scholars.

Teilhard de Chardin postulated a 'noosphere,' a realm of reality beyond the biosphere which has been created by human culture and largely consists of all that we know, and which will eventually lead to the conclusive evolutionary step that will integrate everything into a mystical vision of finality. While I'm not big on mystical visions, I like the idea of the building of the noosphere, in which I think the Forum has an important role to play. Not only are there philosophers in the computer industry, there are poets doing construction, artists in the secretarial pool, historians in the boardroom, each doing their equivalent of distillery data bases.

While the Forum and I lurch about trying to do what we are trying to do, we are, in our infinitesimal way, adding to a noosphere which, if it will lead anywhere, can only be somewhere good.

Wiggins's Term Ends; Robert Thimmesh Becomes President

David Wiggins's term as president came to an end in the winter of 1992 as he left to become program manager for the Saint Anthony Falls interpretive program. Wiggins was succeeded by Robert Thimmesh. Thimmesh, a real estate investment manager, art gallery owner, and writer, had been a member of the Scholars since 1983. He had been an occasional member of the board.

Introducing himself in his first presidential message, Thimmesh offered a perspective on education and its meaning and value:

> As Forum members, we generally place a high value on education, as it is a significant aspect of our status as independent scholars. We tend to give credence, however, to a wider range of education and educational values than does the educational establishment.[49]

In January of 1993, at Thimmesh's first meeting, the Scholars adopted a brief statement of purpose: "The Minnesota Independent Scholars'

Forum is a non-profit organization formed to encourage and promote inquiry, research, discussion, writing, and publication by independent scholars."[50] This statement is an abbreviated version of a longer statement of purpose which has been part of the bylaws (although somewhat edited from time to time) from the beginning of the organization. Its current form can be found in chapter 7.

In this same issue of *The Forum,* writing about the tenth anniversary of the founding of MISF, Brian Mulhern, the archivist of the Scholars, summarized the first ten years of the organization's life, and made a comment that shows the Scholars' self-awareness. After describing the awarding and distribution of the NWAF grant, Mulhern observed:

> ... the major project outcome [of the NWAF grant] was deemed to be refinement of the notion of independent scholarship. Through matching-fund requirements, the Northwest Area Foundation funding marshaled over $200,000 of resources for individuals engaged in significant scholarly work without benefit of full-time support from academic institutions.[50]

That is, the organization that might have replaced the academy instead became a parallel to the academy. This identity crisis is also implied in Bob Thimmesh's presidential editorial in the autumn of 1993, when Thimmesh and Harold Orlans, editor of the publication of the National Coalition of Independent Scholars, had an exchange of letters about the meaning of independent scholarship. Orlans seems to have insisted that a Ph.D., or publication, was necessary to demonstrate "scholarship." Thimmesh used his epistolary exchange with Orlans as the basis for his president's message and in so doing added further definition to the Minnesota version of independent scholarship.[51] It is important to note here that Thimmesh is defining MISF as something different from academic scholarship; articulating this difference was an important step in the evolution of the organization.

A Scholar Writes

President's Message
Robert Thimmesh, 1993

I wish to talk about independent scholars and speculate on why we desire to be associated with a group call MISF. These thoughts are prompted, in part, by a letter of inquiry I received from Harold Orlans, the new editor of the *Independent Scholar,* the quarterly national publication for independent scholars. Harold is responding to a comment I made in a questionnaire sent out by the national group seeking information about independent scholars' groups around the country not formally affiliated with the national group, groups such as ours. I stated (with the Board's concurrence) that I thought the national group (NCIS) had an excessively narrow focus which excludes independents, and that they did not seem to have an independent approach to scholarship.

Insofar as our discussion of scholarship and scholars is usually done in the context of the American university system it seems appropriate, perhaps necessary, to consider independent scholars in relation to this context. It seems to me that an independent scholar may be independent institutionally, culturally, and methodologically. Institutional independence usually hinges on employment—whether or not one is employed by a university or college. Methodology is about doing scholarly research and writing—accepting, and using, those standard scholarly methods which have been accepted and institutionalized by academia. Culture encompasses the overarching system of values through which we assess the methodology, the standards, and the institutions. This value system may become self-referential by introspectively examining the culture and its values.

Independent scholars may work for a university, and they may use many (perhaps all) of the methodologies used by the academy. I believe independent scholars are distinguished from academic scholars primarily along cultural lines, by the values adhered to and believed in. (I am not talking about those scholars who may be marking time on their journey to academia by joining an independent scholars' group, but who in their hearts subscribe to the academy's values.) It seems to me that independents differ (thus making concrete the label "independent") from academics by accepting and utilizing scholarly methodology outside the standardized canon institutionalized by the academy, and by explicit recognition that beliefs and values, including feelings and other emotional states, play an important part in scholarship and the pursuit of truth.

I do not think the academy's pursuit of truth is wrong, but that their pursuit is not the whole story, contrary to the academy's beliefs. The academy is generally uncomfortable talking about beliefs, theirs or others', unless it is a "rational analysis" of belief; they do not like to accept the reality of belief on its own terms. Thus, the Forum welcomes artists and writers, two groups not usually considered to be scholars by the academy, as well as others who consider themselves to be scholars. The idea of scholarship is an open concept, in a constant state of change and evolution. We are reluctant to impose boundaries, which tend to be exclusive by definition, and we like to believe that scholarship is where you find it, sometimes in surprising places. This approach tends to be inclusive.

It may be objected that such an inclusive approach, because it imposes no standards of scholarship, includes a lot of second-rate work. This may be true, but all of the work should be evaluated on its merits without a priori assumptions that a work will be inferior before the work is examined. Adopting standards is no guarantee of superior scholarship—witness the large amount of second-rate scholarship by members of academia. Whether there is a larger amount of second-rate scholarship from independents or from academics is a factual question and a matter of degree. One hurdle faced in deciding this question revolves around defining "second-rate," a question intimately connected with the values brought to the table of analysis.

My comment that the national group was excessively narrow and not particularly independent was focusing on this cultural aspect. It seems to me that they are unduly concerned with having the proper credentials, an exclusionary viewpoint, although they claim advanced degrees are unnecessary as a condition of membership. The national group appears to have adopted the values of the academy, thus distinguishing themselves from the academy primarily by their name and perhaps by their employment.

Now I have no objection to the NCIS's concept of independent scholarship. But it seems to be a limited viewpoint, unable or unwilling to contemplate a broader perspective. It is unfortunate, since not only does NCIS handcuff itself, but the resulting organization tends to look like the academic organization, except that it is not such an institution. It tends to look like a pale imitation of the real thing.

Thimmesh Establishes Fiscal Agency for MISF Members

Midway through his term as president, in early 1994, Thimmesh set several goals for the organization.[52] Among these goals was cooperating with a virtual university, hosting Forum programs at coffee houses, publication of a quarterly "date certain" newsletter, and a semi-annual journal. Tom Abeles, a futurist and founder of Metanet,[53] was appointed editor of the journal, which lasted one season. As will be seen, the quick rise of the internet and electronic communication basically changed the scope of newsletters and the need for them.

By all accounts, Thimmesh's most far-reaching achievement was the establishment of a fiscal agency account for MISF members with National City Bank. Through this account, members are able to receive grant money from agencies which require a 501(c)(3) administrator for granted funds. This membership benefit has proven to be a lasting boon both to members and to the organization of the scholars. Fiscal agency has brought legitimacy to independent scholarship and new members to MISF. Further information about fiscal agency can be found in chapter 9.

In December 1994, Thimmesh wrote a letter announcing the formation of two new study groups: Religion and Culture, to be run by Curt Hillstrom and Susan Smith, and Philosophy, to be run by Hillstrom and Thimmesh.[54]

One of the things that is fascinating in writing a history such as this one is to watch the world through the lens of the organizational details on which one is concentrating. Thus, we have watched the rise of women in leadership roles, concerns about government policies, and the advent of personal computers. And now we see, clearly, the rise of the internet. The May 1994 issue of the *Forum* is full of articles about the internet: "Surfing the Internet," "The Meta Net Connection," and "Internet Marginalia." Even the President's Column (moved to page 4 in the new layout) is entirely addressed to the "electronic age":

> The technology will not make a good writer out of a poor one (although some spelling may improve), it will not deliver a "eureka" (the flashing lightbulb signifying an intellectual breakthrough), but it may deliver you more time in which to become a good writer or to have an "eureka" attack.[55]

Notes for Chapter 3

34 Smith, Susan, Independent Scholarship Enters a New Era, *The Forum* 1, no. 1, Spring 1989.

35 Bennett, James, Independent Scholars: An Interim Report, *The Forum* 1, no. 2, Summer 1989.

36 Sween,Roger, Librarians and Independent Scholarship, *The Forum* 1, no. 3, Fall 1989.

37 Smith, Susan, Message from the President, *The Forum* 2, no. 2, Winter 1990.

38 *The Forum*, Winter 1990.

39 *The Forum* 2, no. 1, Winter 1990. Claire McInerney taught information management at St. Kate's; John Wickre was a manuscript cataloger at MNHS; David Shupe was a reference librarian and an administrator at Control Data.

40 Ibid.

41 Message from the President, *The Forum* 2, no. 2, Spring 1990.

42 Message from the President, *The Forum* 3, no. 1, Spring 1991.

43 Jill Waterhouse is a sculptor and 3-D installation artist. She brought a unique voice to the board in the years that she served.

44 Wiggins, David, Scholars' Forum Five Year Plan, July 1, 1991. Manuscript in MISF files.

45 T*he Forum* 3, no. 3, Fall 1991.

46 President's Message, The Distant Voice of Scholarship, *The Forum* 4, no. 1, Winter 1992.

47 *The Forum* 4, no. 1, Winter 1992.

48 *The Forum* 4, no. 2, Summer 1992.

49 *The Forum* 5, nos 1&2, Winter/ Spring 1993.

50 Ibid.

51 *The Forum* 5, no. 3, Autumn 1993.

52 President's Column, *The Forum*, May 1994.

53 *The Forum* 6, no. 2, May 1994. Abeles described "Metanet as a node on the Internet. In actuality, it is a seminar or conferencing system."

54 Letter from Thimmesh to membership, December 14, 1994.

55 *The Forum* 6, no. 2, May 1994.

CHAPTER 4

Growing Pains (1996–2000)

Ross Corson Wants to Go "Back to Basics"

Ross Corson became president of the Scholars in 1995. Corson was a writer and reporter connected with Metronet and the Minnesota Center for the Book. In his president's message in February 1995,[56] Corson said that he wanted to go "back to basics." Corson proposed that the newsletter be published on a quarterly schedule. (The idea of a newsletter and a journal had evaporated and the newsletter had returned to a 12-page format.) Corson also proposed one or two major public programs a year (possibly in cooperation with other organizations). He also initiated the idea of Works-in-Progress talks, which would allow independent scholars to discuss their work "with a thoughtful group of people." At the time of Corson's writing, three Works-in-Progress talks had been scheduled. Works-in-Progress talks have remained an occasional feature of MISF programming.

In the same issue (2/95), Tom Abeles, the editor of the *Forum*, said that he hoped to have "this newsletter appear in cyberspace as well as hard copy [...] The newsletter needs its members to create [a] virtual reality lens for their colleagues and the larger community."

Controversies in the *Forum*

If the internet was a preoccupation of the first issue of Volume 7 of the

Forum, history and historical accuracy were the focus of issues 2 and 3. These editions appeared in the wake of Newt Gingrich's takeover of the Republican leadership of the House of Representatives and what Corson called "terminal amnesia" about the social mechanisms of the past. In this milieu, the *Forum* published a long article (actually a speech for the American Society for State and Local History) about the necessity for truth-telling in museum exhibits and the importance of knowing the context of the items being exhibited. Carolyn Gilman, director of exhibits and design at the Missouri Historical Society, described the dilemma posed by the application of political correctness. Her summary said:

> [Museum professionals] are paid to analyze and contextualize, to supply perspective and explanation, to represent the true complexity of the past . . . to exercise intellectual authority. If we abdicate that, we are faced with a Pandora's box. Once the science museum discards the scientific method as the criterion of truth, it can't say no when the creationists come knocking on the door. Once the history museum agrees to censor history to spare one group's feelings, it can't say no to the people who deny the Holocaust."[57]

The Scholars continued the historical theme into Vol. 7, no. 3 of the *Forum*, when it reported on a conference jointly sponsored by MISF and the Minnesota Historical Society. The main speaker was Arthur Naftalin, a former mayor of Minneapolis. He addressed the subject of revolutions under the title "30s, 60s, 90s: A Century of Revolution?" (This speech is quoted in full in chapter 10 of this book.) He characterized the 1930s as a period of communitarianism, the 1960s as a period of plebiscitarianism, and the 1990s as a period of individualism. Wise politician that he was, Naftalin was unwilling to predict the future. The rest of this edition of the *Forum* was filled with enthusiastic and cautionary remarks about the "Internet" (still being capitalized, by the way).[58] In spite of financial inducements, the Forum was not able to muster enough members to take advantage of a special offer for organizational internet connection. At this time, the Forum had just under 100 members.

Throughout this controversial period, several people in the Scholars kept working at the basic task of setting up, promoting, and nurturing study groups, which had been a mainstay of the organization since its beginning. A long article by Curt Hillstrom in February 1996 reported that there were three study groups in operation: Philosophy (the "oldest"), Religion and Culture, and Science and Humanities. The article concluded with information on how to start your own study group. [59]

David Juncker Continues Works-in-Progress Programs

Ross Corson resigned from the presidency in the fall of 1996 to pursue an out-of-town job opportunity. David Juncker, the vice president, finished Corson's term. Juncker encouraged and expanded the works-in-progress initiative. Juncker was an academic physiologist and a freelance consultant to many institutions. With the assistance of several board members, Juncker got out a short newsletter, organized an annual meeting, and developed programs. In addition, several fiscal agency requests were reviewed and the decision was made that MISF could not administer more than two grants a year without administrative help. Juncker also initiated the formation of a functioning, working board with regular meetings.

At the close of 1997, at the end of his term, David Juncker wrote a reflective president's report that summarized the accomplishments of the organization. Although Juncker felt that his particular concern was with establishing works-in-progress programs, it is notable that he also discussed the survival of MISF in terms of numbers and dollars. This article serves as a useful summary of where the Scholars had been.

A Scholar Writes

Support of Independent Scholars: An Eight-Year Journey
David Juncker, 1997[60]

As a longtime member of the Minnesota Independent Scholars' Forum it has been my privilege to have served on the Board of Directors for eight years. In leaving the presidency and board duties (our bylaws, wisely, limit continuous board participation to eight years), it seems a good time to reflect on our voyage together.

Lucy Brusic and I joined the board at roughly the same time. We both wished to help maintain a strong newsletter, to support programs providing timely information and mental stimulation, and to institute an active fiscal agency service that would enable members to obtain larger outside grants. We both felt that the future for MISF was tied as much to grants, computers, and well-researched and reported information as it had been to ready access to area libraries and private collections.

The Board under Susan Margot Smith and David Wiggins helped me gain an appreciation for perseverance. Change, no matter how necessary, seems to take a bit of time to accomplish. The newsletter regained its place as a major organ of the Scholars, due mostly to Ms. Brusic's efforts, and we moved on to try to design a new journal. Later, as personnel changed, we had to face the task of rebuilding the newsletter once again (the journal had to be shelved). I'm happy to report that under the care of editor Helen Watkins the newsletter has been revitalized.

The Bob Thimmish and Ross Corson boards were instrumental in defining a practical fiscal agency policy while enlarging the study groups, and initiating the Works-in-Progress project while broadening the lecture series, respectively. Speaker/Panel discussions were re-instituted, and we began to use more public locations in both Minneapolis and St. Paul.

When, mid-term, Mr. Corson faced an imminent move East, I was asked to pick up the reins. We focused our efforts toward a monthly working board, strengthening the successful "Works-In-Progress" program, announcing the fiscal agency support program, and building membership.

Officer and Board Committees' duties and responsibilities were reviewed and further developed in order to more easily understand and complete the annual Forum work. Curt Hillstrom completed the first computerized member data base and mailing list, which made mailings much easier and member interests more readily available to board and members alike. John Bessler continued to provide lecture/works-in-progress programs of interest to members and the community at large, mixing St. Paul and Minneapolis sites.

As 1997 began, it was evident that MISF fiscal agency, with a required lecture or Works-in-Progress presentation, might prove useful to the wider community. We began to get referrals from Metro area granting agencies as well as member interest. Within a very short time, the first two grants with MISF fiscal agency were successfully submitted and initiated. Ms. Brusic, as treasurer, and I formed a separate financial accounting system and divided the advisory function between us. An independent advisory committee, reporting to the board, is being considered to take us to the next level as we seek to build fiscal agency from two to six or eight contracts per year.

Roger Hammer, as Publicity Chair, began to develop a more

comprehensive MISF publicity program than we had seen in years. Roger has completed a demographic questionnaire which will soon be sent to all members. The board also located a lecture site at the Uptown Walker Library that has proved useful in attracting non-members. The challenge will be to translate the increased publicity and public awareness of MISF into a larger membership.

In the near future, I feel, we must keep our newsletter and programming as strong as possible. Overcoming annual ups and downs has proved difficult for us in the past. The continued emphasis on fiscal agency services and the works-in-progress series can position us well for a future in which more and more grant work is performed by independent scholars. The striking increase in government grants going to independent scholars over the last few years is a fact. Many recipients are from our region. It may be time to again review membership in NClS (the National Coalition of Independent Scholars) in a way that lets us connect more readily with other independent scholars and potential independent scholars. Several of our members are already involved nationally, attending regional and national NCIS conferences.

I'm excited by the opportunities facing us; I know Ms. Brusic and I are interested in supporting the board by continuing to work with MISF fiscal agent grant recipients. It will be interesting to see how well we as an organization continue to adapt and grow.

Pat McDonough Redefines Newsletter

Pat McDonough succeeded Juncker as president in the winter of 1998. McDonough was a speaker, author, and consultant in the areas of development and banking. One of her goals was to continue to tighten up the operations of the board. In addition, she hoped to encourage more people to attend MISF meetings. Of the 80 or so members of MISF, only a few showed up at public programs.[61] McDonough announced a regular schedule of meetings and advocated for more user-friendly meeting places. (There had been various problems with parking, amenities, and refreshments.) In the summer of 1998, McDonough wrote the first budget for the Scholars.[62]

At the same time, the newsletter was redefined as a journal. Helen Watkins, with training in law and English, became the editor during this redefinition. She employed a layout professional and announced themes in advance. Elevating the journal from a newsletter was a significant accomplishment; at least one major regional publisher said that he read the MISF journal to find possible writers for a future book-publishing agenda.[63]

In late 1998, MISF applied for and received a network grant from the Minnesota Humanities Commission. This grant paid for a speaker at the annual meeting, supported the publication of the expanded journal, and enabled the Scholars to set up a website. The website was important for advertising programs and keeping in touch with people who were interested but not formal members of MISF. Although the nature of the website has changed over the years, the Scholars have kept a presence on the web since this time. The web address continues to be mnindependentscholars.org.

National Coalition of Independent Scholars Meets in Twin Cities

In October 1998, the annual conference of the National Coalition of Independent Scholars took place in the Twin Cities. Among the 45 people who attended was a large contingent of MISF members.[64]

Ginny Hansen, loyal member of MISF and dedicated scholar, wrote this engaging report of the National Scholars conference. It is notable for her frank discussion of the fact that many unaffiliated scholars were having trouble pursuing their interests and getting published. The wide geographic spread of the attendees also shows that other groups similar to MISF were in existence.

A Scholar Writes

National Scholars Coalition Conference Held Here
Ginny Hansen, 1998

The 1998 Annual Meeting of the National Coalition of Independent Scholars was held at the Minnesota History Center in St. Paul from Friday, October 2, through Sunday, October 4. About 45 people attended, including an impressive contingent from MISF. Alice Schroeder, MISF 1999 Board member, remarked on her delight at making so many new friends. "I felt I was among a lot of people very much like me. Although they were obviously committed to good, thorough scholarship, they were totally approachable, glad to discuss their work and yours."

Registrants were welcomed at dinner Friday by NCIS President Ellen Huppert (San Francisco historian of 19th-century Europe). The keynote speaker was Anne Lowenthal, Ph.D. in Art History from New York City, who talked on "The Star of Independence." Saturday's sessions began with NCIS Past President Patricia Farrant (Iowa City, Iowa, electronic publisher of scholarly journals) moderating a panel called "Independent Scholarship and the Academy: Status Reports." The panel included Toni Vogel Carey (Lansdale, Pennsylvania, author of *It's Only Logical: Your Old Habits Won't Tell You How to Change Your Old Habits*). Her talk was on "The Noble Legacy (and Present Eclipse) of Independent Scholarship." Alice Goldfarb Marquis, Ph.D. (LaJolla, California, author of five books on 20th-century

American culture) talked on "Scholarship: Navigating a World in Chaos." Jean Cameron of Minneapolis (University of Minnesota, CLA analyst of college entrance assessments) asked, "Do Independent Scholars Know Something the Rest of Higher Education Doesn't?"

Alice Schroeder said Ms. Cameron's talk underlined interesting trends related to her own work: (1) flexible degree programs for adults with jobs; (2) more program control for older students and ethnic minorities; (3) more specifically job-oriented degrees; (4) an increase in "distance learning"; and (5) evidence that demands for change will be initiated by the public, not by the colleges; e.g. welfare-to-work training, self-determined degree programs, interdisciplinary programs, and lifelong learning. Saturday continued with two concurrent sessions. Nela Schleuning (Mendota Heights, Minnesota, author of books on Meridel LeSueur and the Hormel strike) handled "Transitions and Balancing Acts," a panel which included Jane Ford, Ph.D. (LaJolla, California, in publishing) on "Making It in Two Worlds: Developing the Strategies"; Bill Engel (Nashville, Tennessee, author of *Slips of Thought* and *Education and Anarchy*), on "Let No One Belong to Another Who Can Belong to Himself"; and Joanne Lafler (founding member of NCIS, theater-historian and author) on "The Biographer as Participant in the Story: Writing the Life of My Husband's Father."

Session II late Saturday morning was moderated by our Rhoda Lewin, Ph.D., (author of *Witnesses to the Holocaust* and *The Reform Jews of Minneapolis*). The panel was called "What Are We Doing? (Individual Research Reports)". Presenters were Herbert Posner (Durham, North Carolina, NIH biochemist/pharmacologist, and degreed city/regional planner) and Isabel Samfield (Durham, North Carolina, music teacher) on

"Creative Inquirers: The Poetry of Scientists"; Georgia Wright (Berkeley, California, medieval art historian/videographer) on "A Pamphleteer in the French Revolution"; and Yaffa Claire Draznin (Chicago, Illinois, researcher, author, and compiler of correspondence of Olive Schreiner and Havelock Ellis), who asked "But What Did She Do All Day? The Life of the Middle-Class Matron in Late Victorian London."

Concurrent sessions Saturday afternoon began with one on Virtual World Interactions, moderated by Margaret DeLacy, Ph.D. (a founder of NCIS, President of the Northwest Independent Scholars Association in Portland, Oregon, and webmaster for NCIS, working on a book on contagion in 18th-century England). Presenters were Thomas Jepson (Chapel Hill, North Carolina, telecommunications systems engineer/historian, NCIS Board member, and biographer of Ma Kiley), who spoke on "Deconstructing the Global Village: Scholarship in the Information Age"; and Laura Garces, Ph.D. (Washington, D.C., author, self-employed in international affairs), who focused on "Globalization and Violence."

"Scholarly Publishing and the Tiger Traps Along the Way" was moderated by Yaffa Claire Draznin. Panelists were Elizabeth Welt Trahan (Amherst, Massachusetts, retired scholar in German literature) on "Kafka's Castle Revisited: Finding a Publisher for My Holocaust Memoir"; Rhoda Lewin on "The Good, the Bad, and the Indifferent of Getting Published"; and William Murphy (editor at University of Minnesota Press) on "If It Is Good, It Will Be Published."

Late Saturday afternoon, our own MISF presented "Mind Games" (a "scholarly pursuit" game). June Dale (food research & development and writer) worked up some advance publicity. Roger Hammer (independent publisher) kept score, while Alice Schroeder (the Bakken Museum) and George Anderson (chemist and Shakespeare scholar) were judges of answers. Cheryl Dickson, Executive Director of the Minnesota Humanities Commission, moderated. Over 20 participants had a grand, fun time, and many prizes were awarded. A concurrent session, "What We Are Doing: Reports of Individual Research," was moderated by Catherine Reed (St. Paul entomologist, prairie conservationist). Presenters were Jeane Olson (Washington, DC), "Some Spiritual Aspects of E.M. Forster's Disbelief"; and Edith Ehrlich, Ph.D. (Amherst, Massachusetts, Philosophy/German Literature), "Choice Under Duress: Jewish Councils During the Nazi Period."

The conference ended with two sessions on Sunday morning. The first, "Constraints and Realities," was moderated by Elizabeth Trahan and presented Paul Finkelman (Akron, Ohio, legal historian and coauthor of a constitutional history of the U.S.) on "Independent Scholarship and Academic Freedom—A Conundrum"; Charles Shrader (Carlisle, Pennsylvania) on "Problems of Intellectual Property"; and Patricia Farrant on "The Scholarly Journal in the Digital Age." Session II was a "Conversation with the NCIS Executive Board," moderated by President Ellen Huppert, designed to encourage voicing of concerns, questions, and suggestions.

Due to family responsibilities, Pat McDonough did not run for a second term and was out of office before the network grant given by the Humanities Commission in 1998 was completed. In order to avoid a repeat of the problem of the grantees leaving before the grant was completed, the date of the annual meeting was amended in the bylaws from the last quarter of the year to the second quarter of the year (that is, from November/December to May/June) and the terms of board members were staggered.[65] The grant evaluation submitted to the Minnesota Humanities Commission noted under Other Comments: "We would like to say that the difficulties caused by having the project manager/president decide not to run for office before completing the terms of the grant have caused us to revise our bylaws to create better continuity for the organization."[66]

George Anderson Tries to Increase Membership

George Anderson was elected president in late 1998. Anderson is a freelance chemist with a special interest in the Periodic Table of Elements and an avocational interest in the authorship of the Shakespeare canon. Anderson stated his objectives for the Scholars in his first president's article.[67] He was especially concerned with issues of academic and intellectual freedom, and with the rise of the political conservative right.

A Scholar Writes

Reckoning MISF's Past With its Present
George Anderson, 1999

It is an honor to be elected President of the Minnesota Independent Scholars' Forum. I trust my service in 1999 will match in some ways the expectations of those who attended the Forum's November annual meeting. Personally, I have found calm dedication in MISF members, order in its records, cooperation from previous board members (notably past-President Pat McDonough), and a sound financial base on which to grow.

Treasurer Curt Hillstrom has summarized MISF's membership trends and expenses over the past several years, and this data appear in the graph below.

A History of the Minnesota Independent Scholars' Forum

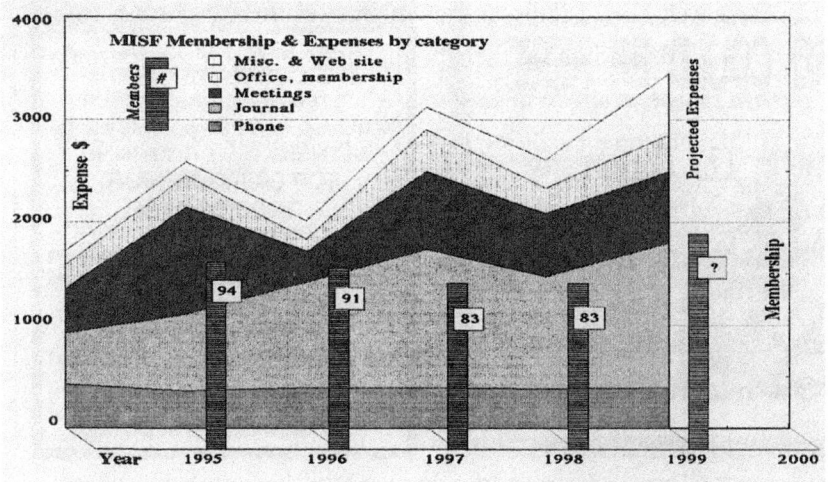

Using data supplied by Curt Hillstrom, George Anderson graphed trends in membership and expenses in early 1999. Noting that expenses were not the real problem, he challenged members to try to increase the membership numbers which had been falling.

Membership "bars" are important to notice. Our numbers have gradually declined, dropping off 10 percent over the past four years. This trend needs to be reversed, and I think we can do it. MISF expenses, however, have been growing over the years, primarily due to (1) cost of increase in the size and quality of the journal and (2) cost for the anticipated website in 1999. These two investments, in the journal (the *Forum*) and in a website, should help attract new members. Both items were included in a 1998 grant from the Minnesota Humanities Commission, and this grant is allowing our operating 1999 budget to stay in the black. Our savings account, approximately three thousand dollars, is roughly the size of our annual budget. As a friend from Lake Wobegon might say, "That's not so bad."

The challenge to MISF may not be in our size (though membership needs to grow), nor are we stymied by a budget; the challenge lies in addressing the obvious, coming to know what we do best, and then doing it. MISF members are known to have well-honed skills, and many have claims to scholars' trophies. We read about their publications in the MISF journal. We saw an example in October, when we hosted a conference of the National Coalition of Independent Scholars. Yes, we all have heard notable lectures by members. But the tougher questions are: Why should new members join? What sets MISF apart from other Minnesota organizations? How do we define ourselves, in terms both of what we are for and of what we are against? What does "independence" mean to us?

In the broader sense of identity, I feel the Forum's "independence" hearkens back to a long established sanguine guard against institutional orthodoxy, against the abuse of power, and against "art made tongue-tied by authority" ("Sonnet 66" by Shakespeare). Members of MISF must stand ready to defend and protect scholarship as a flower of liberty, wherever it grows, not only for ourselves but for generations to come. In pursuing original work, in research and scholarly efforts, authority remains diffuse. It may be subtle or blatant, encoded in software or on the Web, but heedless authority is known to encroach upon those who challenge current thinking and ideas, as well as upon minorities and the powerless. The only moral response to silencing is to provide access to a forum for diverse voices. As scholars, we have rights that come tightly bundled with obligations to those from whom our rights are derived. Shakespeare's "Sonnet 94" was composed about four hundred years ago, but it resonates with today's struggles over issues of power. It presents an image of authority, whose force and essence are expressed in self-containment, in granting to all others the same autonomy of which it itself is the supreme example. As "authors" of our own scholarship, we can have no better model to follow:

They that have power to hurt and will do none,
That do not do the thing they most do show,

Who, moving others, are themselves as stone,
Unmoved, cold, and to temptation slow,
They rightly do inherit heaven's graces
And husband nature's riches from expense;
They are the lords and owners of their faces,
Others but stewards of their excellence.
—William Shakespeare, "Sonnet 94"

Reckoning our past with challenges to liberty may be scant framework on which to rest further articles on the "Future of Independence," but we will try. Beginning with this issue of the *Forum*, we will include [. . .] journal articles that cover specific encroachments on intellectual freedom.

New Position on the Board

A new position on the board under Anderson's leadership was a business editor for the journal. Board member Alice Schroeder was appointed to this position. Schroeder's efforts meant that the budget ran slightly ahead of projections and the journal had tasteful ads (many for bookstores) and article illustrations, both photographic and drawn. For a time, the journal was laid out by a professional designer. (Desktop publishing was not a layman's job as it is today.)

Board Member Ginny Hansen and Editor Helen Watkins coauthored the article "On Nurturing a Flow Chart for Learning" in Watkin's last issue (1999–2000). They offered an impassioned justification for independent scholarship, in light of institutional academia's rigid narrow-mindedness. The specific context was a conference that took place at the University of Minnesota in 1994. In spite of its inviting title, "Knowledges: Production, Distribution, and Revision," the conference was dismissive of independent scholarship groups like MISF.

A Scholar Writes

On Nurturing a Flow Chart for Learning
Ginny Hansen and Helen Watkins, 1999–2000

The social climate has to be prepared before seeds of knowledge can be nurtured to fruition. What then of scientia that does not carry the DNA of an existing discipline, does not function within an acknowledged epistemological institution, and does not structure its rhetoric to address the inquiries/audiences already socialized? Leonardo da Vinci wrote his logs backwards and buried them because he knew the world was not ready to receive them. Today, however, as in Umberto Eco's *The Name of the Rose*, the institutional barricades are being stormed: the public insists on knowing.

The technological revolution, making the internet a more viable tool than printed textbooks (which often cannot be imported, for example, by inquirers in mainland China), challenges the whole idea of a restricted audience of specialized cognoscenti. Knowledge has become, in the age of information, a cache that can be dipped into not only by budding Einsteins, Bohrs, and Feigenbaums, but also by hackers in Silicon Valley, ninth-graders on their school's internet, budding Picassos prior to Gertrude Stein's patronage, and Chinese students taking instruction in "feng shui" as well as in pharmacology.

One can only be trained in yesterday's knowledge. Columbus could not get a federal grant to discover America, only to find China. We cannot "train" Bohr to see quanta nor Picasso to see multiple dimensions. Those storming the barricades of established knowledge from within or without may, however, be able to "train" us to inquire in revolutionary ways after unheard-of knowledge.

A History of the Minnesota Independent Scholars' Forum

One of the ideas behind the Independent Scholars movement in America is that new areas of knowledge require that old wineskins be replaced by vessels that can handle new wine. Often this is a matter of a single, multidisciplinary scholar working on an unfunded fringe or as a retired "éminence grise" who is indulged his bit of old foolishness; or, in many cases, of a scholar working quite outside academia, with funding scrounged from the common work-a-day world.

When in 1994 I read an announcement of a conference, to be held at the University of Minnesota, on "Knowledges: Production, Distribution, Revision," sponsored by the "Group for Research into the Institutionalization Professionalism of Knowledge-Production," it seemed to me that they should hear from an active group such as the Minnesota Independent Scholars' Forum. I thought they would be eager to hear about us and our "knowledge-production." Alas, they were not, for they had no classification for this kind of new wineskin. I don't know what kinds of "new wine" they fancied themselves producing. But I do know that the kinds of new knowledge we in MISF are happily researching were nowhere to be seen among their kinds of "knowledge production": no sociology of the Miao Chinese (Hmong) in original situ, no rediscovered works by women philosophers of ancient Greece, no rediscovery of the crafts of ancient Irish harper/bards, no chaos-science, no radical new 3-D periodic table of chemical elements, no quantum physics of the mind (no brain), no inquiry into how the rocks at Stonehenge were placed, no archaeology of Minnesota, no ornithological influences on Columbus's voyage, no inquiry into the power of choreography in the court of Louis XIV of France, no women poets in colonial America. Progress in all these fields has been presented in programs or study groups by MISF members, but the Ivory Tower apparently will not be interested in them any time soon. Without specific departments to give them context in already delineated fields, these discoveries did not exist for those conferees.

Yet as a member of MISF, I believe passionately not only that they do exist, but that these kinds of inquiries are our future. These researchers' new methods, required by new questions on new materials, will provide the necessary tools for yet-uncatalogued coursework that students will demand, and that academia will then "discover" and teach, as it "discovered" jazz in their music departments 50 years after it had become common knowledge. Knowledge is being produced all the time, outside of "professionalized, institutionalized" structures, as are new tools like the internet.

The Minnesota Independent Scholars' Forum has the capacity to act even more on the cutting edge of knowledge than we have realized. When will the public beat down the doors of academia and demand the processes, not just the products, of thought, the knowledge that is a search as well as an end point? I hope this comes far sooner than Leonardo da Vinci's vision of 500 years into the future. In the meantime, I see MISF, with its public programs and interdisciplinary sharing of questions, doubts, and wonder, as a kind of "first call for help" for inquirers who have a need to know. With luck, our members will cease to be volunteers, and become paid for their ability to navigate toward a continent some have seen only in their dreams.

Rich Thompson Becomes Editor of the Journal

As of the spring of 2000, Rich Thompson, a civil engineer with an interest in craftsmanship and old buildings, was the editor of the journal. He announced an ambitious series of topics for the journal, several of them referring to the idea that the university and education in general were becoming tools for the furtherance of capitalism. This was the era of "online universities" and "virtual degrees."[68] In the same issue, MISF tried to mount a discussion and defense for the teaching of Humanities at the University of Minnesota. The Humanities Department at the University had been phased down to one professor on the grounds that it was interdisciplinary and students could get an overview of Western thought in other departments. The Scholars' initial plan, announced in the spring of 2000 for the fall of 2001, called for four lectures on the place of humanities in liberal arts education.[69]

Nonetheless, by fall, "[f]or a multitude of reasons, MISF [. . .] had to abandon its anticipated four-part program on the humanities as taught at the University of Minnesota." However, the prospectus of the one program that did take place— "Changes in the Citizens' University," by Dr. Ann Pflaum—gives a feeling for the upheaval of the period. Pflaum, the University historian, had written a book, *The University of Minnesota 1945-2000*, based on in-depth interviews with over 200 students, faculty, and staff as well as archival research.[70] She announced that she would speak about "broad cultural changes" such as the influx of students after World War II and the civil rights movement.

George Anderson continued to be president of MISF until the winter of 2000. Under his leadership, further steps were taken toward an MISF website with the registration of a domain name and the possibility of individual webpages. The host for this version of the website was Twin Cities Freenet.

Notes for Chapter 4

56 *The Forum* 7, no. 1 (February 1995).

57 *The Forum* 7, no.2 (August 1995).

58 *The Forum* 7, no. 3 (November 1995).

59 *The Forum* 8, no. 1 (February 1996).

60 *The Forum* 8, no. 3 (Autumn, 1996).

61 *The Forum* 10, no. 1 (Spring 1998).

62 *The Forum* 10, no. 2 (Summer 1998).

63 *The Forum* 10, no. 3 (Autumn 1998). See also Autumn 1997.

64 The National Coalition for Independent Scholars [NCIS] came into being at about the same time that MISF did. MISF has had a long relationship with NCIS, although the membership requirements are different between the two organizations. (See the Thimmesh discussion with Orlans in chapter 3).

65 Bylaws, adopted November 21, 1999.

66 Project Director's Evaluation for Network Grants filed January 14, 2000.

67 *The Forum* 11, no. 1 (Spring 1999).

68 *The Forum* 12, no. 1 (Spring 2000). In April of 2000, the program committee reported to the MISF Board that "The University Administration's polity is one of neglect, hoping the Humanities Program will soon "wither away." (Program committee report April 4, 2000).

69 *The Forum* 12, no.1 (Spring 2000).

70 *The Forum* 12, no. 2 (Fall 2000).

CHAPTER 5

The New Millennium (2001–2004)

Shirley Whiting Emphasizes Collaboration

Shirley Whiting was elected president of the Scholars in the winter of 2000, for the term from January 2001 forward. Whiting, a former teacher and librarian, had been a member of the Scholars for many years and had served in various capacities on the Board.

Whiting's goals as president included increasing membership and creating collaboration with other organizations. The first of these collaborations included sponsoring Philocafes, also called "Coffee with a Scholar." Tom Abeles, a new board member, was the host of the Philocafes. The Scholars also embarked on long-range planning with Alice Schroeder as the chairperson of the committee. On the other hand, the editor of the journal resigned and the journal went silent. In addition, Freenet, which had been the host of the MISF website, went under.

9/11

Then 9/11 happened. The newsletter returned to life as a journal under the editorship of Lucy Brusic. She asked then-president Shirley Whiting and longtime board member David Juncker to write pieces reflecting on the September 11 attacks. Juncker, a frequent contributor to the journal, tried to relate the World Trade Center bombings to the larger world of science and history. His article reflects the confusion and uncertainty that the bombings brought to the beginning of the twenty-first century. (He had just attended the Nobel Conference in Saint Peter, Minnesota.)

A SCHOLAR WRITES

MAKING SENSE—MOVING FORWARD
DAVID JUNCKER, 2001

11 September 2001

New York's World Trade Center and the United States Pentagon were fire bombed using innocent passengers in four separate, hijacked planes. It was the largest initial act of war to occur on American soil and one of the largest worldwide. Hundreds of civilians in the planes and thousands in buildings and on the ground died. Advances in the sciences of real-time, visual, and sound communication added to the horror of the events. Photographers, TV cameras, and personal cell phone calls from almost all possible locations brought terror out of the closet to a world-wide audience.

The first responses were defensive: the successful diverting of one of the planes to reduce wider death and destruction, and the mobilization of firefighters and police to save individuals from the dying buildings. Our heroes (individual and service) were the New York firefighters and police forces which directed evacuations and aided the injured. When the dust and smoke subsided, we all felt the desire, as several religious and political leaders would put it . . . "to bomb the perpetrators back into the Stone Age."

Broad, rapid sleuthing provided evidence suggesting that the perpetrators were a small set of loosely joined, highly trained graduates of an exiled, wealthy, religious terrorist's training camps. This perpetrator and his assistants had a recent history of several successful operations including the destruction of at least one commercial plane, a US military barracks in Beirut, embassies in Kenya and Tanzania, and the US destroyer *Cole* in a Yemen harbor. Admittedly, the events were "over there" and casualties were relatively few. They didn't command our attention or focus.

Little noted was an additional fact: these same adversaries had received their covert operations training from US forces during the height of the Cold War. We had then provided them with millions in funds and equipment to enable them to covertly terrorize Russian forces fighting in Afghanistan.

It soon became evident that the world had changed since the time of more "regular wars." President Bush made a statement that he couldn't see using $1,000,000 [worth of] bombs to destroy small collections of empty tents. Additionally, the country in which the terrorists were hiding was already devastated from prior wars; there were no "good" targets. And, it would be necessary to differentiate between friends and foe, between civilians and perpetrators.

We Were Experiencing a New Kind of War

Over the past decades, significant changes affecting the technology and strategy for war have been recognized by many worldwide. One change that I recall occurred in 1986, following the USSR's Chernobyl accident. Within two days, the USSR was pleading before the United Nation's Vienna-based, International Atomic Energy Association (IAEA) Board for the same two to three weeks to "get their house in order" that had been used by the US following the Three Mile Island accident. IAEA Board Representatives collectively said, "No!" Information and working plans would be necessary within 24 hours, due to the potential international effects of any substantial radioactive disbursement.

Almost as an aside, it was noted that Europe now had an extensive patchwork of nuclear electric power plants, which, if a second incident occurred, could spread their radioactive cores throughout the region.

Another change has resulted from the devastating effectiveness of modern munitions and weapons. Not able to be contained within small boundaries, weapons had become increasingly dangerous to both sides. Now "precise" weapons with well defined damage [targets] are the weapons of choice.

Finally, during the 1990s, worldwide accessibility and economic development created international companies and organizations, with headquarters in multiple countries and installations spread across the globe. The interconnectedness of commerce, recreation, religious bodies, and currencies worldwide has begun to blur the definition of national borders and national interests.

A New Order
Collectively, these changes may have dragged us, kicking and screaming, into a new era in which classical wars are no longer possible. We may be facing the need for police and police actions rather than war. We may need to convert our classical war machinery into multiple local, national, and international police forces. Any society needs police, as there will always be a few aberrant individuals and organizations which focus only on themselves, to the detriment of those around them.

Our Own House

To be sure, we have religious and non-sectarian fanatics on our home front. One religious leader recently made a point of focusing on President Bush's use of the word "war," saying that it meant civilian deaths were okay. He also took the time to say [that] the Bible condoned killing under certain circumstances, as when Peter cut off the ear of a soldier in the garden of Gethsemane. Somehow, he missed Jesus's response. This same person and several other leaders have stated that God allowed the United States to be attacked because of Vietnam War dissenters and a growing US acceptance of lesbians and gays. It isn't too far to the nearest fanatic.

Our neighbor, a retired Japanese woman married to an American World War II pilot, hosts one of our local coffee shops. She confided in me that she felt great sorrow for the loss of innocent life on September 11. [. . .] She then went on to explain that she had lost many family members and friends in the bombings of civilian Hiroshima and Nagasaki. There followed a silent moment that I won't soon forget. We can't even imagine that Ground Zero.

It seems that world history is replete with questionable uses of both the highest and lowest technologies of any given period. Advances seem invariably tied to misuses and overuses. Even in a civilly policed society, new discoveries will present the opportunity for new uses, both good and bad.

Scientists and Scientific Discoveries

Okay, what about these scientists and all their new discoveries? On the first day of the Nobel conference, it was apparent that the scientists were questioning and redefining themselves as well. Scientific discovery was once again under close scrutiny, this time by leading adherents.

Notable points included: "There is fear . . . of the side effects of the medicines we take, of genetically modified foods or irradiated foods, of what is in the air." There was acceptance of uncertainty in research [. . .] ". . . that (in science) there is no absolute truth." This, of course, hasn't kept scores of physicists and mathematicians from continuously trying to find a single "Unification Theory" for the universe.

My favorite point was the gun laws as revisited by molecular scientists: Nobelist Roald Hoffmann [American theoretical chemist who won the 1981 Nobel Prize in Chemistry] spoke on "Science and Ethics: A Marriage of Necessity and Choice for This Millennium." He asked whether there could be "bad molecules" or merely "bad people" manipulating molecules. He noted that as societies may need to ban certain types of guns, they may also need to ban, or otherwise restrict, certain molecules—perhaps the ones used to manufacture the PCP drug, Angel Dust.

It was acknowledged that scientific work can't be entirely "ethical-neutral." Scientists' work has the potential of wide effects and needs to continue to adhere to societal rules and ethical concerns. Several scientists reminded their fellow members that scientific inquiries most often arrive at a discovery different from the one envisioned by the researcher at the start. A professor from England used the Columbus example: Columbus was trying to find the shortest route to India when he "discovered" land. (Those are my quotation marks, as I found the example interesting. I'm quite sure the indigenous tribes felt their lands were already well discovered.)

Conclusion #1— that the consequences of discovery are rarely clear-cut—led to Conclusion #2—"It is up to society to decide how to use [a new discovery], and we hope they will do that wisely." A statement that, I'd wager, will continue to be worth a little worry on all our parts!

What is becoming evident is that we are also entering an age of increased review, or police work, concerning societal and ethical controls for selected discoveries. Good examples of the need would include the banning of lead additives in gasoline (which poisoned thousands of children near highways—even though it was great for smoother-running automotive engines)—and the more recent tire manufacturing fiascos.

From Here

I am reminded of that ancient Chinese curse, "May you live in interesting times."

Likewise, Shirley Whiting reflected on the national tragedy. Her reflections, like David Juncker's, give a feeling for the confusion and dismay that the attack brought to this country and to the struggle that everyone faced in trying to comprehend the tragedy.

A Scholar Writes

President's Column
Shirley Whiting, 2001

With all the events since September 11, I feel I should be writing something both moving and profound. Yet I have nothing profound to say. We all see the images. We all share the fears. We know we face the danger of engaging in a struggle where one misstep could lead to the end of civilization. This knowledge is all the more frightening when we consider that the enemy we face may not care whether civilization is destroyed, may even relish the opportunity to "serve God" by destroying it. Let us hope we have elected leaders who are capable of managing a situation of such delicacy, complexity, and ferocity.

I'm accustomed to looking at events in psychological and symbolic ways. Perhaps it is my background as a teacher. If you teach long enough you come to realize that the differences in people are superficial compared to the similarities. We all have the same needs for food, shelter, acceptance, and a way to work out our spiritual life. We all take the religion and culture we grew up with for granted until we are forced to examine them. Then we are likely to hear the small, still voice within, the voice that says, "What if?"

What if my way is but one of many ways? What if I have an obligation to learn about others, to better understand them and, in understanding them, better understand myself? What if each of us is but a part of a larger entity that we call God? What if God is not "out there" somewhere, but here inside each of us? What if the same is true of evil?

In our lifetimes, most of us will never encounter the dramatic forms of terrorism we witnessed in New York City. Yet in our daily lives, we are increasingly aware of insidious kinds of terrorism that contaminate familial and communal life.

What, for example, is domestic violence but a form of terrorism on a smaller scale? Yet some women, and many children, live in an atmosphere of violence for much of their lives. Drug use and suicide rates among our young people bear witness to the dysfunction that exists in parts of our society.

Perhaps terrorism is simply another name for extreme behavior without regard for the rights of others. If that is so, then perhaps we can each fight terrorism in our own way, by championing the rights of victims of violence, by teaching respect for self and others in our schools, and by fostering a return to that old fashioned concept of 'love they neighbor,' examples of which were there aplenty in the rescue teams in New York City.

We certainly must fight terrorism by increasing our vigilance. But widening the kind and scope of that vigilance is important also. The internet and globalization have shrunk the planet and we are much closer to our neighbors than ever before. We export our culture all over the world so people know about us, yet we're often ignorant of other cultures, learning about them only when we are in conflict with them.

The learning curve will be high for all of us in the times ahead. Our debates about reforming our educational system will take on new meaning as we are forced to educate our children about the world they are to inherit. We must teach them to be vigilant without being timid. Above all, we must teach them to recognize the kind of behavior that breeds bullies, and that includes our own.

We've often heard the comment in the last two weeks, "The world has changed since September 11; it'll never be the same." I'm wondering if we have changed since September 11, and if we'll ever be the same.

Boundaries of Knowledge

In line with the perceived importance of having regular meetings in order to attract members, MISF planned a series of meetings in 2001–02 called "Boundaries of Knowledge." These meetings were jointly sponsored by MISF, the First Unitarian Society, the Department of Cultural Studies and Comparative Literature at the University of Minnesota, and the Department of Philosophy and Graduate Liberal Studies at Hamline University. Subjects included Science and Religion, Humans and Non-Humans, and Medicine vs. Alternatives.[71] The speakers for this year were Dr. Robert Tapp on "Science and Humanism"; Dr. Ken Keller, "Technology and Human Values"; Dr. Sam Imbo, "Oral Traditions"; and Dr. Harvey Sarles, "Can the University be Saved?"

"Boundaries of Knowledge" evolved into a second series, "Voices of Concern," in 2002–2003. Abeles was again the leader of these seminars. Abeles wrote the following reflection in the spring of 2002 to publicize the "Voices of Concern" lecture/discussions. He was on the MISF Board and had been active in organizing the Philocafes which preceded the "Voices of Concern." Abeles is a futurist with a varied portfolio, including training in chemistry. He is also involved in sustainability studies and strategic planning.

A SCHOLAR WRITES

EVERYONE'S A PHILOSOPHER
TOM ABELES, 2002

I have a coffee mug with, of course, a cat and a saying: "Don't take life so seriously; it's not permanent." But we humans do take life seriously, and many of us are very sure that we have the answers (like Keillor's Guy Noir) to life's persistent problems, from global warming and the nature of the universe to the best burgers in town and how to balance the state's budget.

At the same time, we have a schizophrenic relationship with those "experts" whose voices grace the academic podiums, the shelves of the local bookstore, or any number of other "bully pulpits." We stand them up in order to shred their arguments over a beer during half-time at the local sports bar. We raise them on pedestals when they can be cited to validate our critical and insightful analysis of US foreign policy or the nature of the universe.

Such exchanges have taken place for centuries, from the "Socratic" dialogues that ended with a cup of hemlock to exclusive "salons" and all-night sessions in college dorms. More formal discussions have also provided venues, from itinerant lecturers bringing enlightenment to the frontier of major seminars and symposia presenting world-class thinkers and those who move nations.

Of course, these exchanges have never been universal platforms for the "vox populi." Greek "democracy" was not inclusive. Discussions and lectures tend to segregate by a variety of standards and criteria, often self-imposed, implicit rather than explicit, and ranging from religion and politics to economics and social class. Christopher Philips, in his wandering through the United States, attempted to show that Socratic exchanges could be held with groups ranging from grade-school children to those who were incarcerated. Earl Shorris, in his work with the fiscally disenfranchised, showed that there were no barriers to prevent even high school dropouts from engaging with world-class philosophical ideas at a scholarly level. In fact, Shorris's conclusion was that such skills were more important to assure the disenfranchised a "seat at the table" than the traditional job training route which emphasized practical skill sets.

"Voices of Concern" is the theme adopted by the Minnesota Independent Scholars' Forum (MISF) for its 2002–03 season of philosophical discussions, designed to meet a growing interest in the Twin Cities area in holding hosted exchanges between community members on issues of substance. These moderated discussions blend the formal lecture/presentation with a Socratic exchange. Hosted by the First Unitarian Society in Minneapolis, these once-a-month meetings feature a guest expert in a moderated discussion. The fall program will cover issues ranging from business ethics to technology and society.

These public forums have attracted a broad spectrum of individuals, from university students and faculty to independent scholars and members of the lay public.

MISF hopes that these short engagements will result in an extension to a more permanent group interested in carrying out discussions on a topic over an extended period. MISF has supported similar discussions, many of which have had a life extending over several years on [. . .] topics as diverse as "philosophy and religion" and "technology and human values." Many of these [discussions] have used works of members while others have drawn from internationally recognized works in their respective arenas.

MISF is one of a number of organizations across North America, from Vancouver to New York City, that are sponsoring such exchanges. The formats and venues vary from public after-dinner meetings in restaurants to small, invitation-only meetings in more intimate settings. What is interesting is not only the growth of these venues but their persistence over several years with a consistent core membership. Vancouver's forums will be a feature during the meeting of the National Coalition of Independent Scholars to be held in that city in the late summer of 2002.

As independent scholars, it might be interesting to speculate as to why these venues arrive at this moment in history. While these engagements have a bearded history and the arrival of the internet has created similar exchanges on a global basis, it is interesting that these semi-formal venues are persistent and insistent in their very presence. And many of the more active forums, for example Vancouver, Minneapolis/St. Paul, and New York, exist in spite of or in addition to similar opportunities on the many university campuses present in these communities.

Some have speculated that the academy has lost its hegemony or intellectual luster. Others suggest that there exists a need to engage with issues of significance with others at a more local level.

Is it possible for scholars to thrive outside of the academy? Is, as Orwell suggests, everyone equal, or are some more equal than others? Is—or can—everyone be a "philosopher"?

In the winter of 2003, the theme for "Voices of Concern" was "Democracy in Contemporary Society." The announced topic was exploration of "concerns about individual rights and freedoms versus restrictions on those privileges needed to provide security." The group also looked at the "privileges commanded versus responsibilities expected in a democracy."[72]

Twentieth Anniversary Celebration

In Whiting's second year as president, she was joined by Alice Schroeder as vice president. Schroeder took charge of planning the twentieth anniversary celebration of the founding of the Scholars, which took place in November of 2002. The main speaker at this celebration was Cheryl Dickson, the former director of the Minnesota Humanities Commission, and the person most directly responsible for the beginnings of the Minnesota Independent Scholars' Forum. Dickson recounted the beginnings of the organization. Her account, the best single account of the beginnings of MISF, is quoted at the beginning of this book (see chapter 1). The Minnesota Humanities Commission helped with a funding grant for this celebration.[73] Lionel Davis provided a recorder solo. Other speakers included essayist Judy Yeager Jones, who offered a reflection of thanks for Dickson's foresight, and poet Morgan Grayce Willow.

In introducing her poem, Willow, who holds an M.A. from Colorado State University, and is the winner of several awards from the McKnight and Jerome Foundations, remarked that, "In recent decades, poetry has found itself at the center of controversy. It has been accused both of being too self-referential and of being too political." Willow wrote "All That Fiddle" in partial answer to the question of what poetry is all about.

A Scholar Writes

All That Fiddle
Morgan Grayce Willow, 2002

There is no use
for it.
    Except
when recycling old ones
for fresh drafts of prose,
poetry's more saleable cousin.
Or for holiday gift wrapping:
Longfellow papers
on a great aunt's package;
Shel Silverstein swaddling
a toddler's toy;
moist pages from Gertrude Stein
packing stems of roses.

Use poetry in the home
to line kitchen cupboards.
Cut poems in strips
for to-do lists:
buy plums at the coop,
find receipts for the IRS,
select perennials
for next spring's
planting. Jot down
screw sizes needed
to fix the storm door,
measurements for new

window blinds. Put down
names of potential parents
for the stray cat
in your alley.

Poetry's narrow stalks
of color add interest
to your bookshelves,
breaking up those wide columns
of fiction. On your refrigerator
poems adorn, entertain,
enlighten. Fold a poem
to mark your place
in *Prevention* magazine.
Use one to relieve eye strain
caused by ads on billboards,
buses, bumpers, and TV.

Poetry. It's what we search for
when we read.
It's the one clear sound byte
rising sharp above static.
It's music whose sole instrument
is language.
        Use poetry
to help babies sleep.
Use it to teach them
to read. Use a poem
as recipe for surviving
lost love. Use poems
to clear away clutter
in your mind. Use them
as greetings; save money
on cards. If your camera

is stolen, let poems
replace snapshots,
souvenirs from your trip.
Let a poem find the words
when you stand beside a grave.

Let poetry stir your soup
of language, adding spice
to an everyday cadence.
Steal liberally from poems
when your own words fail.
Use them as your getaway
car. Let poems
be your umbrella when harsh
words hail.
Use them
at work. If you
are a physicist, search poems
to name new particles you discover.
If a pipefitter, let poems model
the tight line. If a cabbie,
set your meter to the Rubaiyat
of Umar Khaiyam.

Because metaphor
means miracle, use poetry
to heal. Let poetry escort you
through your valley
of madness. After centuries
of experience, it knows
the way out. Follow Rilke.
With poetry, live in
the questions. Or,
Mickey Rooney.

Let poetry prove
there's still stardust
in life's dirty old pan.

Following the Celebration

The mood of the anniversary celebration was upbeat; the celebration had demonstrated the staying power of MISF. As Shirley Whiting expressed it early in her tenure, "The Scholars [are] a viable organization that serves people who work without academic support on projects that have captured their interest and imagination . . . [W]e are carrying on a fine tradition and [serving] a worthy purpose in this age of the rapid explosion of information."[74] Nonetheless signs in the first decade of the 21st century were sobering for scholarship. In November of 2002, Tom Abeles circulated an article from the *Chronicle of Higher Education* titled "Scholarly Publishing Struggles with Shrinking Audience and Growing Pressure," in which four editors described the difficulties of finding a broad audience for scholarly books.[75]

Loss of Academic Library Privileges

Then, in the spring of 2003, news came that the library at the University of Minnesota would no longer allow free borrowing privileges for MISF members. (They cited budgetary constraints for their decision.) While we have no idea how many people were using these privileges, their loss was a blow to membership numbers.[76] Access to the library had been a draw and a selling card. No amount of negotiation on MISF's part (several people tried) would persuade the library management to change its mind.

Roger Sween, a librarian and library consultant, tried to soften the blow in a *Forum* article by pointing out that much specialized library access was now available on the web. His long article gave many helpful pointers for scholars who were losing library access. I had at first intended to cite Sween's full article here, but so much has changed in the digital world since 2003 that copying the whole article would be nostalgic if not pointless. Instead, I quote the last paragraphs of his article to show how far we have progressed in the past thirteen years, exactly as Sween predicted.

The information industry and libraries are in the first stages of what is a slowly burgeoning forest of digital access to text. Gradually, but increasingly, more titles will be available online in their digitized substitutes. Minnesota is one of the states where advocates of digitization have come together to work out a plan for digitizing valuable, rare, and unpublished resources and making them available on line.

In summary, libraries are going beyond their walls. The public can still go to libraries and use them in-house, but increasingly libraries will be used at a distance but delivered up close.[77]

Shirley Whiting's last year in office was disappointing to her. She had tried very hard to develop cooperative relationships with other organizations, but with the single exception of the journal (see next chapter) not much resulted from her efforts. Alice Schroeder, who had been in line to be the next president, died in 2005 after a long illness. Whiting's last presidential column, written in the middle of the 2004 election, summed up the mood.[78] "We are in a time, it would seem, of a shift in our perceptual abilities. The planet is shrinking. Problems are mounting. Leadership is uncertain," she concluded. Nonetheless, the organization persisted.

Notes for Chapter 5

71 *The Forum* 12, no. 2 (Fall 2000). Sam Imbo was a professor of philosophy at Hamline University; Ken Keller, a chemical engineer, was a former president of the University of Minnesota, and a professor of public policy at the Hubert Humphrey Institute; Harvey Sarles taught Cultural Studies and Comparative Literature at the University of Minnesota; Robert Tapp was dean of the Humanities Institute at the University of Minnesota.

72 *The Forum* 14, no. 2 (Winter 2003).

73 *The Forum* 14, no. 3 (Spring 2003).

74 Shirley Whiting to David Juncker, June 25, 2001.

75 http://chronicle.com/daily/2002/11/2002112203n.htn "Scholarly Publishing Struggles with Shrinking Audience" by David Glenn. November 22, 2002.

76 One member wrote as she withdrew her membership: "... the best benefit of MISF membership has been the University of Minnesota library card. Without that benefit, MISF membership is hard to justify." *The Forum* 15, no. 2 (Winter 2004).

77 *The Forum* 14, no. 3 (Spring 2003).

78 *The Forum* 16, no. 1 (Fall, 2004).

CHAPTER 6

New Journal, New Initiatives (2006–2011)

It could be said of this period in the history of the Minnesota Independent Scholars' Forum that, in spite of a dispirited ending to the preceding decade, the Forum began a new era. Although members were still concerned to define themselves, they nonetheless had arrived at a point where their writings were no longer solely concerned with their identities as scholars. There are several possible reasons for this change:

1. The Scholars were seasoned as an organization, with patterns in place that more or less assured their survival economically and socially;

2. They had a leadership core who were willing to take on the basic tasks of running an organization;

3. The societal crisis of the wave of unemployed scholars has passed with the retirement in the early 1990s of a pool of older professors.

David Juncker's Second Term

David Juncker assumed the presidency for the second time in November 2004. Writing in 2005, Juncker's first presidential message described MISF in the following words:

We, in MISF, are such a group: diverse, inquiring, fumbling along at times, willing to subject current mores, belief systems, and our pasts to a closer scrutiny. We are an eclectic admixture, combining respect for significant parts of our collective pasts, futurists actively planning for a better tomorrow, practitioners of both global awareness and local action [. . .] with desires to remain active participants in the present. Trudi Juncker puts it thusly: "MISF is an acronym for 'misfits.'" Maybe there is more truth to her description than we care to admit. Yet, an organization that fosters the initiation and continuation of thoughtful analyses of life and civilization from one generation to the next is additionally useful to humanity and our little world.[79]

A National Perspective on Independent Scholarship

In spite of various setbacks, the National Coalition of Independent Scholars (NCIS) carried on with annual conferences. Rhoda Lewin, the first president of the MISF, was a member and sometimes an officer for NCIS. She frequently attended the national conferences. This report about the fourteenth biennial conference of the NCIS appeared in the Winter 2005 issue of the *Forum*. It is noteworthy that she begins with attention to fellowships and grants for independent scholarship. Lewin is honored for her support of MISF in the annual meeting lecture in June, now named the Rhoda Lewin lecture.

A Scholar Writes

A Report on the NCIS Conference
Rhoda Lewin, 2005

One of the highlights of the National Coalition of Independent Scholars' seventh biennial conference in New York City, October 15–17, 2004, was the 2004 update of NCIS's 28-page "Fellowships and Grants for Independent Scholars." It includes a long list of foundations and other grant sources, and extremely helpful information on how to apply for grants and how to access other funding, as well.

Conference sessions, and a display of members' published works and other items, were at a historic building, the General Society of Mechanics and Tradesmen Building, a short walk from our low-cost Day's Inn hotel. More than 60 people attended, including NCIS founders, long-time friends, and newcomers from Canada, Switzerland, and all over the United States.

In a feature story in that weekend's *New York Sun*, NCIS founder Ron Gross said that being an independent scholar gives you "freedom to follow your own bliss, and freedom from papers to grade and departmental meetings to attend." Other highlights were the fact that academe is beginning to "accept" independents; the Modern Language Association and American Jewish Historical Society's Academic Council now invite independent scholars to serve on committees. Another interesting statistic was that a majority of current NCIS members are women!

Although there were too many wonderful conference speakers to list here, Ellen Huppert shared useful details on how to organize a successful scholars' group; her San Francisco group has 501(c)(3) status, so they can sponsor members' grant requests. [In addition] their "Works in Progress" group evaluates members' projects; they have monthly writers and play-reading group meetings; and they've taped and plan to publish members' "intellectual biographies."

Several speakers talked about networking groups. There are an estimated 100 groups like Evan Sinclair's New York City "Socrates Café," whose members range in age from teenagers to 80-year-olds. They meet at cabarets, vote on topics to discuss, and talk about things like: "How do we know if we're happy?" "What is art?" and "What is the value of nonsense and the absurd?" Joseph Wosk of Vancouver, B.C., has organized "café chat groups" in Australia, Canada, and the U.S. which are hosted by local restaurants; in the summer, they also meet for "Philosophy on the Beach." And last but not least, Bernard Roy has organized a student "chat group" funded by CUNY, and Café Philo, a concept that began in France in 1992. Members include teachers, auto mechanics, software writers, professors, and so forth. They meet every other week in a local restaurant "to eat, drink, and talk [...] Nobody has authority [...] We're all open to criticism, and can test what we think. And we choose the next meeting's topic before we leave, so we can think about it and maybe do some research."

NCIS meetings also give you many things to think about, and many stories to tell. For example, Stephen Wheatley, vice president of the American Council of Learned Societies, said that before 1946, Americans were winning one out of seven Nobel Prizes; since then, they've won one out of two. He then asked a provocative question: Did this change take place because the Nazis killed so many German and other European scholars, and so many others fled to the U.S.? Other speakers focused on finding a publisher, negotiating royalties, publishing on the internet, and how to target your audience. And there was so much more—but I'm out of space.

New Journal, *Practical Thinking*, Begins

Shirley Whiting's efforts to have MISF coordinate with other organizations bore fruit in a new publication in July 2005. Replacing the *Forum* as an MISF publication was a new journal called *Practical Thinking*; it was a joint publication of MACAE (Minnesota Association for Continuing Adult Education) and MISF. The MACAE editor was Vic Klimoski, a poet and, at that time, spiritual director for the Benedictine Monastery of Saint Paul. The MISF editor was Lucy Brusic, a long-time member of MISF.[80] Principally concerned with teaching, MACAE's focus was on the diverse areas of adult education, ranging from adult basic education through extension programs, community education, and volunteer programs. MISF kept its focus on research and scholarship outside the academy. Nonetheless, the two organizations drew from a similar pool of educated, adult-concerned communication.

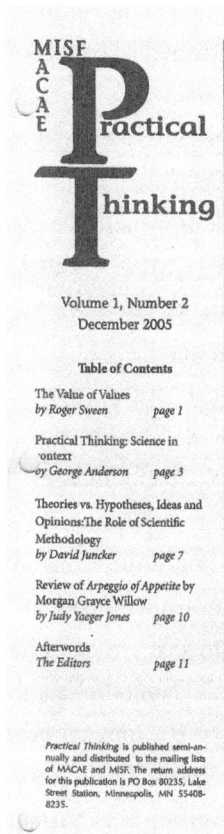

In July 2005, MISF launched a new journal named *Practical Thinking*, usually abbreviated to *PT*. *PT* was a joint venture with MACAE (Minnesota Association for Continuing Adult Education). The format usually involved two articles from MACAE and two from MISF. When the cooperative venture ended in 2008, MISF kept *PT* as the name for its journal.

Usually the new publication featured two articles from Scholars and two from members of MACAE. The advantage to MISF was a new stable of writers, some of whom covered new subjects, such as "Knowledge and Information in a Media-Saturated World" and "Rethinking Adult Education in a Pancake World."[81] The disadvantage to the Scholars was that the journal had less space for articles about organizational business, meetings, and personal information. The joint effort lasted for about two years. In the summer of 2008, with the retirement of the MACAE editor, Vic Klimoski, it seemed best to end the publishing venture. MISF retained the name *Practical Thinking* when it assumed sole editorship.

New Initiatives to Increase Membership Include a New Logo

As ever, the problem was how to find and enroll new members. In 2006, under Juncker's leadership with Hillstrom's help, MISF created a new logo for its membership brochure. The new logo, designed by Hillstrom's daughter, Molly Hillstrom, featured a group of scholars sitting around a table, presumably talking about philosophical issues. The old logo (which had been in place since 1987) had featured "The Lonely Scholar" by Bernardo Bellinzone, with a quotation from Samuel Johnson: "To talk in public, to think in solitude, to read and to hear, to inquire and answer inquiries, is the business of a scholar."[82] Several board meetings were devoted to discussing the new logo, which was not universally accepted. One member wrote on an evaluation form: "Since when does having a centuries-old tradition register as detrimental?"[83] Nonetheless, the new logo was adopted and is still in use on stationary, the journal masthead, and the membership brochure. Its official use certainly underlines the shift from individual scholarship with which the group began to the more community-and meeting-based organization it is today.

A History of the Minnesota Independent Scholars' Forum

This logo of the "Lonely Scholar" by Bellinzone was symbol of the Scholars from about 1988 to 2008.

In 2008 this new logo representing scholarship as a cooperative venture was adopted by the MISF board. The logo was created by Molly Hillstrom.

In 2007, MISF lowered its dues to $25 a year for individuals. The rationale was that the membership was not worth quite so much without borrowing privileges at the University of Minnesota and that a lower membership fee might encourage new members. At the same time, a year-end appeal for funds was instituted.

In 2007, still under Juncker's leadership, the organization tried to raise its public image. Curt Hillstrom, a longtime member and advocate for the Scholars, reported that people kept asking him when and where MISF met. Hillstrom saw this question as a reason to push for regularly scheduled meetings in a regularly scheduled place: the group had been meeting at three-month intervals in various places, usually determined by the convenience for the speaker. Although there was hesitation, the group agreed in November of 2007 that we should have a meeting at least every other month.

The same month returned a good report on a mini-conference in the fall of 2007, "Henry David Thoreau: His Journey to the 21st Century." The conference was jointly sponsored by the Thoreau Society of Concord, Massachusetts, the Minneapolis Athenaeum, MISF, and Walden University. The theme, promoted and organized by MISF's resident Thoreau Scholar, Dale Schwie, concerned Thoreau's connections to the 21st century. One of the speakers took as his subject a description of how the Thoreau journals have become the "base line for a long-term study of climate change."[84]

The Wireless Pond

At the same time, MISF was planning a much bigger conference under its own name. "Afloat in the Wireless Pond: Minnesotans Reflect on Living in Digital Days" took place March 1, 2008. Sponsored by MISF and the Minnesota Coalition on Government Information with funding from the Minnesota Sesquicentennial Commission, this conference tried to bring into focus the many ways in which the internet was altering our lives.[85]

The following report comes from Charles Cubrimi. Charles Cubrimi is the pen name of an engaging writer and musician of minor repute. He grew up in New Jersey and moved to Minnesota a score of years ago. This conference was notable for the fact that MISF was no longer thinking about its image as a scholarly group but rather addressing itself to concerns outside of the organization.

This frog was the symbol for the 2008 MISF conference, Reflections from the Digital Pond.

A Scholar Writes

Reflections from the Wireless Pond
Charles Cubrimi, 2008

It wasn't Kermit, but it really was a green frog on the poster croaking the thesis of a one-day conference Saturday, March 1, 2008. Entitled "Afloat in the Wireless Pond," the event was sponsored by the Minnesota Independent Scholars' Forum and the Minnesota Coalition on Government Information, organized by Lucy Brusic and Mary Treacy and funded in part by a grant from the Minnesota Sesquicentennial Commission. Throughout the day, about 60 people were on hand to hear an exciting array of speakers at Luther Seminary in St. Paul.

Setting the tone with a suggestive image, Laura Waterman Wittstock, CEO, Wittstock & Associates, evoked the [analogy of the] "long house" as a place for discussion. The discussion taking place there, however, was not just to deliberate on issues for the present moment, but to decide what would encompass seven generations forward. Wittstock urged us not just to think in a "now"-centered way, as if we had no future. Rather, she coaxed us to enter the [figurative] "long house" and think of matters that have consequences for the future, for seven generations.

Kenneth Brusic, editor of the Orange County Register (Santa Ana, CA) and the keynote speaker of the day, did have the future in mind in his illustrated talk about the role of newspapers in the present and in times to come. Evoking a Minnesota songwriter, Brusic intoned the editors' lament: "The Times, They Are a-Changin'." He was referring, it seems, to the *New York Times*, the *Star Tribune*, and his paper the *Register*; but he was also speaking calmly (but with a hint of anxiety) about the sea changes affecting information gathering in general and newspapers in particular.

Disruptive technology caused the demise of Western Union, Brusic observed. Similar forces are at work disrupting the newspaper industry: things like Craigslist, Google News, and other media advances. "The *Daily Show*," he noted wryly, "is a major source of news for a sizable portion of the younger population. Substantial sources of revenue (like the Want Ads) have migrated to faster and less costly electronic servers." Erosion of credibility, he lamented, has hurt the industry as well.

Questions abounded: how do we sort through the glut of information? Do we really need professional journalists? How do we persuade people to read views that challenge—rather than support—their already-existing views? Brusic offered few answers, but he did point to some ways in which newspapers are struggling to sail the waters of changing times and evolving technology. For one thing, he noted, newspapers need to redefine themselves as executive summaries of the flood of—often conflicting—information. Further, local and more focused news features need to be developed to reach diverse populations and neighborhoods. Finally, he concluded, changing technology doesn't have to be the enemy. On the contrary, efficiently integrated, it can encourage newspapers to be more efficient, timely, and informative.

A panel composed of Peter Shea, Morgan Grayce Willow, Tom Eland, Marion Rengel, and Helen Burke concluded the morning session. With different styles and skills, the panelists dived into the digital pond and created a drenching series of thoughtful splashes. Rengel, public spokesperson for the Digital Library Project, talked about how a digital library is in our future with access being the primary goal. Eland, director of information at Minneapolis Community and Technical College (MCTC), called the audience to think in different ways, with information literacy being the basic concern. He challenged the notion that Google gets to set the agenda about what and how we learn. The structures we see developing do not build sustainable and caring communities; and that should be a concern for us all. Willow, a poet who also teaches at MCTC, made a plea to restore vitality to the use of language. She talked about poetry sites on the Web and how helpful they can be. But she cautioned us to cast a wide net in what we read: one should not be solipsistic and read only what one likes. Burke, senior librarian of government documents for the Hennepin County Library System, summarized her thinking with a thoughtful, cautionary, and proverbial statement: just because we send emails doesn't mean we communicate.

Shea, who teaches philosophy at Gustavus Adolphus, gave a dramatic four-point presentation in which he outlined (in low tech on a white board) "ignorance" (we are not only ignorant, but we are ignorant of our ignorance); "surprise" (we need to be surprised); "generosity" (if we lose generosity in this respect, the game is over); and "curiosity" (you've gotta think about stuff you've never thought about—that's why libraries are important). Further, we should not be pessimistic because we are ignorant; but we need to use not just our eyes but our other senses as well. Luther Seminary has good janitation, Shea sniffed, because, by using the nose, one can tell how clean the restrooms are.

Following a substantial lunch and a generous door prize giveaway (including the signature green frog), the group reconvened for several demonstrations. Tim Hoogland from the Minnesota Historical Society gave an encouraging summary of History Day as a life-transforming experience for the 30,000 kids in Minnesota who participate. While affirming that the Web helps young people do research, he warned against "Googlepedia: click/point/file/paste." He introduced a History Day student, Sophie Naylor, who placed second nationwide in the History Day competition. Naylor described and then showed her film project on the Starvation Study in 1944. Not only was this video a moving presentation, it also demonstrated the capacity of the digital pond to provide vast and varied research material.

Jim Ramstrom from the Land Management Information Center demonstrated that accessible maps can tell stories and teach important lessons. With a series of map illustrations, for example, Ramstrom showed how Benjamin Franklin did his homework and influenced the map of the newly forming United States. Franklin successfully made the case for drawing the US/Canada border substantially farther north than it might otherwise have been.

Later in the afternoon, Carol Urness, map historian and former head of the James Ford Bell Library, reviewed the history of printing and pointed out that information is not necessarily knowledge. She also referred to Benjamin Franklin's use of maps in setting the northern border of the United States so that it would include Isle Royale. Tom Leighton, principal city planner for Minneapolis, described his work in the revitalization of West Broadway in Minneapolis and raised questions about the usefulness of technology in urban planning. Some technology, such as the telephone, is so widespread that we no longer think of it as technology, while other technology is perceived as a threat by some populations. He questioned whether increasing access to the Web would increase community involvement.

The final speaker for the day was David Wiggins, National Park

Ranger with the Mississippi River National Park. Urness offered various reflections in an eclectic presentation that covered a good deal of his life and his connection to the history of Minnesota. His conclusions demonstrated that the Web is still many things to many people: for some it is a great connection to the rest of the world even though its organization sometimes seems akin to chaos theory; to others, the Web is problematic because it robs us of time to think and integrate the vast amount of information it brings to us. The diversity of Wiggins's presentation underlined the diversity of the various viewpoints explored during the day.

The day was long and fruitful. One came away bursting with new ideas and worries, with a cautious but informed appraisal of the treasures and pitfalls of the electronic/ information age in which we live. It seems that, like the frog on the poster, we can dive into the pool and swim in the waters or we can just sullenly sit on the lily pad—and croak.

Twenty-Fifth Anniversary

Still under Juncker's leadership, the Scholars celebrated their twenty-fifth anniversary on June 14, 2008. A lunch at Maria's Cuban Restaurant was followed by a talk from early member Peter Shea. About thirty people attended.

Shea was the editor of the *Humanities Science News* [HSN], from which we have drawn early reports about the beginning of the Scholars. His talk, "Celebrating Thoughtful People," illustrates how much MISF had moved away from its beginnings as an organization for out-of-work Ph.D.'s. The reporter is a retired Lutheran pastor.

A History of the Minnesota Independent Scholars' Forum

David Juncker, a past president of MISF and Brian Mulhern, archivist of MISF, show off the 25th anniversary cakes. Photos by Tom Dukich

A Scholar Writes

Celebrating Thoughtful People
Robert Brusic, 2008

To celebrate the twenty-fifth anniversary of the Minnesota Independent Scholars' Forum, a group of over thirty inquiring minds gathered at Maria's Cuban Restaurant in Minneapolis on June 14 to eat and to hear Peter Shea talk about "Celebrating Thoughtful People." Shea began by saying that going to the bathroom during his talk was permissible. In non-linear fashion, he spoke for an hour, affirming the notion that thinkers can precipitate intellectual revolutions and save civilization. There is, he affirmed with passion, a need to spread a vital intellectual culture, for we are guardians of ideas, responsible to the community at large and to the next generation.

Throughout his engaging presentation, Shea wandered along a number of provocative paths. He noted, for instance, that ideas rarely migrate from a bookshelf to the mind. Shakespeare and Dickens are dead letters unless someone, such as a speaker at the right time, can impart the thoughts and ideas of significant people. Ideas that are connected to lives go down better. Encounters with lives are inextricably bound to encounters with ideas and vice versa.

These fertile encounters are what he meant by celebrating thoughtful people. Celebrating, in Shea's mind, is to make accessible, to make people think and act. Accessing the lives and ideas of people is important to promote thoughtfulness and action.

Philosophy Camp

Shea illustrated his point by referring to a course called

"Philosophy Camp," an experience he coordinates at Shalom Hill Farm. There, in southern Minnesota, people have a chance to "dry out" from the frenetic pace of modern life. In this experience, people have the freedom to explore and experiment, to raise the issue of what's worth thinking and talking about. It's a celebratory practice, making minds available and accessible to one another. It is, in short, an experiment in access.

Expanding on his work with young people at Philosophy Camp, Shea noted that we all need a place where we can go and think. Public television, he said, used to provide some of that before it became captive to invasive economic and cultural forces. He likes television and wants to rescue it from its current bondage, hoping that it can once again make people's lives accessible to one another by the healthy and stimulating flow of ideas.

What has this to do with Independent Scholars, which is celebrating its quarter-century anniversary? Well, here is a broad public space that has access to ideas and lives across the generations. Shea, an early member of MISF, advocated a forum where the young and the elderly can meet and interact. The youth are the hope of the elderly; and the elderly know what it takes to live life over time. Sharing interests with the next generation is crucial. In that creative forum minds can be opened to science, literature, poetry, and much more. He noted how exciting it is to see how even fifth graders, properly approached, can wake up and interact with intellectual activity.

In listing the options for thoughtful lives, Shea spoke about creative education, the possibilities latent in television, and the role of the church. The latter, he said, has been in a living dialogue with the past for two thousand years; it has a perspective that can be helpful in the larger conversation he advocates. We must keep reminding ourselves and the larger public how big the tent is as a meeting space. Meetings as such are boring, he concluded, but ideas are exciting. Shea invited us to put on our thinking caps, join the intellectual revolution that is brewing, and act. There is a lot of unused potential to be harnessed and set in motion.

Curt Hillstrom Institutes Regular Meetings

Curt Hillstrom's term as president began in July 2008. Hillstrom, as we have seen, has been an active member of the Scholars since 1986. He has often served as treasurer for the board and has maintained a database of present, past, and potential members. He has also been the convener and director of the Philosophy Discussion group and has recently formed, with Emily Pollack, the History Discussion group which he also leads (See chapter 8). In the first edition of the journal after he had been elected president, Hillstrom reflected on "The Underground Scholar."

In the article below, Hillstrom's first after becoming the president of the Scholars, he reflects on the importance of the continuing existence of the Minnesota Independent Scholars' Forum—even though the organization seems more or less invisible to the general public.

A Scholar Writes

The Underground Scholar
Curt Hillstrom, February 2009

The density provided by cities creates new sets of human dynamics. Consider the thriving theatrical scene in the Twin Cities; the existence of small, semi-obscure dance companies; the small churches of parochial denominations; the many business networking opportunities; the really good shopping. I once happily counted two dozen cross-country ski trails within a half-hour drive of my home.

One consequence of this density is the existence of an "underground." Underground, that is, as contrasted with mainstream. It is something—an event, a person, a movement—not commonly talked about or reported on. You must seek it out; it does not come looking for you. The quintessential example of this phenomenon is underground music.

Virtually all musicians start out unknown; some never get beyond that. And some actually prefer that. Punk bands, for example, started underground not just because they were unknown, but also because they were contemptuous of mainstream values. Other musicians are offering up music that appeals to a limited audience, suffering low attendance and low funds. Some may have talent, but with lives busy in other arenas, they simply don't have the time to develop the talent they have. Not a few are just mediocre and will manage to stay underground in spite of themselves. But there are two things that are common to all underground musicians: they are doing music for its own sake, and, for the most part, they are very happy to be doing it.

Before I go any further, I want to point out that "underground," like most such terms, is slippery. It is more of a non-linear continuum from mainstream to underground, and where any musical style or group falls is subjective. Nonetheless, music that was at one time clearly underground does sometimes become mainstream. Disco, punk, and hip-hop all existed with small audiences before catching on with widely popular support; the Grateful Dead used to sell their CDs from the trunk of their car.

Most independent scholars do not think of themselves as being underground, but I think it can be argued that they—most of them—fit the definition. (We are going to define academia and popular writing on intellectual topics as the mainstream here.) Independent scholars, like underground musicians, have small, perhaps specialized audiences. If you want to find them, you must seek them out; they will not necessarily come to you. There are other parallels with underground music here, too. Like the original punk bands, some just don't want to be a part of the mainstream, because of philosophical differences or because they simply want to avoid the pressures and politics of academia. Others are interested in topics with a limited focus that would not ordinarily interest academia, such as local history or sports trivia. [. . .] For the most part these scholars are intelligent, capable people with busy lives that don't always allow the time to develop their ideas as they would like. There are some who may never produce a satisfactory intellectual product. But, like underground musicians, they have two things that are common to them all: they are pursuing knowledge for its own sake, and they are very happy to be doing it.

But even for independent scholars, total independence is not desirable. Networking can be useful and an audience is desirable. This is where MISF comes in. In the midst of the city, we want to find independent scholars, including those who don't realize that they are such, and bring them together. Moreover, in the age of the internet, we can reach beyond the borders of the city to independent scholars who have been traditionally more isolated and include them in our circle. We want to connect independent scholars and help them find an audience and expand their opportunities. We feel that this is one of those cases where the parts add up to more than the whole. We also want to make it possible for the genuinely talented scholar, like the pioneers of disco and hip-hop, to emerge into the mainstream. But mostly we want to be here to pursue our intellectual interests because, after all, it's something we love. And that's reason enough.[86]

Regular Meetings Begin

In addition, the February 2009 edition of the journal announced on the back cover, "MISF now has regular meetings and some great talks." In this edition of the journal the organization was able to announce a lineup of four meetings in the beginning of 2009. These programs included Richard Fuller of Gustavus College on "Physics Encounters Consciousness"; Glenda Eoyang, executive director of the Human Systems Dynamics Institute, on "Complexity and the Pragmatism of Time"; Tom Dukich, philosopher and scientist, on "Life After the Bailout: Transition to Resilience"; and Dennis Schapiro, businessman and education writer, on "Children as Pawns in Public Policy."

Hillstrom continued to write about scholarship in his twice-yearly president's column—nearly always pointing out that MISF needed more members. For example, his president's message for December 2009 began, "When I became president of the Minnesota Independent Scholars' Forum a year and half ago, I had several goals. The most important one was to increase the amount of face-to-face time between members. I also wanted to raise our profile on the internet and to increase our membership."[87]

Although Hillstrom lamented the fact that the membership goal had not been met, he took some pride in the fact that MISF had instituted regular Saturday meetings at Hosmer library and established a presence on meetup.com. In addition, the History Study Group had joined the longtime Philosophy Group as an extension of the regular Saturday meetings. Aside from a small core of diehard members, there was not much overlap between these groups. In addition, the fact that anyone could attend any meeting without becoming a dues-paying member meant that MISF membership continued to hover right around 50 persons.

Hillstrom continued his presidency into 2010. In September 2010, *Practical Thinking* published "Yes, But Is It Health Insurance?" by Lee Wenzel.[88] (The entire article appears in chapter 11.) This article created more demand (there are no more copies) than any other article MISF has published in its thirty year existence. The article was written in the hopeful glow of the ACA legislation, but predicts in its second paragraph the problems that we now understand to be inherent in universal insurance:

> The purpose of this article is to make explicit the implicit abandonment of insurance implied in the recently enacted national health care legislation. When everyone can obtain coverage and premiums are not related to risk, that is no longer insurance. To the extent that the concepts of insurance guide implementation, the system might well implode for lack of outcomes and uncontrollable costs.[89]

In spite of the timeliness of this article on health insurance, divining what topics might be timely and finding writers to address such possibly relevant topics was a consistent problem for the editor of the journal. In her editorial of March 2011, Brusic remarked that it was hard to predict what ideas would be attractive six months out. When the 2011 journal was planned (in the wake of an earthquake in Haiti and a market meltdown in September 2010) the editorial committee had hoped that the theme of the journal would be survival. By the time the journal was printed some three months later, other concerns had driven out these topics and the journal came to be about the survival of ideas, such as Islam and the idea of God.[90]

Most presidents serve for two consecutive two-year terms—a total of four years—and Hillstrom completed his second term in 2011. During the years of his presidency, the articles in the journal show a kind of double vision. Some articles focused on scholarship. "How to Use an Editor"[91] by Virginia Hansen, "Defend our Archives" by Mary Treacy,[92] "How to Use a Research Library" by Tim Johnson,[93] and "Collecting and Archiving in a Digital Age" by Lucy Brusic[94] all discussed traditional scholarship. Other articles reflected the experience of being in a revolution initiated by cell phone ("Side Effects of a Communication Revolution" by David

Juncker)[95] and advances that had been made in modern astronomy ("A History of Astronomy" by Ed Ferlauto), as reported by Bill McTeer.[96] In general, these articles show MISF moving away from purely scholarly concerns to look at and reflect on the larger world.

Thoreau Society

In the middle of all this whipping back and forth between the present and the past, MISF took a definite step into the past on June 18, 2011, with a trip on the Minnesota River in Thoreau time. The trip, sponsored by the Bloomington Historical Society and the national Thoreau Society, with support from MISF, commemorated Henry David Thoreau's trip to Minnesota in 1861. Dale Schwie, a member of the Scholars, a Thoreau scholar, and a board member of the Thoreau Society, was instrumental in planning and promoting the trip.[97] Fifteen members of the Scholars were among the 150 people on board the *Jonathan Paddleford*. The importance of this event was in putting the Scholars into a larger context, in which they shared a program and a "meeting space" with another organization. Several presidents have felt that this direction would be a good one for the Scholars to pursue,[98] though it must be said that this boat trip, while fascinating and mind-broadening, did not obviously result in any new members for MISF.

Fifteen Scholars joined members of the Thoreau Society and others on board the *Jonathan Paddleford* to replicate a trip made by Henry D. Thoreau in June 1861. Our trip took place June 18, 2011. We were accompanied by Richard Smith as Thoreau and Newell Chester as Governor Alexander Ramsay. Photos by Bob Brusic.

Notes for Chapter 6

79 *The Forum* 16, no. 2, Winter 2005.

80 The *Forum*, as a journal/newsletter, ended at this time with Vol. 16, no. 2.

81 "Knowledge..." by Tom Eland, *Practical Thinking* 1, no.1, July 2005; "Rethinking Adult Education..." by Terilyn C. Turner, Vol, 2., no. 2 (January 2007). *Practical Thinking* is abbreviated as PT.

82 The citation is from "The History of Rasselas, Prince of Abissinia: A Tale" by Samuel Johnson (1759). This is a work of fiction about the effort to try to decide what to do with life. Rasselas is assumed to be relaying Johnson's feelings, but he is a fictional character.

83 Ginny Hansen to Curt Hillstrom, letter June 14, 2006.

84 *PT* 4, no. 1, (February 2008).

85 *PT* 4, no. 2, (June 2008).

86 *PT* 5, no. 1 (February 2009).

87 *PT* 5, no. 2 (December 2009.)

88 *PT* 6, no. 1 (September 2010) The entire article is reprinted in Chapter 11.

89 Ibid.

90 *PT* 7, no. 1 (March 2011).

91 Ibid.

92 *PT* 7, no 1 (September 2011).

93 Ibid.

94 *PT* 7. no. 1 (September 2011). One of the problems of publishing an occasional and sometimes irregular journal is that the editor neglects to change the masthead. The dates on these journals and following are different and *correct*, although the issue and volume numbers are the same.

95 *PT* 7., No. 1 (March 2011).

96 *PT* 7, No. 1 (September 2011). See note 16 above with regard to numbering.

97 An article by Schwie on Herbert Gleason, a photographer of Thoreau sites, is included in Chapter 11.

98 Ibid.

CHAPTER 7

MISF Comes of Age (2012–2016)

Michael Woolsey Increases the Visibility of MISF

In the fall of 2012, Michael Woolsey began his first term as president. Woolsey had been a lead analyst in information technology for 3M. Lucy Brusic continued as editor of the journal. Woolsey's main goals as president were:

1. To revamp the organization's mission statement in a form more definitive of its purpose;
2. To make explicit the organization's Scholarship Standards;
3. To increase the visibility of the organization by updating its website, mnindependentscholars.org;
4. To change the name of the journal to something more descriptive than *Practical Thinking*;
5. To encourage members to apply for grants to support their scholarly projects, in particular grants from the Minnesota Legacy Fund[99] for historical research.

Grants

By 2014, only ten grant awards had been made involving MISF, and none since 2006. Each of these had been with MISF acting in the role of Fiscal Agent. David Megarry, as board member in charge of the MISF Fiscal Agency administration, described this benefit as follows:

One of the benefits of membership in the Minnesota Independent Scholars' Forum is the Fiscal Agency feature. A Scholar can apply for a grant as an individual and use the Scholars' Forum as the Fiscal Agency to satisfy the fiduciary needs of a grantor organization. Those grantor entities can be more comfortable giving monies to a Scholar if there is an intermediary organization to manage the funds. The MISF Fiscal Agency is such an intermediary organization.[100]

In 2014, at the initiative of a group of unaffiliated history scholars headed by Barb Sommer, two new grant awards were made involving MISF. One was from the Minneapolis Foundation to an individual scholar, with MISF acting in its accustomed fiscal agency role—that is, taking a percentage for administration of the grant. The second grant was from the Minnesota Historical Society's Legacy Fund to MISF. By the rules of the Legacy Fund, grants are made to organizations, not individuals. The organization administers the grant by finding contractors to execute it. The grantee organization does not receive any remuneration for its project administrative costs. With this first Legacy grant, MISF began an expanded role in support of grant projects. This new role has the effect of involving MISF more deeply in grant projects than it had been in administering non-Legacy projects. It has also strengthened its relationship with the grantor. The Minnesota Historical Society's Legacy Fund Office has made five grant awards to MISF in the last three years, one of which funded the production of this history.

Website and Media Connections

Thanks to internet connections, MISF is fairly well known. Its meetup.com membership is around 500 and it has a sign up/internet mailing list of at least 150. The paid membership has stabilized at around 60.

Woolsey did not consider paid membership a top issue. "I've always operated under the assumptions that MISF fills a unique societal niche, and if outsiders perceive the need and quality of its several offerings, membership will follow. Besides . . . we don't require membership for two of our four functions; and it's even three of four [functions] if you consider that we sometimes give away copies of the journal to the general public at monthly meetings."[101]

Mission Statement Revision

As Woolsey continued in his presidency, he identified a stronger online presence as a top consideration. As a part of this work, the board rewrote the mission statement for publication on the website. The new mission statement reads:

> The Minnesota Independent Scholars' Forum exists to foster scholars, whatever their formal credentials or academic involvement. MISF strives to be encouraging and critical, always aware of what distinguishes good scholarship. We encourage all projects of disciplined intellectual inquiry.
>
> Our membership is open to anyone who shares this goal.
>
> To achieve its mission, MISF provides scholars with:
>
> 1. Opportunities to collaborate with other scholars of similar interests;
> 2. Regular opportunities to exchange ideas on designated topics in small groups;
> 3. Opportunities to present, to the critical eye of other scholars and the public, the fruits of study, both in oral and written form;
> 4. Fiscal agency for scholarly grant submissions.
>
> In an age of ever more sophisticated means of communication, MISF promotes face-to-face interaction among scholars as an irreplaceable means to scholarly excellence.

Marketing Strategy

William McTeer, independent computer consultant and board member, volunteered to take on the task of figuring out a marketing strategy. His findings echoed the importance of identifying prospective members from a large field, such as educated retirees, members of compatible non-profits, subscribers to some journals, and readers of certain online blogs and journals. Suggested ways to reach prospective members included being present on various online venues (such as our website, as well as meetup.com, Facebook, GiveMN.org, and Guidestar.com), as well as coordinating with other organizations. Basically, McTeer's suggestions for increasing membership boiled down to broadening the definition of what scholarship is: (1) intense interest that involves research though not necessarily in academic fields, and (2) highlighting the environment that encourages such scholarship. By this definition, programs, study groups, grant support, networking, and moral support all constitute support of independent scholarship.[102]

Eventually, McTeer was asked to revise and revamp the Scholars' website to make it a better marketing tool. McTeer and Mike Woolsey published a revised and upgraded website in early 2018. It can be found at mnindependentscholars.org.

Although MISF stays fairly steady in membership, its resources have grown. The organization has participated in GiveMN every year since the inception of the fund-raising drive in 2009, and has realized a small amount of money each year. In addition, the death of longtime and founding member Rhoda Lewin in 2012 caused the board to dedicate a lecture in her name, which in turn brought a memorial gift.

The *Minnesota Scholar*

Woolsey's goal of changing the name of the journal to something more appropriately descriptive than *Practical Thinking* was accomplished when the journal began a new run as the *Minnesota Scholar* in July 2015. The older journal was commemorated by the numbering—the *Minnesota*

Scholar begins with Vol. 10, no. 1 (July 2015). The renamed journal continued the patterns of the previous publication: several articles by scholars on topics of personal interest; reports on the Saturday meetings; occasional remarks on MISF business; announcements of upcoming meetings; and a short editorial essay.

One of the evidences of the increased maturity of the organization is that it is less self-conscious about its definition and more inclined to take on subjects of scholarly interest. Thus, the second issue of the *Minnesota Scholar* (June 2016) had an article by Gus Fenton on "Pursuing Family Roots" and a review of *Who Owns History* by Mike Woolsey. Fenton is a semi-retired biomedical engineer, whose interests include wolves and international travel.

A Scholar Writes

Pursuing Family Roots
Gus Fenton, 2016

The title question perhaps should better be phrased as "When genealogy?" since at some phase in most people's lives they become interested in their roots. This may take the form of talking with a fanatical relative whose life goal is to document every last scrap of familial history, or, in more serious cases, you might actually become that crazy person. Get worried when you start thinking that family vacations spent walking four abreast through graveyards looking for the tombstone of a fourth cousin multiply removed (once or twice forcibly) sounds reasonable. DSM-IV codes have not yet been developed for this condition.

Becoming a genealogy freak sneaks up on you. For me, the switch turned on in my 50s while clearing out some files in the attic. I came across an old postcard, written in Finnish, dated

1910, that my mother had given me years ago. It was sent from Vadsø, Norway, by my future grandmother to my future grandfather who was living here in Minneapolis. Prior to the postcard my only awareness of their lives was that they were Finnish immigrants and that they lived in Milwaukee, Wisconsin. Why was my grandmother in Vadsø, Norway, and my grandfather in Minneapolis? I don't understand Finnish, so I didn't know if this was a steamy love note or a "Hi, how are you?" kind of thing. Unfortunately, it was the latter, but I get ahead of myself. Certainly, it was a puzzle. And engineers like me are attracted to puzzles. Moths to a flame is what it is.

I told my siblings that I was looking into why Kustaa, my maternal grandfather and namesake, was in Minneapolis for a year or so in 1910, and for whatever other information could be found. I naively assumed this would result in five pages of material, a quick project, done and done. The reality, as you may have guessed, was otherwise. Telling my siblings of my project also caused them to send me all the stuff they'd been saving along the lines of family memorabilia. Boxes of it.

As I looked into Kustaa's life, I started encountering more and more information about him, all of which was news to me. News because I probably wasn't paying attention as a kid, and nobody thought I needed/wanted to know—likely possibilities. First, there were the census records where I had to sort my Kustaa out from a same-name, same-aged doppelganger who emigrated from Finland to the same place (Wisconsin) at about the same time. From that, I was somewhat disappointed to learn that I neither owned 40 acres in northern Wisconsin nor was descended from a bigamist. Then I started reading my mother's writings, where literally half of her 90 vignettes related to her childhood, speaking volumes about the times. I learned about the five different places my grandparents lived in

Milwaukee, each time horse-trading one piece of property for the next, preserving capital since they probably didn't have any. Then there was another old postcard sent by my grandfather to his relatives back in Finland circa 1911 when he and my grandmother were, likely, just engaged. The picture on the postcard showed my grandmother sitting on a donkey, looking a bit concerned, with my grandfather standing next to her. Kustaa had written in Finnish on the picture, "Oh, poor donkey!" At last, the source of my misbegotten sense of humor was identified.

Needless to say, the writing project burgeoned beyond five pages to become a 234-page book now safely archived amongst relatives, the Library of Congress, and ten other repositories. And that was just the start. Having finished my mother's side of the family, I went on to do the same to my dad's side. Most of his folks had been on this side of the Atlantic since the early 1700s, pursuing dreams or escaping nightmares or perhaps a bit of both. Given no further sides of the family to document, I turned to a journal my great-great-grandfather had written in the late 1860s about his life and times growing up in Vermont and then moving to the "wild west of Michigan." Over three hundred pages he wrote and never felt the need for a period or paragraph break. I edited the Jack Kerouac out of him and annotated the historical incidents he cites, which, though common knowledge to those of his time, are forgotten to us. A pity.

Where do you go from here? It was obvious to one in the throes of genealogy withdrawal, but perhaps not to all, that the history of our house, built in 1906, needed to be documented. For this one, I learned about how Minneapolis property listings work, but the paperwork is still just confusing. With the census data, we found that our house, which we view as comfortably full with two people, once held seven people (husband, wife, two daughters, two of the wife's sisters, and a roomer). From the

1934 Minneapolis Building & Housing Survey we know we had running water inside the house, but whether the toilet was indoor or out is not clear. And then there are the plat maps and Sanborn insurance maps which draw me in inexorably due to my acute cartophilia. (Side note: per the OED, a cartophile is also one who pursues ". . . collecting, arranging, and studying cigarette-cards and similar items." What exactly are cigarette-cards? Oooh, the next research project?!?!)

I've now walked all around the "why" of genealogy without providing a direct answer to that question. Having mostly retired from the engineering world, I needed to do a bit more than play guitar, exercise, read *Scientific American*, and drink beer. For me, the searcher and organizer and finisher within emerged. "Emerged" is too mild a term. More like the thrasher within started aggressively demanding projects to research, coordinate, and complete. What's the next stop? Who knows?!?!? And that's the great part about it.

"Pursuing Family Roots" became the beginning of a new series about particular pursuits—whether scholarly or personal—that scholars enjoy. This series helps us find out who our members are. Klein has continued with articles such as "The Belonging Addiction" by Stephen Miller (December 2016) and "Why Art?" by Robert Brusic (December 2017).

Another frequent feature of the journal has been book reviews. We have tried to review the works of any author who is a member of the Scholars, but we also include reviews of important books such as the following.

A Scholar Writes

Who Owns History?
Mike Woolsey, 2016

Foner, Eric. *Who Owns History?: Rethinking the Past in a Changing World.* Hill and Wang, 2003.

Who owns history? Hmm ... you didn't think anyone "owned" it? Well, think again, according to this distinguished historian, Columbia professor, and protégé of legendary historian, Richard Hofstadter. History has been the political tool of many an exploitive government, three of which are subjects in this collection of lectures and essays spanning the years from 1989–2002. The people of the Soviet Union, South Africa, and (lo and behold) the United States have each been victimized by historical narratives that served the political purposes of a power elite. As the Soviet Union crumbled and apartheid ended, those narratives had to be rewritten, it being a hallmark of political liberty for a people to have access to the true history of their country.

But United States history? What has been fabricated about that? Take for example the events and meaning of the Civil War and the subsequent period of southern Reconstruction, the latter of which happens to be this author's historical specialty. D.W. Griffith's early-1900s film *Birth of a Nation* is one of the more familiar artifacts of the Reconstruction myth, but it was also "the complicity of scholars" that legitimized the mythical and nostalgic perspective of the war and Reconstruction. They constructed a narrative that popularized the notion that the war was one fought between "brothers" for the purpose of preserving the Union rather than of transforming it, i.e. that it was to heal a conflict within the national "family" rather than to enfranchise one fifth of the population that had had no place in that family. However, it is as transformative that the events of war and Reconstruction are best understood. The effect of the mythical narrative continues to be felt in our own day, as, since the 1980s, the US Supreme Court has consistently retreated from the enforcement of civil rights, leapfrogging the 14th Amendment to take its bearings by the prewar version of the Constitution. In doing so, it has taken an "ahistorical" approach to interpreting the Constitution. This charge may strike the reader as debatable, but the author supports it with compelling evidence.

So, historical truth matters. It matters a great deal. "We can forget the past, but the past, most assuredly, will not forget us" (Foner, 108). To be sure, every historical narrative is a selection, and ordering, of facts; and every selection and ordering of facts constitutes an interpretation. So how do you get to the truth if there are as many different interpretations as there are historians? Can any recorded history be expected to have captured the past as it actually happened and for what it means? This historian-author answers that it is difficult for laymen to comprehend "that there often exists more than one legitimate way of recounting past events" (Ibid., Preface, xvii), and it is "the constant search for new perspectives" that is "the lifeblood of historical understanding" (Ibid., xvi). For this reason, "There is nothing unusual or sinister in the fact that each generation rewrites history to suit its own needs . . ." (Ibid., xi). In fact, it "must" rewrite history (Ibid., xvii), as society changes—a seemingly hard-to-digest hypothesis, but not so much when you think about it. Approximation to historical truth is the best we can hope for, and that is an effect best achieved by constant reevaluation and reordering of the known facts from fresh perspectives.

Thus may be understood to be an to the titled question, "Who owns history?" or rather, who rightfully owns history? "Everyone and no one . . .," (Ibid., xix) he writes. It's "everyone" in that each one of us is the inevitable product of the past, and "no one" in that "study of the past is a constantly evolving, never ending journey of discovery" (Ibid).

Monthly Programs

For the past several years, since Hillstrom's presidency, the Scholars have carried out an ambitious series of monthly public programs covering such subjects as "War and Art: Russian Artistic Expression During WWI" by Carol Rudie of the Museum of Russian Art and "Never Again—Genocide Prevention in the 21st Century" by Kathleen Laurila of the Nonviolent Peaceforce. Most meetings take place in a local public library and are advertised by internet notices to members and other interested individuals. They are also posted in the library. The involvement with a public library is to MISF's advantage, because we are required to line up our programs several months in advance so they can be announced by the library. This advance planning is greatly recommended in any organizational structure.

Occasionally, meetings take place outside of the public library, such as art museum tours and a summer picnic. These meetings are advertised to all members and interested individuals through the internet. All are welcome.

We try to incorporate talks by our members on projects they are exploring (works-in-progress) or subjects in which they have become more or less expert. We have an annual poetry meeting in either April or May, now named in honor of the late Virginia "Ginny" Hansen.

A ten- or eleven-member board meets once a month to make policy and financial decisions, but most board communication is done through the internet. Most decisions revolve around keeping members and others aware of our meetings, with the hope that they will attend them.

We try to cooperate with outside organizations. At the suggestion of the late Dennis Schapiro, we had a joint program with the League of Women Voters on Civil Discourse. We have kept up our membership in the National Coalition of Independent Scholars, and support events at the Minnesota History Center, though generally our numbers do not stretch to involvement in outside events.

Conclusion

What this narrative is designed to show is that independent scholarship in general and MISF in particular have evolved beyond the status of trying to replicate the academy.

Essentially, we have "come of age" as a free-standing organization. We offer an established set of services such as our journal, fiscal agency, regular meetings, as well as a web presence. We have an established process for providing these services: regular meetings and an elected board of directors. We have a clear mission statement. And we have been able to create a unique societal niche, in which people who have scholarly leanings and interests are encouraged to pursue subjects that intrigue and inspire them. We are not a substitute for the academy, but are rather functioning as a complement to it.

Accordingly, the following chapters highlight various aspects of the Minnesota Independent Scholars' Forum's organizational life: study groups, fiscal agency, monthly meetings, and our journal.

Notes for Chapter 7

99 Legacy grants are grants administered by the Minnesota Historical Society's Grants Office for the purpose of preserving the history of the state.

100 *PT* 8, no. 1 (March 2012).

101 Woolsey to Brusic, email, February 22, 2017.

102 This material, a reworking of Curt Hillstrom's report by a promotion committee, is abstracted from McTeer's report to the board. This material was reported in a MISF Marketing meeting in 2012.

PART 2
The Present: What MISF Does Today

NOTE: This book is built on writing by scholars. In the first seven chapters and in chapter 12 the writings are organized chronologically. The selections in chapters 8–11 are organized topically. For the convenience of the reader who might wish to read all the essays in the order in which they were written, a chronological listing is provided in the appendix. See page xx.

CHAPTER 8

STUDY AND DISCUSSION GROUPS

Study/discussion groups have been a vital part of MISF from the beginning of its existence. At the opening meeting, November 6, 1982, six reading/discussion groups were established:

1. A late eighteenth century study group headed by Sandra Sandell;
2. A study group in twentieth-century German literature;
3. A historiography group headed by P. J. (Patricia) Kulischek;
4. A discussion group on Richard Rorty's Book *The Consequences of Pragmatism*;
5. A discussion group on Roger Jones's book *Physics as Metaphor*;
6. A downtown luncheon group on children's literature.

People who were interested in other topics were encouraged to contact the then-president of the Scholars, John Butt.[103]

By the middle of 1983, these groups were still functioning, though the leadership had changed. In the summer of 1983, the Religion and Culture group and "A proposed mail order group for writers to try out their ideas" (headed by Carol Bly) had been added to the lineup.[104] By the end of 1983, the Late Eighteenth Century group reported that it was a group of five to seven people, meeting every four to six weeks. The Roger Jones group had become the Science/Humanities group, and the Richard Rorty group had become the Philosophy group consisting of "mostly philosophers." The Children's Literature Group had morphed into a Philosophy and Children's Literature group and the Historiography group was discussing social history. [105]

Study groups were so vital to the young MISF that they were the program for the 1984 Annual meeting, at which a "representative from each study group [discussed] the major problems or topics that [the] group explored during the past year or so."[106] After this annual meeting, four new groups were added to the roster: "Gender Roles and Culture," "China, History, and Culture," "Social Change," and "Politics and Aesthetics."

Six of these groups were still meeting a year later in 1985, although the headline that announced their activities was "Study Groups Sluggish."[107] The same six (more or less) were still meeting in 1986, although "Gender Roles and Culture" had become the "Group on International Feminism" and "German Literature" had become "German Literature and History."[108]

In 1987, a group studying American women and art had been added to the roster. Many other groups were, however, inactive by the time the Forum began to publish in 1989. In the first issue of the Forum, an entire page was given over to study groups, with the explanation that "[s]tudy groups provide members the opportunity to explore ideas through reading and discussion. [. . .] Anyone interested in 'sitting

Sidebar on Peter Shea and the *Humanities Scholars Newsletter*

One could write a considerable discussion about the intellectual ferment present in the Twin Cities in the middle 1980s using Peter Shea's *Humanities Scholars Newsletter* (HSN) as a primary source, but that insight is not the primary (or even the secondary) object of this book.

in' or joining currently established groups is welcome."[110] Nonetheless, the only two study groups that continued to be active in 1989 were "Science and Humanities" and "Eighteenth Century."

By the winter of 1990 a "Chaos" study group had been added, as had a group on "Patterns in Women's Spirituality." In the spring of 1991, reflecting the rise of the computer, the lineup again expanded to include "Communication and Information Technology" and "Intercultural Diversity."

Still, it is interesting to note that copies of HSN are a fascinating snapshot of the early 1980s. Shea attempted to list notices of "lectures, conferences, and presentations in the humanities (mostly in the metro area)"[109] on a monthly basis beginning in October 1982. His newsletters, which were stamped and mailed to subscribers, were always four and often six pages long, in 10-point type, full of all the information about speakers, meetings, and other happenings that Shea could squeeze in. His work is a glimpse into the intellectual ferment that characterized the era and reminds us of the importance of the humanities. It also reminds us that we do not now get the broad spread of information from the internet that we might from a humanities clearing house. And it reminds us that there was money available for the humanities and humanities programs in the early part of that decade. I am impressed at how much work Peter Shea put into his monthly publication, how hard it was for him to keep up with everything, and what a valuable insight into the period the *Humanities Scholars Newsletter* is.

The Science and Humanities Study Group

The Science and Humanities Group is an example of the Scholars' interdisciplinary spirit. The "Sci/Hum" group, as it came to be known, was the brainchild of Roger Jones. It apparently morphed out of the Chaos study group. Roger S. Jones was a professor in the Department of Physics at the University of Minnesota. He had a long-standing interest in the conflict and connection between science and the humanities. The group was active when the newsletter began in 1991 and continued until 2000, when it ceased to be sponsored by the Scholars (although it appears to have continued by private invitation). As Rhoda Gilman said of Roger Jones, the leader of the Sci/Hum group: "[He] spoke on physics as metaphor. Jones was in the physics department at the University of Minnesota. The physics department was looking for material research. Jones felt that his interest in seeing physics in relation to philosophy 'shut him out' of the department."[111]

In an interview with David Megarry in the summer of 2015, David Wiggins commented on the importance of Roger Jones and the Science and Humanities group.

> The Sci/Hum group was a fascinating blending of science and the humanities. Rhoda [Gilman] brought the Sci/Hum group together. She brought Roger Jones in, as she knew him through Zen circles. Rhoda knew about science through humanities. [The group brought] sciences up to a different place in the organization. Most independent scholarship did not incorporate sciences. [It was] too hard of an academic discipline. [But] both Megarry and Juncker came in with science backgrounds. Neither of them was narrow. They were fluent in humanities disciplines. Meta-message from the beginning [was to] keep and strengthen science. [I] hope it can continue. [I hope we can] keep and strengthen that component. We don't have a science discussion group at the moment. [We] need to pay attention to that, given current science issues.... There is definitely

plenty to talk about. Maybe [it is] a place where independence is significant.[112]

Roger Jones Writes

This article by Jones appeared in the *Forum* in the winter of 1991. Jones, a professor of physics at the University of Minnesota, had published a book, *Physics as Metaphor*, on the conflict between the humanities and science. Jones was a charter member of MISF.

A Scholar Writes

Science and the Independent Scholar
Roger S. Jones, 1991

A few months ago, I tuned in to the middle of a radio talk. The topic was science, and since I'm a scientist, it caught my attention. But this was not your everyday science talk—this guy was condemning science. He said (and I'm paraphrasing), "I used to think that science could get us out of our troubles. I really believed that pollution of the environment, nuclear weapons, information overload, and so on, were all technical problems that science would eventually solve. But with the passing years, I've lost my faith in science. If we don't stop science, it will stop us. The problems are multiplying much faster than the solutions, and we can no longer wait for the ethics of the scientific community to curb the researcher's obsession to do a thing simply because it's possible or because human curiosity must be satisfied." "Strong language," I thought to myself. And yet, the guy didn't sound like a kook. He knew what he was talking about.

Despite his radical message, he reasoned carefully and agonized over the enormity of his position. Who was he, anyway? l wondered. Could a scientist be so openly critical of science?

As the speaker concluded, he wisely proposed no simplistic solution, but urged serious thought about the future consequences of unbridled scientific research. The announcer came on: "You've just heard a talk by Pete Seeger." (I knew that voice had a familiar ring.)

"Pete Seeger," I mused. "Where does he get off advocating an end to science? What right does he . . ." But I caught myself. After all, Seeger has certainly spent most of his life struggling against the forces that oppress humanity. He is profoundly committed to using his art and fame [against] what he sees as antihuman trends in our civilization. He's thought about such matters as much as, if not more than, most Americans. Besides—and perhaps of greatest importance to me—I believe that, as a reasoning and intelligent person, Seeger has as much right as any scientist (perhaps more!) to critique and evaluate science in the light of its effect on modern life.

Now, Pete Seeger may not be an obvious model for an independent scholar. (He'd surely chuckle at the very idea.) But in his way, he's certainly a wise and seasoned student of history, politics, and human nature. His voice deserves respect and consideration. And so do the voices of thousands of people—who may or may not call themselves scholars—but whose positions as outside observers and students of science give them an advantage over insiders in objectively judging the consequences, import, and influence of science.

Independent scholars (not to mention independently minded people), whose principal interests lie in the humanities, and who have studied science from a conceptual, philosophical, historical, and aesthetic point of view, are in a position to make valuable contributions to the long-avoided (and even taboo) cultural and ethical evaluation of science. Unfortunately, we are unlikely ever to get such an evaluation from within the scientific community itself. Scientists need prodding and guidance, although they are often too arrogant and self-centered to see it. Here is an opportunity and an obligation that the community of independent scholars cannot afford to miss.

Other Study Groups

Study groups rose and fell until 1994, when for reasons that are by now obscure, President Bob Thimmesh announced in a letter titled "Dear Independent Scholar" that two new study groups would be forming. One would be a Religion and Culture study group chaired by Curt Hillstrom and Susan Smith; the other would be the Philosophy study group chaired by Curt Hillstrom and Bob Thimmesh.[113] The importance of this announcement is not so much that two more study groups were formed, but that Curt Hillstrom became formally involved with them, which he has been ever since.

The Philosophy Study Group

Hillstrom has shepherded the Philosophy study group since 1994. It has grown from a group of four or five participants to a gathering so large that Hillstrom is presently running two sessions, one on Mondays and one on Wednesdays. The group is advertised on meetup.com, where it has 550 followers, and by group email to a select mailing list.

Although the group is now reading books, such as *The Cave and the Light: Plato Versus Aristotle and the Struggle for the Soul of Western Civilization* by Arthur Herman, for many years it read and discussed papers and articles such as this one (below) by Hillstrom.

Hillstrom wrote this account in response to a request from the editor of *Practical Thinking*, when it was sharing its publication with MACAE (2005-2007). The broader audience suggested a slightly broader frame of reference.

A Scholar Writes

The Curious Case of Recurring Philosophies
Curt Hillstrom, 2007

Except for a couple of brief intervals, the Minnesota Independent Scholars' Forum has hosted a Philosophy study group for all of its nearly twenty-five years. As its coordinator for the last dozen years or so, I have marveled at the variety of opinions people express at our meetings. (Perhaps this should not be surprising. After all, the history of philosophy is cluttered with widely divergent ideas.) I recently had extended conversations with two of our members. These two have worldviews which were arrived at through considerable reasoning, although the conclusions they have come to are quite diverse.

Even though Phil majored in physics in college, he was never quite satisfied with the scientific explanations of the universe. Yes, scientists can tell you that magnets attract, and they can even use sophisticated mathematics to predict exactly how it will happen. But they cannot ultimately explain how magnetism works. Even after fancy theories of electromagnetic waves and quantum particles, there always seems to be another level that science needs to go to provide a more adequate explanation. After college, Phil worked at a variety of jobs, including ones dealing with computers. Impressed with the power and flexibility of these machines, he concluded that the universe works much the same way. What we regard as the natural world is actually a virtual world. The laws of the universe work the way they do because that is the way that God programmed the cosmos. Human beings are like characters in a video game, manipulated not by some evil or indifferent entity, but essentially by themselves. That is, by their souls, who exist in a different world—the real world—with God. Goals, drives, hopes, and ambitions lie with the soul, but the soul is constrained in this operation by the virtual character it controls. Mental illness, physical limitation, or an unfavorable environment are something over which the soul does not have control.

Rich, by contrast, has no trouble accepting the world we experience as an independent, objective reality. But to determine exactly what this world is, and to come to some kind of general agreement about it, requires careful reasoning and precise procedures. The best of these procedures is the scientific method. This involves carefully collected data and well-tested hypotheses to come to conclusions which, unfortunately but inevitably, are always heuristic. Nonetheless, this procedure has acquitted itself well over the last five centuries. Critical listening and Socratic reasoning can also give us confidence in the probability of something being true. The emphasis here is on probability, not certainty. And when it comes to gods and supernatural powers, these can be pretty well eliminated by Occam's Razor, which awards the less complicated system the honor of being most likely true, as well as the lack of any objective way to verify such powers.

Similarity to Enlightenment Philosophy

At about the same time I was talking with these gentlemen about their beliefs, I was also reading about Enlightenment philosophy. One thing that struck me about these two diverse ways of looking at the world was how much they paralleled the dominant philosophies of the Enlightenment: rationalism and empiricism. Phil's philosophy would be the rationalist one. Dissatisfied with scientific explanations, he, like the rationalists, used his mind, imagination, and experiences to posit a whole new system that he felt more comfortable with. His worldview is unorthodox; some would probably call it bizarre. But is it really so different in this respect from that of Gottfried

Wilhelm Leibniz, the influential Enlightenment philosopher who came up with the idea of monads[?] According to Leibniz, a monad is a point in space (though he denies that there is anything like space as we presume to know it), an indivisible entity with, essentially, just a long list of experiences. A human being is one sort of monad. Monads do not physically interact with each other, though we seem to, since our experiences are coordinated with the experiences of other monads through the pre-established harmony created by God.[114]

Rich's philosophy would, of course, represent empiricism, since he is, simply enough, an empiricist. He feels that what we know comes basically from what we experience in the world around us: the sights, sounds, and other phenomena that reach our senses, along with the data that we obtain from our scientific instruments. The mind is important in utilizing this data and turning it into theories and useful predictions, but the mind cannot reliably go beyond what this data tells us. Reason by itself does not contain any magic kernels that, simply through contemplation, can be expanded into philosophical insights of profound importance. Unlike Phil, Rich feels that science has done a marvelous job of explicating the universe. According to Rich, the scientific method is far superior to what even a brilliant mind can come up with on its own.

While the coincidence of talking to Phil and Rich at the same time as I was reading about Enlightenment philosophy led me to see these parallels, it soon became apparent that this dichotomy between rationalists and empiricists has always existed, though they have not always used those names. It is more like a division between, roughly (very roughly), believers and skeptics. The former are people who look at the world and say, "This can't be all there is!" and promptly begin looking for, and finding, the meaning of things beyond the obvious. Reality is not appearance. Skeptics, on the other hand, are people who look at the world and say, "Okay, this is what we have, and any claims about something beyond this cannot be reasonably justified." Their philosophies try to deal with the world as it directly appears to us. This doesn't mean that skeptics have no beliefs or theories, just that their beliefs cannot transcend what can be confirmed from experience.

Perhaps the clearest example of this split is between Plato, with his eternal Forms which epitomize everything from circles to goodness, and Aristotle, who rejected the Forms and, by fourth-century BCE standards, did some pretty good science. But the split starts even before that time, as philosophical questions first began to be raised in ancient Greece. Pythagoras and Heraclitus argued for, respectively, a mathematical mysticism and the universally controlling principle of logos, while Democritus and Empedocles presented physical elements (atoms for Democritus; earth, air, fire, and water for Empedocles) that defined the world for them. Later, during the Roman Empire, Saint Augustine became the first great Christian philosopher (in the process adapting Heraclitus's logos), while the Epicureans and Stoics resolved problems on how to live on an earth that holds the only life we have.

After the Enlightenment, a particularly interesting example of the split showed up in the nineteenth century. Georg Wilhelm Friedrich Hegel believed that mankind's pursuit of this reality-beyond-mere-appearance (for Hegel another logos) is the driving force that, along with a law of historical process, will ultimately reveal the Absolute. Karl Marx then "turned Hegel on his head" and proposed a historical process in which labor and the laws of economics will eventually create an earthly workers' paradise. But one has to be careful with these broad generalizations. There are philosophers who are hard to categorize.

Still, as Bertrand Russell commented regarding one's attitude toward God, either you believe or you don't.

History and Philosophy

Significantly, there have been times in history when either the believers or the skeptics have gained political control. In medieval Europe, Christian philosophy so dominated that anyone who advocated a philosophy that was significantly at odds with the Scholastic ideas of the time risked losing their freedom to present opinions, their position, or even their life. Copernicus waited until he was on his deathbed to publish his theory of heliocentric astronomy; Galileo was forced to apologize and placed under house arrest for agreeing with Copernicus; and Giordano Bruno met the ultimate fate at the burning stake for his outspoken ideas of a universe, ideas contrary to those held by the church. In this environment, while the church provided succor for the souls of citizens, the overwhelming majority lived in appalling poverty. So little scientific or philosophical investigation was allowed that this period has come to be known as the Dark Ages.

More recently, communist revolutions, inspired by Marx to hurry along the workers' paradise, occurred in many countries. Once in control, the communists employed their interpretation of the scientific method (including Marx's economic theories) to determine how things should be done. The church was suppressed; capitalism and many related freedoms were constrained. The citizens, while guaranteed the material necessities for a reasonably comfortable life, were left with a kind of spiritual void.

The leaders of both medieval Europe and twentieth-century communism genuinely had the best interests of the populace at heart. But the believers did not want the skeptics to undermine the real truth, and the skeptics did not want the believers to infect the public with preposterous ideas. To thrive, a society needs both. When the believers are allowed to present their case without fear of suppression; when the skeptics are allowed to critique the believers; when the religious and the artistic are allowed to inspirit the people; when the scientific and the technical are allowed to propose and test their ideas—only then will a society exist which can shelter and feed its citizens as well as care for their souls. Such an ideal society may be historically inevitable or it may not. Regardless, it is one worth pursuing.

History Study Group

Since 2009, MISF has also sponsored a History Study Group. Hillstrom is assisted in this group by MISF member and board member, Emily Pollack. This group has recently read such books as *Washington's Farewell* by John Avlon and *Alexander Humboldt and the Invention of Nature* by Andrea Wulf. Usually the discussion of long books is spread over two or three months' meetings. The group is small, but it has a loyal core. As with all MISF activities, attendance is open to the public whether they are members of the Forum or not.

Notes for Chapter 8

103 *HSN* 1, no. 3 (December 1982).

104 *HSN* 1, no. 9 (Summer 1983).

105 *HSN* 2, no. 4 (December 1983).

106 News and Views (November 1984).

107 News and Views (November/ December 1985).

108 News and Views (April 1986).

109 *HSN* masthead.

110 *The Forum* 1, no. 1 (Spring 1989).

111 Brusic interview with Rhoda Gilman, July 3, 2017.

112 Megarry interview with David Wiggins, July 7, 2016.

113 Letter to members from Robert Thimmesh, December 14, 1994.

114 The idea of the universe as a computer or an information processing system has been around since at least the mid-nineteenth century. Phil says the most recent proponent is Seth Lloyd, whose book, *Programming the Universe: a Quantum Computer Scientist Takes on the Cosmos* (Knopf, 2006), makes the same argument, though without any God. [footnote to original article]

CHAPTER 9

Grants and Fiscal Agency
by Michael Woolsey

Longtime MISF member and former president David Juncker indicates that the idea of providing administrative support and fiscal agency for grant awards to individual scholars has been part of the MISF mission since its early years, and certainly since 1987. But actual steps to set up a fiscal agency structure were not taken until 1994, when a fiscal agency bank account was set up at National City Bank of Minneapolis. Then it was not until 1996 that MISF, acting as fiscal agent for the grantee, received the first grant award.

Since then, there have been a total of sixteen grant awards made under the auspices of MISF, from four grantor organizations: Minnesota Humanities Commission, Minnesota Historical Society, E.L. & E.J. Andersen Foundation, and the Minneapolis Foundation. Initially, the grant awards went to individual scholars, with MISF acting as fiscal agent, but later awards from the Minnesota Historical Society have been made to MISF itself as the grantee. In this case, MISF has been responsible for all aspects of the projects, its member-scholars serving as either volunteers or paid contributors.

Here is descriptive information on each of these grants.

1. Nuer Journeys: Narratives of War, Flight, and Resettlement in a Twin Cities Sudanese Refugee Community

Date: June 1996
Grantor: Minnesota Historical Society
Grantee: Jon Holtzman
Grant Amount: $4,640.00

Based on research funded by this grant (together with funding from a postdoctoral fellowship of the International Migration Program of the Social Science Research Council and the Andrew Mellon Foundation), Holtzman published a book, *Nuer Journeys, Nuer Lives: Sudanese Refugees in Minnesota* (Pearson Education, 2000), that juxtaposed elements of Nuer culture, which are well known within anthropology (and featured in most anthropology textbooks), with new developments arising from the immigration of many Nuer to the US in the 1990s. They came as refugees from a civil war in southern Sudan.

In addition, Mr. Holtzman presented his research results to a meeting of the Minnesota Independent Scholars' Forum at the Minneapolis Walker Library in May, 1997.

2. Songs, Heroes, and Legends: The Cultural Side of Rural Public Education in the Cokato, Minnesota Community (1910-1935)

Date: June 1996
Grantor: Minnesota Humanities Commission
Scholar: Gloria Morris-Grothe
Grant Amount: $2,000.00

The project explored the way public schools functioned in a community of the past to help students of an immigrant population achieve goals, reach aspirations, and develop character traits compatible with a democratic society. The project was an extension of documentation for the researcher's M.A. thesis about the relationship of Swedish songs to immigrant experience both in the Swedish homeland and in this country. The project involved a case study of rural Minnesota schools near the town of Cokato, 1910–1935. During that period, public schools placed much emphasis on Americanization, the US became involved in World War I, and the Great Depression followed.

In 1997, Morris-Grothe made two public presentations of the research results, one at the Cokato Museum/Historical Society, and the other for the Minnesota Independent Scholars' Forum at the Walker Library, November 1997, in Minneapolis. In 1998, research results were sent to both Education Committee members of the state legislature and to the University of Minnesota's Center for School Change.

3. A Comparative Study of Religious Architecture in the Old and New World

Date: May 1999
Grantor: Minnesota Humanities Commission
Grantee: Marilyn J. Chiat
Amount: $2,500.00

The project researched questions and proposed answers about the appearance of places of worship built by immigrants and their descendants who settled in the United States. Questions included: How did immigrants decide on the appearance of their places of worship in a new world? Why were certain decorative, religious, and architectural elements replicated in the new world while others were not? What factors led to the choices? What were the underlying changes made over time between first- and second-generation religious buildings? What cultural, social, technological, theological, and liturgical reasons contributed to the choices and later, the changes? A comparative study of the appearance of places of worship left behind in the Old World with those built in the New revealed what was retained and what was discarded and led to answers as to why choices and changes were made. The study contributed to a more complete understanding of the complexities associated with the Americanization process experienced by all the nation's newcomers.

Dr. Chiat is an architectural historian with a doctoral degree from the University of Minnesota. She has been a member of the Minnesota Independent Scholars' Forum since its very early days and was the recipient of a Scholar of the Year award in 1988 (See chapter 2). She reported on her research in the winter 1999–2000 issue of the *Forum*.

A Scholar Writes

A Comparative Study of Religious Architecture in the New and Old Worlds
Marilyn Chiat, 1999

Research is a journey, a journey that often takes unexpected but productive detours. This is what happened to me this fall as I began research for my proposed publication, *Sacred Quotes*, a project funded in part by a grant from the Minnesota Humanities Commission and administered by the Minnesota Independent Scholars' Forum.

Work began on the project, "A Comparative Study of Religious Architecture in the Old and New Worlds," in September 1999. In the process of developing criteria for the selection of sites to be included in the study, I became increasingly aware of the need to examine not only the architectural style and plan of a place of worship, but also the religious objects and artifacts selected by the congregation for decoration and/or veneration. In visiting a number of Lutheran and Roman Catholic churches erected by differing ethnic groups, I observed on display, usually above or behind an altar, two similar images of Christ. One is a copy of the Danish sculptor Bertel Alberto Thorwaldsen's *Christ*, either in pure white plaster (the original dating to ca. 1830 is in white Carrara marble) or painted in lifelike colors. The second is a somewhat similar figure of Christ, but with his hands raised, showing his stigmata, and a bleeding heart displayed on his cloak.

The question these two images raise is why these particular figures of Christ were selected out of numerous choices by these congregations, regardless of their ethnic roots or religious faith. Adding another layer of complexity to the question is the fact that unlike many images of Christ in the Old World, where his physiognomy often reflects the ethnicity of the worshippers, in these churches Christ's image has been romanticized to conform to an ideal of a Nordic man. Who produced these images, and how did they come to appear in so many diverse places of worship, placed there by immigrant settlers in the United States?

I brought these questions to Professor Rudolph Vecoli, Director of the Immigration History Research Center (IHRC) at the University of Minnesota. The IHRC is one of the project's cosponsors, and Professor Vecoli, along with his staff, has always been supportive of my research. Professor Vecoli's suggestion was to research Italian figurinai. The makers of figurinai were artisans from the Media Valle of the Serchio and the Val di Lima, a region north of Lucca in western Italy. They were trained in small village ateliers to make plaster figurines. These artisans then fanned out all over the world producing and peddling their wares: images of domestic animals (their first casts were of goats and dogs, produced in about the sixteenth century), various types of garden statuary, nativities, and mythical, heroic, and religious statues. Those who emigrated to the United States founded companies that produced a large percentage of all the religious statuary in American churches. One of those companies is St. Paul Statuary, located in St. Paul, Minnesota.

Professor Vecoli provided me with names of scholars in Italy who could give me more information about the figurinai. I arranged to meet with the scholars in October. In Rome, I met with Regina Soria, Professor Emeritus at the College of Notre Dame in Maryland. Her major area of interest is the artistic interrelations between Italy and the United States, as published in her book *American Artists of Italian Heritage* 1776–1945 (Associated University Presses, 1993). I spent a very productive day with Professor Soria. As I turned to page 80 of my signed copy of her book, I found information about John Garatti, a marble carver born in 1881 in Torino, Italy, who settled in St. Paul ca. 1911 and produced, among other work, the group of the twelve Apostles on the facade of the St. Paul Cathedral.

I then traveled north to Lucca, where Dr. Lucilla Briganti, an expert on Italian immigration and former research fellow at IHRC, had made arrangements for me to visit the Museo della Figurina di Gesso Emigrazione at Coreglio Antelminelli, a small hill town north of [the city]. It was in this small village that the art of making plaster figurines originated, where it became the principal occupation of the local people. The museum not only displays over a thousand plaster statuettes, but also has rooms showing the methods employed in the manufacture of the figurines. Of particular interest to me was the exhibition of religious subjects which, according to the museum's director, during the second half of the nineteenth century made many an artisan's fortune. There, displayed in a catalog of a statuary company in the United States founded by

Italian artisans, were the two Christ figures I saw in so many American churches.

My plans include further investigation of churches that have this particular statuary, and the companies that supplied them. This detour on my journey has proved to be very rewarding, and the information I have uncovered will, I am certain, be included in my published work. But I must now return to the main road of my research and finish compiling the list of potential sites that will make up the format of my book. In December, I have travel plans to discuss German churches with Dr. Patricia Eckhardt in Iowa, and to look at Volga German churches in Kansas' rural areas with Professor Diane Thomas Lincoln from Wichita State University. I also intend to continue my research at the Getty Research Institute in Los Angeles.

I am very grateful to the Minnesota Humanities Commission for providing partial funding for this project, and to the Minnesota Independent Scholars' Forum for agreeing to administer my grant. It is only with this kind of support that independent scholars, such as myself, can pursue our research.

4. Production of The *Bat of Minerva*—A Philosophy Show

Date: December 1999
Grantor: Minnesota Humanities Commission
Grantee: Peter Shea
Amount: $2,000.00

Mr. Shea produced 30 hour-long episodes of *The Bat of Minerva* cable TV show, in the period from January 30 through December 15, 2000. The episodes raised and explored philosophic questions in a variety of personal and professional contexts. At least ten of the episodes involved professional philosophers. The others explored philosophic issues with articulate people reflecting on their personal and professional lives. The show was a one-hour discussion with one to three guests. Mr. Shea was the host for each episode, which was cablecast throughout the seven-county metro area of Minneapolis and St. Paul. The grant award paid the cost of cable access through Metro Cable Network. Mr. Shea concluded the project by submitting the following Final Report to the Minnesota Humanities Commission.

A Scholar Writes

Media Grant Production
for *The Bat of Minerva*
Peter Shea, 2001

The Bat of Minerva produced and distributed programs containing philosophic reflection on diverse human experiences. Our guest list included established philosophers, beginning philosophers, and reflective people with a variety of experience and expertise. We had the great privilege of featuring some important public philosophers: Senator Eugene McCarthy consented to an interview, and Martha Nussbaum agreed to let us cablecast her "Mitau" lecture at Macalester. We also arranged an interview with May Ellen Petrisko, a philosopher now working as Deputy Commissioner of Higher Education for Maryland, and finally broached the University of St. Thomas philosophy department with an interview with the distinguished Catholic philosopher, Thomas Sullivan.

Our academic interviews outside of philosophy were wide-ranging. We had a wonderful session with the state microbiologist, John Hunt, on the epistemology of medical testing, and two fine sessions with public sculptors and professors of art,

Andrea Myklebus and Stanton Sears. Mary Rose O'Reilley, an English professor, discussed and read from her recent book *The Barn at the End of the World*, and Juanita Garciagodoy, who teaches Spanish literature at Macalester, did sessions on Mexican spirituality and Day of the Dead rituals. Other guests this season represented the academic disciplines of anthropology, library science, geography, and theater.

The world outside of the academy was also well represented. We were pleased to invite Deborah Martin, the director of the Minnesota Folk Festival, to discuss folk music. Sandra Meyer, a professional clown, talked about clowning. Other non-academic guests included a chaplain, a bookstore owner, an architect, an alumni relations director, a retired high-school English teacher, a science-fiction author, a liturgist, and an Australian traditional healer.

It was a very rich season.

5. Minnesota Women in Sports

Date: January 2000
Grantor: E.L. & E.J. Anderson Foundation
Grantee: Kathleen Ridder
Amount: $6,000.00

In the spring of 1999, sixteen women agreed to participate in a book, a collection of essays titled *Minnesota Women in Sports*. The authors attached great importance to the project because they believed strongly that women's sports history, of both individual and team competition, along with the history of women's sports organizations, should be preserved for future generations.

Each essay tells a distinct and compelling story of the aspirations, achievements, and frustrations of a career, and exhibits the author's personal commitment to equality for women. It describes what motivated the author to join the sports arena (e.g. family, school, the women's movement, coincidence, money, and/or mentors) and when she became visible in the sports world. It reviews the inequities that the author faced in the sports field, including both overt and covert discrimination, the specific conflicts that arose, the absence of sufficient funds, and the lack of media support.

This collection of memoirs adds a new and significant dimension to the record of Minnesota women's experience in the twentieth century. The media has covered highly visible athletic achievements of women when they happened, but has rarely provided background material that elucidates the hurdles that women athletes overcame to achieve victory. The stories in this book are intended to remedy that deficiency.

The sixteen women who contributed to the book are: Janet Allen (figure skating), Jeanne Arth (tennis), Margaret Chutich (research), Gertrude Fink (bowling), Jean Freeman (swimming), Marion Bemis Johnson (basketball), Eloise M. Jaeger (University of Minnesota), Judy Mahle Lutter (sport and health), Dorothy McIntyre (high school athletics), Sandra Peterson (recreation), Patricia A. Stringer (softball), Beverly Vanstrom (golf), Chris Voelz (intercollegiate athletics), Jean A. Brookins (editor), Barbara Stuhler (editor), and Kathleen Ridder (introduction).

The project resulted in the publication of a book of memoir-essays by fourteen women athletes, *Minnesota Women in Sports: Leveling the Playing Field* (North Star Press, 2005).

6. The Spiritual Traveler: Chicago and the Great Lakes

Date: March 2001
Grantor: Minnesota Humanities Commission
Grantee: Marilyn Chiat
Grant Amount: $2,500.00

The purpose of the project was to expand the research and information available in the author's previous book, *America's Religious Architecture: Sacred Places for Every Community* (John Wiley & Sons, 1997), so that a greater variety of sacred sites could be made known to the public. Because of the more limited geographic parameters of this book, the author was able to explore a greater variety of sites in more detail. These structures and sacred sites are important historical "documents"—texts with important stories to tell about the people who came to settle in this country. The project attempted to make people aware of these sacred sites, both the built and the natural. It explains how to "listen" to the stories that make these places special to others. Exploring a sacred place involves a twofold journey, in both the sense of travel to a site and a journey of enlightenment—gaining a better understanding of our nation's great diversity as displayed in its many spiritual spaces and the stories they embody.

The project resulted in the publication of *The Spiritual Traveler: Chicago and Illinois: A Guide to Sacred Sites and Peaceful Places* (Hidden Spring, 2004).

7. The Development of Psychiatric Nosology in Minnesota State Hospitals 1885-1910

>Date: July 2001
>Grantor: Minnesota Humanities Commission
>Grantee: Patricia A. Ross
>Amount: $2,500.00

Current categories used to identify and treat mental disorders have developed out of the diagnostic classificatory systems (called nosologies) that arose in the state hospitals and asylums of the late nineteenth and early twentieth centuries. While contemporary scientific work acts to refine and provide a physiological basis for some of these categories, a vast part of the current system remains a direct product of the developments that took place during this historical period. However, these developments have not been carefully explored. This project examined documents from Minnesota's state hospitals during this time period. The general purpose was to investigate the types of categories for diagnosing and treating mental health [being used] in Minnesota's state hospitals. There were, at that time, as there are today, competing theories regarding the causes and processes of mental disorders. The research addressed which, if any, underlying theory of mental disorders these diagnostic categories suggest, with intent to provide a better understanding of the historical development of current psychiatric nosology from the perspective of Minnesota's state hospitals and to compare Minnesota's history with that of other areas.

Questions are continually raised concerning the validity of diagnostic concepts as well as the degree to which such concepts reflect nothing more than the values of the current society. Accordingly, care was taken to note any social, moral, or religious norms that may be influencing all such developments.

The larger project, of which this was a part, addressed the question of how psychiatric concepts are formed and change over time, whether any of these changes reflect a move toward a more objective, less value-laden nosology, and how concepts reflect particular metaphysical frameworks.

The research results were described in two papers—one submitted for presentation at the American Psychiatric Association meeting in May 2002, and another sent to the journal *Philosophy of Science*. Moreover, presentations of the results were made to both the Minnesota Independent Scholars' Forum and the Minnesota Bioethics Center.

8. Revitalizing the infrastructure of the MISF organization

Date: January 2002
Grantor: Minnesota Humanities Commission
Grantee: MISF Minnesota Independent Scholars' Forum
Amount: $2,000.00

The grant supported various functions of the MISF organization, including production of the MISF journal (then known as the *Forum*), website design, annual meeting room rental, publicity ads, etc.

9. Building the Telecommunications and Information Policy Roundtable (TIPR) Framework

Date: April 2006
Grantor: Minneapolis Foundation
Grantee: Mary Treacy
Amount: $2,500.00

The project augmented the Telecommunications and Information Policy Roundtable (TIPR) framework to create a coalition to identify policy players; local effective practices and their policy components; relationships with other working groups; and needs (including research, tools, communication networks, and policy development in other locales).

Concrete outcomes of this project were two multi-organization meetings: one in May 2006, cosponsored by TIPR, the American Society of Information Science and Technology (ASIST), and the Minnesota Coalition on Government (MNCOGI); and the other, a major conference planned for March 2007, sponsored by TIPR, MNCOGI, and the Minneapolis Public Library.

10. Policy Roots of the Digital Justice Agenda

Date: June 2006
Grantor: Minneapolis Foundation
Grantee: Mary Treacy
Amount: $9,500.00

The Telecommunications and Information Policy Roundtable (TIPR) took the lead:

1. To strengthen itself as a venue for identification and discussion of policy issues implicit in technology decisions;
2. To convene information sessions that were readily accessible to community groups currently grappling with technology developments;
3. To establish an online issues alert system;
4. To identify and share existing resources with community action groups;
5. To assist communities of interest to use technology tools and resources, including access to public information, to substantiate their needs;
6. To identify and try to mitigate barriers, including language, geography, physical challenges, and cultural specifics;
7. To craft specific content and tools to be used by communities of interest, particularly communities of color and economically challenged groups;
8. To link existing resources with current needs at the community level.

Organizational partners in this project were TIPR, MISF, MNCOGI, the Minnesota Coalition for Freedom of Information, the Joint Media Committee, and the Minnesota Chapter of the American Society of Information Science and Technology.

As a result of these efforts, a major conference, "Afloat in the Wireless Pond," took place at Luther Seminary in St. Paul in March 2008. A MISF journal report on that conference, by Charles Cubrimi, is included in chapter 6.

11. In Behalf of the Neediest: A History of the Salvation Army's Booth Memorial Hospital, St. Paul

> Date: December 2013
> Grantor: Minnesota Historical Society Grants office, administrating Legacy Funds
> Grantee: Minnesota Independent Scholars' Forum (contract scholar: Kim Heikkila)
> Amount: $10,000.00

The researcher accessed primary source material from local, regional, and national archives, establishing a history (1913–1971) of the Salvation Army Booth Memorial Hospital for unwed mothers. Heikkila holds a Ph.D. in American Studies from the University of Minnesota. The following account of her research appeared in the MISF journal (*Practical Thinking*), December 2014:

A Scholar Writes

To Bear the Mark: Unwed Motherhood at the Salvation Army's Booth Memorial Hospital (A Work-in-Progress Report)
Kim Heikkila, 2014

The building still stands at 1471 Como Avenue in St. Paul. Its red brick exterior, gabled roof, and three-story tower reflect the Tudor Revival style of the early twentieth century. A concrete addition from a later era sits at the east end of the structure. Drivers traveling along Como Avenue have to peer beyond a row of hedges to get a good glimpse of the place. If they pass too quickly, they might not hear the echoes of young women's chatter or babies' wails. For sixty years, from 1913 to 1973, the Salvation Army operated this stately mansion as a home and hospital for unwed mothers. Women from across Minnesota fled to Booth Memorial Hospital to hide their pregnancies and deliver their babies out of view of friends, family, and neighbors. Sometimes, they left Booth with their babies; oftentimes, they left Booth empty-armed, heartbroken, but hopeful that they were giving their children better lives. "It was hard for me to give him up," said a 19-year-old woman of her newborn son in 1963, "but I realized he would have a happy home." Besides, she explained, she was the one who had erred. "It's better that I bear the grief and the mark instead of the child. It was my mark, not his."[115]

I've been conducting research into the history of Booth Memorial Hospital since 2012. In the fall of 2013, some of my colleagues in the Minnesota History Researchers Group and I met with MISF board members to see if MISF could secure a Minnesota Arts & Cultural Heritage Fund (i.e. Legacy) Grant that would help support my research. Mike Woolsey, David Megarry, and I wrote a grant proposal that MISF submitted in October 2013; by the end of the year, MISF had been awarded the grant and, after accepting bids from other scholars, named me as primary researcher for the project.

These funds have been instrumental to my continuing research, allowing me to examine sources at the Minnesota Historical Society, the University of Minnesota Libraries, and the Salvation Army National Archives in Alexandria, Virginia. The records of private charitable organizations, state and county welfare departments and committees, hospital planning commissions, and the Salvation Army Women's Social Services Department show how the practice of maternal surrender of "illegitimate" children waxed and waned over the course of the twentieth century. As such, they help us contextualize the experiences of the young woman who reluctantly placed her baby for adoption in 1963.

Most of the materials I examined reflect the attitudes and practices of experts who took it as their responsibility to help mend the tear in the social fabric caused by unmarried pregnancy. In Booth's early years, Ramsey County social workers and Salvation Army officers alike believed that active motherhood would best redeem the illegitimately pregnant and their offspring. The 1914 annual report for Booth, for instance, emphasized the importance of "keeping the tie between mother and child unbroken." During the post-World War II era, however, explanations for illicit pregnancy had shifted from the moral to the psychological, and professionals believed (at least for the white middle class) that mother and child would be better off if they started life anew, child with a well-prepared adoptive family and mother with a supposedly clean slate. By 1952, 43 percent of unmarried mothers who appeared before the Ramsey County Welfare Board were surrendering their babies for adoption. Practices at Booth followed suit: of the 376 babies discharged from Booth in 1967, only 47 went home with their mothers; 189 went to adoption agencies, 140 to "other" care providers. The trend was reversing itself a mere four years later, however, when 77 percent of unmarried mothers in Ramsey County chose (or were able) to raise their children.[116] Booth ceased to function as a home for unwed mothers in mid-1973 as changing attitudes about sex and single motherhood rendered its services unnecessary.

As illuminating as they may be, statistics gleaned from meeting minutes and committee reports tell only part of the story; they don't provide much insight into the experiences of individual unwed mothers. The general paucity of information about actual unwed mothers makes the Gisela Konopka papers at the University of Minnesota Archives a real treasure. Konopka was a sociologist who studied teenaged girls and, with the help of an assistant, interviewed thirty-three "Booth girls" in 1963; her papers include the edited transcripts of these (and other) interviews, which became the basis of her 1966 book *The Adolescent Girl in Conflict* (Prentice Hall, 1966).

The interviews reveal the struggle these young women faced in deciding their future and the future of their babies. Many of them expressed sorrow at losing their babies alongside a hope that adoption was in the children's best interests. Like the 19-year-old who surrendered her son, a 17-year-old girl believed that her daughter would have a better life in an adoptive family: "She always will be my daughter, but I realize that it is not fair for me to keep her," she told Konopka's assistant, Vernie-Mae Czaky. "She is in very good hands and that's what I want for her." Yet the decisions were not the girls' alone. Many girls surrendered their babies at the urging of parents or pastors, adults who wielded considerable influence in the lives of dependent teenagers. When they did so, however, they faced public censure, as when Hennepin County court referee Alden Sheffield scolded a young mother for being unwilling "to put forth the effort for her own flesh and blood," the result of her "selfish gratification" of desires. Another 17-year-old summed up the sad dilemma: "Most of us really feel we care for the babies, and we love them, and if the older people realize we love the babies, then perhaps there will be less hate for the girls who get in trouble."[117]

The Konopka interviews show Booth's residents wrestling with painful decisions about their babies, a useful counterpoint to the views of external experts. Yet they are only a drop in the bucket; thirty-three voices from one year out of the more than ten thousand girls and women Booth served over sixty years. The weight of the archival evidence I've gathered tips toward the external, showing us Booth from the outside in. Making sense of the past even with an incomplete record is the historian's task, however. In this case, the job has been made much easier with the support of MISF and the Minnesota Arts and Cultural Heritage Fund.

12. Dakota Life in Minnesota in the 19th Century

Date: July 2014
Grantor: Walt and Elizabeth Bachman's Donor-Advised Fund at the Minneapolis Foundation
Grantee: Carrie Zeman
Amount: $5,000.00

A probe of National Archives (NARA) Record Group 217, Records of the Accounting Officers of the Department of the Treasury, to identify the location, type, and scope of the extant record generated by the Federal Government's treaty obligations to Dakota people in Minnesota between 1830 and 1863. The project included research trips to the National Archives in Washington, D.C., digitization of selected records, research in corollary collections, analysis of findings, writing of reports, and presentations on results. It gathered information that allowed the Minnesota Historical Society to pursue incorporating the digitization of select records. This body of 1863 testimony had been sheltered from the vagaries of six generations of historical interpretation. In a very real sense, these rediscovered claims allow Minnesotans to speak in their own voice for the first time in 150 years, and to an audience having both a more sympathetic view of Dakota people and a more nuanced understanding of the push-and-pull factors that led both sides to war in 1862. Further, the claims have come to light in an era when digitization—the only way to navigate the massive volume of testimony—is the standard for reproduction, and when information management technology like databases and digital mapping are routinely applied to history. The study of history now includes quantitative sub-disciplines that scholars will apply to mine these stories collectively, adding macro-value to the 2,800+ narrative parts of this collection.

Project results of this research:

1. Preliminary analysis, description and inventory of the Treaty of 1858 settlement ledgers in E525;
2. Description and location of settlements for earlier Dakota treaties, if extant;
3. Preliminary analysis, description, and inventory of the settled accounts of the Superintendents of Indian Affairs for the Northern Superintendence and of the Agents of the St. Peter's [Dakota] Agency.

Ms. Zeman's discoveries have become a matter of common knowledge at NARA. They are public records, open to all, and the 1863 Sioux Claims have been of so much interest that the LincolnAchives.org (LADP) has begun digitizing the entire collection—2,940 claims, perhaps 50,000 page images. It remains to be seen where they will be hosted online. LADP may put them up, or they may sell the digital manifestations to an entity like MNHS.

13. The Salvation Army's Booth Memorial Hospital for Unwed Mothers Oral History Project

Date: December 2016
Grantor: Minnesota Historical Society Grants Office, administrating Legacy Funds
Grantee: Minnesota Independent Scholars' Forum (contract scholar: Kim Heikkila)
Amount: $9,557.00

The project documents the experiences of women who were at the hospital from the 1950s through its closing in 1971. Oral histories are recorded with nine interviewees, including women who were at the hospital during their pregnancies and others involved in their care during their stay at Booth.

This project builds on the Salvation Army's Booth Memorial Hospital for Unwed Mothers archives research project awarded to the Minnesota Independent Scholars' Forum in 2014. The project identified primary sources about the little-known work of the Salvation Army's Booth Hospital—common in the early and middle years of the 20th century—of caring for unwed mothers during their pregnancies. The standard outcome of this treatment was releasing the children for adoption. Archival research through the 2014 project identified the reasons and purposes for this treatment, but did not include the experiences of the women who were part of it. The memories and insights into their experiences in the Booth Hospital, both in interactions with administrators and in their interactions with one another, are part of the untold Booth Hospital story.

Preparation by the oral historian for the interviews drew on information in the primary source material identified through the preceding archives research project. Based on this research, common interview topics for all interviewees were identified; additional research was then done to develop questions within these topics that met each interviewee's specific area of knowledge.

The suggested interview topics included:
- The basic story of the women's pregnancy and need for care as unwed mothers;
- The information the women were given about Booth Hospital for Unwed Mothers and their decision to go to the hospital;
- The policies of the hospital as understood and communicated at the time;
- Daily routines at the hospital including the chores and responsibilities of the women, the interactions among them, and the relationship between the women and others involved in their care;

- The births of their children and subsequently giving them up for adoption;
- Their thoughts about the work of the Booth Hospital as they look back on that period of their lives.

Project deliverables are oral history recordings, transcripts, completed project forms, question guides, interviewee correspondence, and research notes. The recordings and transcripts, as a set, have been donated to the Social Welfare History Archives at the University of Minnesota Libraries (part of the Migration and Social Services Collections in the Archives and Special Collections Department), where they will be cataloged and made available to researchers.

14. Scholars Without Walls: The History of the Minnesota Independent Scholars' Forum (1983-2018)

>   Date: September 1, 2017
>   Grantor: Minnesota Historical Society Grants Office, administrating Legacy Funds
>   Grantee: Minnesota Independent Scholars' Forum
>   Amount: $7,090.00

Although the research, historical narrative, and initial editing of this book were done by MISF volunteer members, tasks that had to be outsourced to qualified professionals were book design, cover design, photo enhancement, peer review, and final editing. This grant covered the expense of that outsourcing.

This book is designed to serve equally well as part of a greater whole (a series of histories on independent scholarship in Minnesota) or as a stand-alone work. As such, it provides answers to two central questions: what has been the organizational experience of MISF in promoting independent scholarship, and to what extent has it been successful in that endeavor?

15. Seeking Refuge in a New Land: A Pop-up History of Refugees in Minnesota (1967-2017)

Date: January 1, 2018
Grantor: Minnesota Historical Society Grants Office, administrating Legacy Funds
Grantee: Minnesota Independent Scholars' Forum
(contract scholars: Bruce Johansen and Will Matthews)
Amount: $9,999.00

The purpose of this project is to foster an educative, public dialogue concerning issues of refugee settlement in Minnesota over the past 50 years. The medium for effecting that purpose is a "pop-up" (temporary and portable) exhibit that will be transported from one public venue to another throughout the state. The content of the exhibit will be provided initially by research of both primary and secondary source material on the history of refugee settlement in Minnesota, covering 1) state policies and practices, 2) the public's reception of refugees, and 3) the refugees' life experiences. It will be followed later by an implementation project phase (and accompanying grant proposal), during which the exhibit will be transported and displayed and the dialogue begun.

It is expected that, during this subsequent phase, the exhibit will be highly interactive with the public, making for continual growth in terms of relevance and educative quality. As such, the exhibit will be something of a hybrid. It will synthesize and present research like a more conventional history exhibit, but it will also be structured around visitor participation, leaning heavily on varied events (speakers, meals, discussions, etc.) to optimize public participation. Eventually, it could evolve into a digital interface that would allow visitors to record their own thoughts about refugee issues and explore the recorded thoughts of others. Such an interface might allow visitors to upload photographs of themselves, or something else significant to them, and incorporate text or audio. Done successfully, it could be an important feature of the exhibit, amassing an ever-increasing digital "collection" as the portable museum moves from place to place. More importantly, it will allow a discussion to take place across the various exhibit locations, so that diverse audiences and viewpoints could be brought into the conversation. This kind of growing, digital exhibit might even become a valuable record of the historical moment.

The research phase will involve gathering and synthesizing materials, to include existing scholarly research, images, objects, archival documents, and existing oral histories. Personal narratives will be an important component of the project, and the research would leverage digital storytelling work that's already been done by the University of Minnesota Immigration History Research Center's Immigrant Stories project, Green Card Voices, and others. This approach will call attention to and showcase the good work of others, bringing it to new audiences. The researchers will review digital stories and meet with individuals who have been involved with those projects.

Drafting the text or script for the exhibit will be based on the research results. Of primary importance in creating the exhibit will be:

1. Delivering historical information in a clear and compelling manner to diverse community members across the state,
2. Bringing research done by others to new audiences through a new medium, and
3. Supplementing exhibit information with storytelling to give a human face to the information conveyed.

Refugees will be invited to assist with each part of the process, including research, selection of exhibit materials, and (in the subsequent implementation phase) facilitation of community presentations and conversations. Their participation will be essential to ensure an informed and nuanced discussion.

Depending on the direction the research takes, any or all of the following questions could be raised and addressed by the exhibit:

- How have federal and state policies shaped refugee resettlement?
- How consistently has policy been applied to different groups of refugees?
- How do refugees fit into the larger history of immigration to America?
- What does it mean to be Minnesotan? Who can be included? When? Why?
- What are the origins of refugee resettlement in Minnesota? How and when did Minnesota become a home for multiple waves of refugees?
- How do refugees describe their experience of coming to Minnesota?
- What are some common, everyday challenges that refugees face?
- How do challenges differ by generation?
- How have refugee stories changed over time?
- What gave rise to the current refugee crisis?
- What have been the repercussions of this crisis: in Minnesota, the US, and internationally?
- What similarities or differences are there between the experiences of previous groups of refugees and contemporary groups?
- How can the history and experience of refugee resettlement help to contextualize the present moment?

(At the time of printing, this project is still in process.)

16. *We Won't Go! (And We Don't Want You to Go, Either): Oral History*

>Date: June, 2018
>Grantor: Minnesota Historical Society Grants Office, administrating Legacy Funds
>Grantee: Minnesota Independent Scholars' Forum
>Amount: $9,081

The purpose of this oral history project is to document the Vietnam War resistor movement in Minnesota. The project will do interviews with people who broke the law, violating the Selective Service Act, in the late 1960s and early 1970s. Among those will be the "Minnesota 8," the 1970s Selective Service draft board raiders. The individuals to be interviewed will have in common that they were actually tried and convicted of violating the Selective Service Act, by either 1) refusing to be inducted, refusing to report for induction, or refusing to register in the first place; or 2) carrying out a raid on a draft board in Minnesota, or else in another state (two raids by Minnesotans were carried out elsewhere).

Accordingly, the project will be in two phases, a first to interview draft board "raiders" and a second to interview draft "resisters." Each phase will be the subject of its own grant proposal, of which this proposal is the first.

There are copious document records from the period already in hand. They will be used to more fully understand the period, and also to identify more potential interview subjects. More than one Minnesota resistance publication tracked and named those who were convicted and imprisoned.

Although the raiders are commonly grouped together as a unit, like the Minnesota 8, each person has a unique story to tell. Their ages; backgrounds; ties to the University of Minnesota; reasons for risking imprisonment by raiding draft boards and destroying records; responses to their arrests and convictions and years in federal prisons; and commitment as war resistors are the stories of individuals whose actions came to represent Minnesota's role in the antiwar movement. Documenting their stories as individuals will add to the depth of knowledge and layers of information available about this period of Minnesota history.

Although the interview subjects will have their felony convictions in common, it is sure that their motivations and decisions will be widely divergent. Some will have deep and long-held religious convictions as their personal belief foundation, while others will be mainly political.

Questions to be raised in the interviews include:

- What family, social, religious, and politcal environments shaped your views and actions?
- What moved you to knowingly break the law and risk imprisonment? How did you both work and not work in alliance with one another?
- How did your actions affect your later life?
- Do you now regret how you acted back then, are you proud of how you acted, and/or do you wish you had done more to oppose the war?
- Have your political views substantially changed since then?
- Why do you think Minnesota was such a "hotbed" of resistance to the war?

The interviews will be available to local researchers in both audio and transcribed form, and, through the resources of the primary repository and additional repositories, to researchers throughout the world. The primary repository is expected to be the University of Minnesota Archives, which will develop and post the project findings on its website. In addition, copies of transcripts will be offered to the Minnesota Historical Society Archives and other repositories that may be identified in the course of the project, where they will be cataloged and made available to researchers. All repositories will be granted a shared copyright to the transcripts.

It is possible, and within the scope of this proposal, that individuals will be interviewed who have done one or more of the above "qualifying" acts, but have never been identified or charged, or provided support in such a way that they could have been charged and convicted. In such cases, or in the case of others who may wish to be interviewed but remain anonymous, it may be necessary to structure repository and copyright arrangements to protect participant identity, either for a specific time period or indefinitely.

(At the time of printing, this project is in its initial stages.)

Notes for Chapter 9

115 Interview #BH 237, Adolescent Girl in Conflict: Individual Interviews-Booth Memorial Hospital (Unwed Mothers) 1963, Folder 2, Gisela Konopka Papers, University Archives, University of Minnesota, Twin Cities. Hereafter referred to as Konopka Papers.

116 *Annual Report of the Board of Control of St. Paul and Ramsey County 1914*, 144, Ramsey County Welfare Department Annual Reports, Minnesota Historical Society (MNHS) State Archives; *Annual Report of the Salvation Army Rescue Home & Maternity Hospital, 1471 Como Avenue, St. Paul, MN, 1914*, Brochures/Philanthropy, Salvation Army, Folder 25, Louis W. Hill Papers, MNHS; *All That Money! 1952 Annual Report of the County Welfare Board of the City of Saint Paul and the County of Ramsey*, n.p., MNHS; *Salvation Army Annual Report, St. Paul, MN, 1967*, n.p., Vertical File: Northern Division-Greater Minneapolis St. Paul Area, Salvation Army National Archives; *Ramsey County Welfare Department Annual Report 1971*, 26, MNHS. For more information on national trends regarding single mothers' surrender of babies to adoption, see Regina Kunzel, *Fallen Women, Problem Girls: Unmarried Mothers and the Professionalization of Social Work, 1890-1945*(Yale University Press: 1993); Rickie Solinger, *Wake Up Little Susie: Single Pregnancy and Race Before Roe v. Wade* (Routledge: 1992); Ann Fessler, *The Girls Who Went Away: The Hidden History of Women Who Surrendered Children for Adoption in the Decades Before Roe v. Wade* (Penguin: 2006).

117 Interviews #BH 240, BH 250, Konopka Papers. Sheffield quoted in Ben Kaufman, "They Give Away 'Own Flesh and Blood,'" Minneapolis *Star* (August 19, 1965). This article prompted passionate responses from social workers from a number of agencies, including the Salvation Army, that worked with unwed mothers and their children. They were outraged by such "destructive moralizing," and called a meeting with the presiding judge to discuss "ways for the agencies to work even more closely and effectively with the court." T.O. Olson to District Judge, Juvenile Court, et al, August 31, 1965, Hennepin County Community Health and Welfare Council Records, Box 19, University of Minnesota Social Welfare History Archives.

CHAPTER 10

Meetings

Since 2009, MISF has had regular meetings, usually on the fourth Saturday of the month. These meetings are an opportunity for scholars to present information about works-in-progress. They are also an opportunity to hear outside scholars speak on topics of personal or general interest. The range of speakers has been broad and eclectic—ranging from David Wesley on Cold Fusion (April 2017) to Virgil Johnson on costume designs for Shakespeare's Henry II (September 2017).

The meetings of the Scholars, which take place in local libraries, are free and open to the public. Speakers are always offered a year's membership in MISF as part of their compensation, and many accept the offer.

Prior to Hillstrom's presidency, meetings were somewhat more occasional and frequently occurred as part of a special event, such as a symposium cosponsored with other groups.

Former Minneapolis Mayor Arthur Naftalin was the keynote speaker at a symposium on September 16, 1995, cosponsored by the Minnesota Independent Scholars' Forum and the Minnesota Historical Society, and with support from the Minnesota Humanities Commission. This article is adapted from the outline prepared for Naftalin's presentation, in which he offered eleven propositions on the theme of "A Century of

Three Revolutions?" This article appeared in the *Forum* in November 1995.

A Scholar Writes

'30s, '60s, '90s: A Century of Three Revolutions
Arthur Naftalin, 1995

When Ross Corson, President of the Minnesota Independent Scholars' Forum, asked me to keynote the symposium on "the revolutions of the 1930s, 1960s and 1990s," I protested that I was not a student of the "revolutions" and not a proper person for the assignment. But Ross flattered me into accepting, saying I was the only person his committee could think of who might be able to address the subject in an informed way. I had misgivings, but was snared by the flattery and decided I could get by with a few war stories. Soon after accepting, however, I received a further communication from Ross informing me that the planning committee would like for me to keep my remarks to 15–20 minutes. By this time, I had sketched out a vast landscape of ideas and experiences, so I did not find the time limit a congenial idea. But I thought, "Well, I've got so much to say, I'll just wing it for 15 minutes and let the panel take it from there."

But then another communication from Ross arrived, asking me to oblige a request from panel members that I share with them a summary of my keynote address, so they would know how to prepare their responses. Being a good citizen, I obediently acquiesced to Ross's request and prepared a quick-and-dirty set of eleven propositions. They could have been 15 or 20 or 100; they do not constitute a great statement, but they do reveal my deep concern that the successive "revolutions" follow an alarming pattern of civic and cultural deterioration.

Proposition One
The three periods are alike in that they were marked by instability, disillusionment, the rise of violence, and serious political protest. But they differ markedly in context and expression. The earlier two "revolutions" inform our present experience in only a limited way.

Proposition Two
Theories about the cyclical alternation of periods of conservatism and liberalism have, I believe, limited value. I see the three periods as part of a continuum in which our communitarian spirit has progressively deteriorated as the push towards plebiscitarianism has intensified.

Proposition Three
The driving force in the 1930s was economic. The Depression led to severe suffering, and there was wide belief that a responsive government could set matters right. It produced aggressive political movements on both the left and the right, all advocating strong federal intervention.

Proposition Four
The wide-ranging initiatives of the New Deal deflected the "revolutionary" energy, but it was World War II that ended, for the time, the ideological warfare. The spirit of the 1930s was essentially communitarian, a pervasive confidence in the efficacy of government. This spirit was intensified by the New Deal and by World War II, which, despite its costs, led to full employment and a rising sense of shared values as a nation committed to democracy, individual freedom, and the "good life" for all.

Proposition Five
The communitarian spirit reached its apogee in the aftermath

of World War II. Nurtured by sustained prosperity and by a sense of great national strength, the period produced a mood of social challenge that called for the fulfillment of the democratic promise. This unrealized objective unsettled a large section of the public, especially minorities, women, and young people. Expectations for the "good life" and for individual self-realization were rising, but were frustrated by lack of opportunity and by traditional social barriers.

Proposition Six

The unsettled feelings led to a variety of protests—against the barriers to social equality, against practices harmful to the environment, against exploitation of consumers, against conformity in personal behavior. The driving force behind the "revolt" of the 1960s was social. It expressed a deepening sense of individual powerlessness in confronting the big bureaucracies of government and corporations. Small became beautiful. Individuals sought escape through drugs, nonconformist behavior, retreat to nature, and withdrawal into self.

Proposition Seven

The unsettled feelings of the 1960s found no common focus until they collided with the Vietnam War. The resentments generated by the war combined with the growing urge for individual freedom. This produced a sharp disaffection with government, which increasingly came to be regarded as the captive of interests that were not accountable to the public.

Proposition Eight

The communitarian spirit of the 1930s had, by the 1960s, given way to a growing belief in a plebiscitarian form of populism, which held that the government's lack of efficacy could be corrected by direct popular action, such as the political process (initiatives and referenda, presidential primaries, increased voter turnouts, more control of political parties), and by direct individual action (voluntarism, boycotts of offending businesses, acts of civil disobedience).

Proposition Nine
What we witness in the 1990s is, in my view, more accurately described as "counter-revolutionary." The main objective of the present ferment (shared in various degrees by conservatives and neo-liberals) is the dismantling of the programs created in the 1930s and the 1960s.

Proposition Ten
In the 1990s the individual is sovereign; the private market (the ultimate plebiscitarian institution) is in the saddle. The ferment has yet to play itself out. Because the spirit is psychological and essentially irrational, efforts to respond can find no focus. Every public faction has its own cause for discontent—the seedbed for a war of all against all. Faced with such confusion, leaders are totally ineffective, essentially objects of ridicule. (The only respected potential leader—for the moment—is Colin Powell, the perfect Rorschach for the fractionated public.)

Proposition Eleven
Finally, the revolution—counter-revolution—of the 1990s is yet to come. None of our best and brightest, as I see it, has a clue as to what is likely to happen.

Regular Meetings
After MISF moved to regular meetings, it became both possible and convenient to include reports of the meetings in the journal. Virtually all meetings since February 2008 have been reported in the journal. The following article comes from that period.

This essay is the full text of an illustrated lecture that Bill McTeer presented to the Scholars' meeting in November of 2014. McTeer, a computer consultant, has been involved with computers almost since their beginning and has more recently been involved with the MISF website. He also serves as treasurer of the organization. This article appeared in the December 2014 edition of *Practical Thinking*.

A Scholar Writes

Secret Writing
Bill McTeer, 2014

As a boy, I enjoyed reading about heroes stumbling in slimy, dank caves, where they had been left to rot by villains, only to come across a document (map, deed, stock certificate, confession) that solved a mystery and generated a huge reward. This action-story reading diet was probably the beginning of my infatuation with secret writing. In my professional life with information technology, the topic has periodically resurfaced (for example, I spent several years working on the Illiac IV supercomputer, whose design turned out to be optimized for bomb simulations, weather forecasting, and codebreaking). Since MISF is a scholarly organization, I'll put an academic gown on my fun and say (truthfully) that I have a scholarly interest in the history of science and technology, into which "secret writing" fits handily.

This presentation discusses secret writing from early times to the present. It is largely chronological, punctuated by four mini-biographies of people notable in some way. I suspect that secret writing was invented very shortly after humans learned to write. We are a species driven to communicate with each other—but often there are those we want to exclude from the message, whether it be some of our schoolmates, our lover's parents, or the leader we plan to challenge. Although computer cryptography will figure in the story, this isn't an in-depth computer tech presentation. There are many experts far more knowledgeable than I on the intricacies of that area.

Mini-Bio 1: Mary, Queen of Scots, 1542 to 1586; Secret Writing for the Ruling Class

Mary became queen of Scotland after her father died when she was one week old. In 1559, she became queen of France and ruled until her husband, King Francis II, died in 1561. She then returned to rule Scotland. However, she lost the confidence of her court and in 1567 fled to England, where Elizabeth I held her as a perpetual captive. She enters the history of secret writing because, in 1586, her participation in a conspiracy to assassinate Elizabeth and become queen of England was revealed by her secret writings. As a result, Mary was beheaded in 1587. Mary's secret messages were concealed in the bungs of beer barrels and separately encoded for each correspondent. Unknown to Mary, the British were aware of and copied all messages to and from her, but they had to break her coding system to read them.

Before electronics, it was common to attempt secrecy by hiding messages. Although hiding is a wonderful dramatic device (it figures in stories from *A Tale of Two Cities* to *Sherlock Holmes* and *Harry Potter*), by itself it is a weak method of secrecy, because it is easily revealed by espionage. When serious people write things they want to remain secret, they do so by encoding them.

For a thousand years from the time of Julius Caesar, messages were encoded using a technique called alphabet substitution. In this technique, each letter of the message is replaced by a different letter (for example, all instances of the letter "e" might be replaced by "g"). Alphabet substitution was secure until about 800 CE, when Muslim linguists observed that each language has its own inherent natural character frequency; therefore messages coded by alphabet substitution could be decoded (broken) by analyzing the frequency and patterns of the encoded characters. (This is the same method we use to solve the newspaper's weekly CryptoQuip puzzle.) It took nearly 400 years for knowledge of this method to become common in Europe. Once the implications of frequency analysis were understood, various improvements to alphabet substitution were attempted, such as removing spaces, deliberate misspellings, multiple symbols to represent common letters, and extra meaningless symbols ("nulls").

Mary used an encoding system called a "Nomenclature" code, in which common words and phrases are first replaced by an alternate code and then alphabet substitution with nulls was used on the resulting message. The British cipher expert Thomas Phelippes was able to break Mary's code relatively easily by frequency analysis followed by some educated trial and error.

From 1600 to World War I, a number of improvements in encoding schemes were attempted. Most notable are homophonic ciphers, in which the number of alternate symbols for a letter corresponds to its normal frequency, using multiple substitution alphabets. (The Blaise de Vignerère cipher, which used a number of alphabets in a cycle, was proposed in 1586 and was known as *le chiffre indéchiffrable* until Charles Babbage demonstrated how to break it in 1854.) There were also schemes that transposed letters and schemes based on syllables rather than letters. Virtually all of the secret writing schemes through World War I were broken by adversaries. Two notable exceptions, the book cipher and the one-time pad, were too clumsy to be used widely.

Mini-Bio 2: Alan Turing, 1912 to 1954; Secret Writing for the Machine Age

Alan Turing was a British mathematician. In 1937, at age 25 while at Cambridge, he published an influential paper, "On Computable Numbers," in which he explored the characteristics of a universal computing machine. In 1939, he was invited to join the secret British effort at Bletchley Park to break Germany's Enigma coding scheme. He worked there until the end of the war in 1945. Turing's homosexuality was tolerated in the intellectual community at Cambridge and Bletchley, but not in general British society. In 1952, when he naively revealed his homosexuality as a part of filing a burglary report, he was prosecuted for "gross indecency" and stripped of his security clearance. As a consequence, he committed suicide in 1954.

The Germans had been frustrated by the failure of their [codes] to remain secret in World War I and strove to correct that failing. Their solution, which greatly surpassed the complexity practical in a manual cipher, was the Enigma machine developed by Arthur Scherbius and adopted by the German military in 1925. Enigma consisted of a typewriter-like keyboard on which the operator pressed the letter to be coded and a lamp board which showed the letter to be substituted. Complexity was created by a system of scrambling rotors whose position changed as each key was pressed and by a plugboard that could be used to swap letters for the duration of the message.

The British initially believed Enigma could not be broken. However, the Poles were more persistent and developed methods to break the 10^5 rotor settings separately from the 10^{11} plugboard settings, allowing the Poles to read Enigma messages from 1933 to 1938. In 1938, the Germans significantly increased the complexity of Enigma and shortly thereafter invaded Poland. Polish intelligence was able to share their breakthroughs with an astonished British intelligence, jumpstarting the Allied codebreaking efforts. Turing was key to using special machinery ("bombes") to search for patterns ("cribs") in intercepted messages. By 1945, nearly all Enigma traffic could be broken within a day or two.

After World War II, the development of programmable computers and the need to communicate securely between the growing number of them led to a "golden age" of cryptography. Sophisticated techniques were developed:

"Standardized Unbreakable Coding" has been a goal of cryptologists since the 1500s. With computers, there is the ability to implement coding techniques that provide few chinks for codebreakers to exploit other than trying all possible keys. In 1977, the National Institute of Standards with involvement of the NSA endorsed the "Data Encryption Standard." In 2001, DES was replaced with the "Advanced Encryption Standard." AES involves mathematically "stirring" blocks of 16 characters with a key repeatedly. It is used throughout the internet. Some of its variants are certified by the NSA for "top secret communications."

"Public Key Encryption" is a technique that allows parties to verify the identity of their correspondent. It is based on a kind of "magic lock," proposed hypothetically in 1975 and implemented in 1977, that has two different, but paired, keys. When one of the keys is used to lock a secret message, the message can only be unlocked with the other key. Suppose "Alice" (an arbitrary person often used in discussing secret communication) makes one of her two keys public, where anyone can have access to it, and holds the other very privately. With this arrangement, anyone can lock a message with Alice's "public key," confident that it can only be unlocked by Alice using her corresponding "private key." Vice versa, a message locked with Alice's "private key" (and therefore unlockable by anyone using her "public key") must have come from Alice. This technique is used automatically by web browsers to guard against e-commerce imposters.

"Secure key interchange" is a different kind of magic. "Key management" is a problem for most cryptographic systems. Militaries have devoted significant time and expense to distributing encryption keys by courier worldwide on a timely basis—if the same approach were required for all secure communication, the use of secret techniques would be severely curtailed. In 1976, Whitfield Diffie and Martin Hellman developed a technique that, paradoxically, allows the creation of a shared secret using untrusted communications. The technique involves multiple messages between the parties and is similar to the following scenario: Alice wants to send a secret message to Bob, whom she has never met, through an untrustworthy postal service. She locks the message in a box with her own padlock, keeps her padlock key, and sends the box to Bob. Bob cannot open the box, but he adds his own padlock to it, keeps his padlock key, and sends the box back to Alice. Alice removes her padlock and sends the box, still locked with Bob's padlock, back to Bob. Bob removes his padlock and opens the box.

Mini-Bio 3: Phil Zimmerman, 1954 to Present; Secret Writing for Everyone

It was 1989 when ordinary people could get an account giving access to the internet. The World Wide Web was also first specified in 1989. Two years later, Phil Zimmerman, working from his home in Boulder, Colorado, made the "Pretty Good

Privacy" (PGP) software publicly available. With PGP, anyone could use the cryptographic tools developed since the 1970s to send and receive secure e-mail. The result was that in 1993 Phil was investigated for violation of the Arms Export Control Act, an investigation which lasted for three years. The era when everyone could have strongly secret writing had arrived. Civil libertarians hailed an advance in personal freedom. Intelligence agencies decried the threat to societal security.

Between 1991 and today, there has been a massive migration of secret writing from paper form to electronic form. We use secure techniques from public coffee shops to communicate via our smart phones to our bank without a thought (and often without knowing we are doing so). The techniques used are so secure that messages are effectively not vulnerable during transit. The risks now lie in how we store data and in our procedures.

Mini-Bio 4: Edward Snowden, 1983 to Present; Secret Writing Taken for Granted

After a seven-year career in network security, at age 30, Edward Snowden advanced to a position as lead technologist for the NSA's information-sharing office in Hawaii in 2012. There, he copied thousands of secret NSA documents and provided them to investigative reporters before landing in asylum in Russia, where he remains at this time.

The significance of Edward's story to secret writing is how blasé we have become about secret writing. The NSA was apparently so confident in the theoretical impregnability of their systems that they failed to take the steps most businesses would take to protect against excessive exposure to an "inside job."

There are other ways in which we, as a society, have become

careless about secret writing. Mark Burnett of xato.net has analyzed the passwords revealed when a few large sites were compromised. When sorted by frequency of use, the most commonly used password is "password." Fourteen percent of users are using one of the most common 10 passwords and 91 percent of users are using one of the most common 1,000 passwords. Many people use passwords that can be guessed from their Facebook profile. User carelessness is not solely to blame, however. Sites often force us to create passwords according to rules that ensure we must write down our creation to remember it (who can remember "bu2ter_Fly" reliably?). It would be far more secure to use a long and memorable passphrase than a shorter sequence of arbitrary characters.

"Social engineering" is also an issue. Why do we provide our passwords to strangers in situations where we would never consider giving out our safety deposit box keys?

To wrap up, secret writing has had an interesting "story arc" since 1586. What was a special competence (or incompetence) of the ruling class in 1586 is today used thoughtlessly by everyone who uses the Web. During that time, there has been a see-saw competition between codemakers and codebreakers, with the codemakers generally winning in early history, for a while before World War II, and finally in the computer age. At this point, secret writing is most often vulnerable only to our frailty in how we use it.

Dr. Fatma Reda and Maged Makled discuss the Arab Spring for a meeting of the Scholars, February 18, 2012. Photo by Phil Dahlen.

Colleen Moriarty, of Hunger Solutions, spoke to MISF about the 2013 Farm Bill, February 18, 2013. Her objective was to explain the importance of the Farm Bill for people who are "food insecure." Photo by Phil Dahlen.

Dr. Joe Amato addresses the annual meeting of the Scholars, June 15, 2013, on the subject of surfaces. This lecture was the first annual Rhoda Lewin lecture named in honor of the first president of MISF. Photo by Phil Dahlen.

President Mike Woolsey gave his annual report at the annual meeting of MISF, June 21, 2014. Photo by Phil Dahlen.

Evelyn Klein read her poetry for the poetry reading on Earth Day, April 19, 2014. Klein, now the editor of the Minnesota Scholar, is the author of three books of poetry. Photo by Phil Dahlen.

Curt Hillstrom introduces the speaker at 2012 meeting. Photo by Phil Dahlen.

George Anderson spoke to the Scholars, January 21, 2012, about the authorship of the plays attributed to William Shakespeare. Photo by Phil Dahlen.

In this photo, David Juncker, Steve Miller, Ginny Hansen, and Shirley Whiting discuss political discourse with two representatives of the League of Women Voters. September 15, 2012. Photo by Phil Dahlen.

CHAPTER 11

THE JOURNAL: GOOD WRITING BY THOUGHTFUL PEOPLE

A subscription to the Scholars' journal is one of the benefits of membership in MISF. Although the journal has gone through several name changes, it has been in existence since 1989. It was the *Forum* from 1989 to 2005, *Practical Thinking* from 2005 to 2014, and is now the *Minnesota Scholar*. It has also had several purposes.

At first, it was mostly a means of communicating information about meetings, awards, and opportunities. Then, for a period of time, especially when the publication was shared with the Minnesota Association for Continuing Adult Education (MACAE), its purpose was to give scholars an opportunity to publish articles of scholarly importance. More recently, editors have settled into a pattern of scholarly articles accompanied by reports of regular meetings. We make a point of reviewing any book by an author who is a member of MISF. We also publish a list of upcoming meetings and, from time to time, include information about our members.

The journal has also had several editors with varied ideas for its appearance and purpose. For a period of time in the late 1990s, the journal was designed by professional desktop publishers and featured photos and ads. More recently, as desktop publishing has become a household occupation, it has been designed by the editor.

The journal is peer-reviewed with the idea that scholars can present scholarly articles for review. We have several scientists in our membership, so we are able to give critical reading to articles of scientific exploration or discovery. We reach out beyond our membership to experts in other fields if we need to do so.

Although history is a popular subject with many of our authors, we have featured a number of articles that combine disciplines. This section includes a representative group of articles dealing with several scholarly themes: two are interdisciplinary—combining science and humanism. Two deal with politics and modern life, and two deal with historical subjects. Although the articles are chronological within their sections, the sections themselves are not in a particular chronological order.

Interdisciplinary Scholarship

One of the attractions of independent scholarship has always been that the practitioner is not limited to a single field of research but can range widely across several areas of thought. The following two articles give a feel for that endeavor.

George Anderson, a freelance chemist and a former president of MISF, wrote this article in the fall of 2000. One of Anderson's avocations is the poetry of William Shakespeare and the debate on the identity of Shakespeare. He has spoken to our meetings on these subjects.

A Scholar Writes

Broken Symmetry
George Anderson, 2000

Suppose you were at a dinner party where all the guests sat around a large circular table. As salads were served, they were placed evenly on the table exactly between the guests. The surprise was this: no one could remember which salad to eat. Was it the one on the left, or right? After an anxious moment, someone began with the salad on their left. Then, others followed. The symmetry was broken, and happily, the dinner party was able to proceed. Recently, I heard this story on public radio in relation to physics and the evolution of elementary particles after the "Big Bang." Sorry that I didn't remember who spoke, but I trust they will approve my retelling of their good analogy for others to enjoy. Broken symmetry seems to have been important to cosmic events in the past. What do we make of that today?

Big Bang model: If the universe had a beginning, a widely held theory holds that it emerged as a singular event about thirteen billion years ago. It is called the "Big Bang" for obvious reasons: intense heat and radiation were confined to a small space that expanded with enormous velocity—one that continues yet today. Based on the color of distant stars and galaxies, the universe is expanding away from us (earthlings) in all directions. If the universe looks like a balloon, then our solar system is but a point on this balloon. As we watch the night sky, the "balloon" is being inflated, and everything on the surface of the balloon is moving away from everything else. The more distant objects are, the faster they seem to be moving away. In the beginning, when the universe was small and very dense, the temperature was so intense that matter was consumed by radiation.

Elements as we know them did not yet exist, nor did nuclei from which they could be assembled. A particle might appear for a moment but would disappear upon collision with its antiparticle, adding more radiation to the mix. The early universe was poised upon quixotic symmetry. After expansion with time, however, this primordial soup of intense radiation cooled enough that elementary particles would persist—much as hot steam condenses into water drops as it is cooled. Also, each particle was accompanied by an antiparticle, a brew of intense radiation laced with violence, an unresolved alliance between matter and antimatter. Exactly what happened next to break the symmetry is not known, but the standoff was breached. Today we live in a world where matter (as we now call it) has prevailed. Antimatter appears to exist only in small, limited regions of the cosmos. Please pass the carrots.

Biochemistry

Not so fast. Carrots contain protein, and protein is a polymer of amino acids. There are approximately 20 amino acids commonly found in nature, all of one particular molecular configuration. There are 20 other amino acids, mirror images of those naturally found, that are not present and never will be. The stereo chemistry of amino acids has been fully described in biochemistry texts, but the point of this discussion is to acknowledge the broken symmetry these two groups represent. About 3.5 billion years ago, life on this planet evolved in such a way as to eliminate chemical redundancy. The symmetry of stereo amino acids was broken and evolution could proceed more efficiently. The human umbilical cord is one more example of asymmetric specificity. Including the artery and vein, an umbilical cord is always a left-handed spiral. Broken symmetry has been part of biological history for many years!

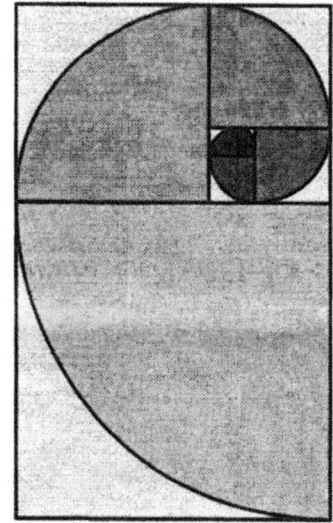 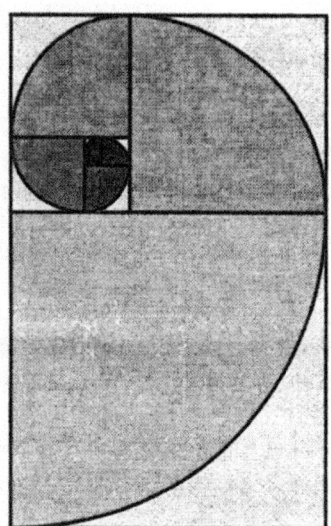

Anderson's article was accompanied by his illustration of broken symmetry.

Broken symmetry may be illustrated by the so-called Golden Rectangle and its mirror image, shown above. Each one contains a spiral extending inward to a point at the "center." The left spiral runs clockwise into the center. The right one runs counter-clockwise. Each rectangle is composed of a series of squares with an arc of a circle inscribed. The length of a side of one square remains a constant ratio to that of its adjoining larger square; by algebra, the ratio of proportion = 0.61803. If nature had rendered Golden Rectangles with some mechanism to "compete" for space or for parts (i.e. squares) from which to "grow," one of the Golden Rectangles might have come to dominate the other. And through some competitive morphogenesis of one with the other, their combined symmetry in nature would be broken. (Cover the right rectangle with your hand.) This may have happened for no apparent reason other than a chaotic event favoring the left rectangle at one instant in time. The symmetry once shared would now be gone. Their beauty would be lost to sight and could only be discerned in the mind's eye.

The point may be this. We live in a world constructed of parts, not broken in ways that need fixing. Yet, neither are these parts symmetric, as creation in its early beginnings had to offer. Broken symmetries have allowed things to happen, avoiding useless standoffs, joining parts together that otherwise wouldn't stick. We have the advantage. With the mind's eye, we see beyond the span of our earthen, sometimes watery, compass.

Thus, if justice in the world is not as we might imagine it, if evil seems to prevail endlessly over good, if gender has an asymmetric bias, if labor and management are mired in endless muck, if liberals or conservatives are the bane of the republic's ills, remember the stuff from which humans are made. In this remembrance, beauty lost is beauty claimed.

David Juncker has been a member of the Scholars for most of its existence. He is trained as a physiologist, with degrees from MIT and the University of Minnesota. He worked for Medtronic Corporation for many years and is an expert in the functioning of frog hearts. He has given many talks to MISF and served both as president and editor of the journal. This article appeared in *Practical Thinking* in December 2005.

A Scholar Writes

Theories vs. Hypotheses, Ideas, and Opinions: The Role of Scientific Methodology
David Juncker, 2005

What makes science or scientific endeavors different from most other logical endeavors is the demand that all findings and opinions be confirmed by repetitious observation and testing before the findings are accepted. The observation, recording, hypothesis, and confirmation steps in scientific practice have themselves evolved over the centuries into what is generally known today as the scientific method: observation, recording, problem identification, hypothesis, prediction, and testing.

It is important to remember that scientists, themselves, are just another group of professional people with the same set of likes, dislikes, and problems as most anyone else. Perhaps an insatiable curiosity provides the difference between them and many other professionals.

Providing a complete historical account of the evolution of scientific thinking is impossible in the space available, but the turning point would most likely be when careful observation and controlled testing were added to the developing logic processes. The earliest scientific endeavors were initiated to find answers to societal "why" questions concerning the origin and meaning of life, and were almost never tested. These attempts, and most thereafter, have been based, additionally, on the strong desire to find answers that can be simplified to basic principles, or to one cause (unification). Over the past few hundred years, scientific research has moved toward finding potential answers for those questions that can be subjected to experimental observation and repetitive testing.

Current scientific methods have been almost overwhelmingly successful during the past hundred-plus years in providing knowledge and advances in the understanding of life at all levels on earth. We are in a period in which the ensuing number of successful new technologies physically assisting or extending our adaptation to earth is rapidly growing, and also entering a period, as a result of recent breakthroughs in genetic mapping and the genetic code itself, which promises to lead to additional aids directed toward our own bodies, bodily functions, and inherited errors.

What Is the Scientific Method?

It is worth looking a bit more carefully at the scientific method. In the scientific method, observations must be made without preconceived ideas or interpretations. It's extremely difficult to enter into scientific efforts without any preconceived answers or interpretations; and therefore, objective, systematic, and very detailed observations and recording have become great aids in finding answers, often dispelling preconceived notions when the data is analyzed. Problem identification tends to be much easier, as it's usually the why-did-that-happen type of question that got one started in the first place. Hypotheses are the attempts at "how" something happened: the educated suggestion of answers to the posed question. Predictions usually precede testing, are based on the scientist's most likely hypothesis, and are most likely posed as "if . . . then" statements. Testing means experimentation. The design and control of experimental tests is neither easy nor always straightforward. Experimental tests must be designed that cover the broadest permissible range of possibilities while evaluating as few variables—preferably one—as possible at a time. Experimental results are, also, often at odds with so called "common sense" predictions. This is due to the fact that common sense is usually based on things that we already hold to be familiar, when, in fact, our results may be trying to tell us something new.

When a hypothesis survives multiple tests under the direction of multiple, independent scientists, it is raised to a theory. Many people confuse ideas, i.e. hypotheses, with theories.

It is very important to recognize, even as earlier scientists did, that the scientific method, as designed and practiced, cannot prove anything. Simply put, it's impossible to perform every possible experiment under every possible set of conditions; and, experimenters are subject to human error, including not having developed the capability of observing everything that goes on in a given experiment. In addition, there are many types of questions for which the scientific method cannot create a theory: Is red better than blue? Are females better than males?

Theories are most likely the highest level of certainty that science can achieve, but it is possible to create additional support for a theory by the accumulation of experiments providing evidence that a given theory is correct. Still, we can never be sure. Electricity, light, cells as the basic unit of life, relativity, the Earth revolving around the Sun, etc.—all are well-supported theories. Nonetheless, some, or all, will eventually change with time and/or place.

A given theory may last for many years and be accepted as truth by most scientists and the general public, and yet be overturned by a new set of contradictory experiments. When this happens, a new theory replaces or evolves from the remains of the old. This process is the reason that science is described as changing, or dynamic. Often, changes in accepted theories follow the discovery and implementation of major new technologies that have enabled more detailed observations and/or tests to be conducted.

A Modern Example

A relatively modern example of this process would be the current understanding of the transmission of electrical signals along nerve cell pathways in mammals, including humans. Through the 1940s, 1950s, and early 1960s, two increasingly antagonistic groups of scientists, worldwide, made hundreds of experiments trying to ascertain if the signals carried by nerve cells traveled "electrically" (electrons, magnetic fields, etc.) or chemically (charged ions or molecules, diffusion, etc.).

The interesting thing about the argument was the fact that both groups, those with strong 'electrical' backgrounds and those with strong 'chemistry' backgrounds, were designing experiments based on their own areas of expertise that gave results supporting their respective theories. Only later was it found by way of an objective and creative new set of experiments that in this case, both had been correct and incorrect; the transmission of the signal within each nerve cell is primarily "electrical," but the signal from the end of one nerve cell to the beginning of the next is almost entirely "chemical." The current theory of nerve conduction has a spot for both prior theories.

The Theory of Evolution

The theory of evolution vs. the idea or hypothesis of either creationism or intelligent design is a nonproblem in the scientific sense, due to the fact that we don't have, as yet, two theories to compare.

A major flaw in what is known today as "creation science" is the fact that it starts the process of scientific justification with the answers known. As we saw with the nerve transmission theory, one cannot enter into a scientific justification with the idea that the answers are all decided, because the act of doing so will influence observations so that participants will begin to see things that aren't there, or miss things that are. Two examples of such a research situation have occurred during the long developmental period and medical use of the light microscope: at first, scientists swore they distinctly saw homunculi in the tissues on the viewing slides and carefully drew them in their notes. This fit their understanding of the human body as most likely made up of smaller copies of itself; it took years, and a junior scientist, to dispel the images. Secondly, we still suffer today with many physiology textbooks featuring four sensory nerve end organs "discovered" by scientists who went looking for four cells to differentiate between touch, pain, heat, and cold (instead of the broad continuum of cell types that accomplish the same purpose and cover even more variables). A second "creation science" difficulty is the lack of comprehensive testing and test results.

One of the newest supporting findings that strengthen the theory of evolution is the recent experimentally derived understanding of the makeup of our individual DNA packages and their resident genes. The fact that each human's DNA is almost entirely similar in its composition and order, yet never identical, and the added fact that sexual reproduction has increased the odds for multiple variations in each individual's genetic code, is additional support for ongoing evolution. Consider the newly established fact that each of us, when we are born, has a distinctly new DNA that is based half on a delivery system (maternal side) that is designed to protect the status quo (least number of errors or mutations) by insuring the minimum number of cellular splits over both time and space[;] with a second half (paternal side) that maximizes cellular splits and, further, rejects the effects of the most recent environmental time period. That is, the successful sperm cell (one of approximately 400 million per ejaculation) was produced within a few days of its pilgrimage (after some 20–30 splits per day during a male's reproductive years) while under the influence of current environmental conditions (heat, radiation, mechanical stresses, hormonal and chemical imbalances, etc.). The sperm carries the most chances for change, both positive and negative. On the other hand, the ovum (egg) penetrated was derived from a cell that stopped splitting at about the 16-cell stage (fourth cellular division) of the maternal grandmother's pregnancy, ending in the birth of the mother, where the pre-ovum then split nine or ten more times to produce some 500–600 potential eggs that sat around until the mother's reproductive period (puberty to late menopause). Thus, our subject egg had to survive only approximately fourteen splits, and its genetic creation was under the environmental influence of conditions some 20 to 50 years ago. In this way, each of us is assured of both a basically unchanged parent DNA and a surely, though most likely very slightly, changed parent DNA from which to make our own brand-new copy. As a living earth organism using sexual reproduction, we get both protected history and guaranteed change.

What I find interesting about the timing of the latest attack on the theory of evolution is that the current attack comes at a time when humans as a species are just beginning to be the first living organisms on earth to move away from a dependence on evolution alone. It is now quite possible, medically, to prolong almost any life until sperm or ova are available to pass on to the next generation, thus freeing us, even those most severely damaged genetically, to pass our "defective" genes on to the next generation. Moreover, it is increasingly possible to correct or synthetically replace mistakes in each individual's genetic expression, i.e. physical body, enabling longer, healthier lives and life spans.

Evolution of Ideas

As new discoveries and information leave the laboratories and become available for use in the public sector, another important set of processes is initiated; that of understanding, acceptance, positive and negative usage, and regulation. Major advances in science always produce change, including possible changes in our beliefs, economy, societies, the world as we see it, and so forth. These changes will always be resisted.

Over the centuries, advances in knowledge are subjected to

this "resistance" process, coming to us (as multiple researchers and philosophers have noted) in three stages:

1. "It's impossible; it can't be done."
2. "It's against the Bible . . . or [the] Koran . . . or xyz law . . . or . . ." Followed soon thereafter by . . .
3. "What do you mean, we've always believed it," or, "Everyone knows that."

Further, as a species we seem to carry within us an anthropocentric viewpoint that most likely has aided our survival in a pool of species. (One sees this same anthropocentric tendency most dramatically in children.) A short list of the many anthropocentric ideas and hypotheses we've encountered, and in many cases ideas with which we must still deal, would include the following:

1. The world exists for one individual, and that one is me.
2. The world exists for my parents and me alone.
3. The world exists for my family alone.
4. There's only one race that counts, and that is my race.
5. There's only one true religion.
6. My country right or wrong. (Note: each nation's two-dimensional representational map of the world tends to have that country's location top center.)
7. Only our species reasons, plans, and carries out actions.
8. The Earth is flat.
9. The stars, our sun, and planets all revolve around the Earth.
10. Our solar system is the only place with life.
11. The universe was designed to make us possible.

Resistance to change, though often seen as damaging and delaying to progress (especially by scientists), has an important positive side that relates directly to the processes of evolution. Each new idea, theory, law, or technology must survive the gauntlet of human resistance to change by proving to be an added gain, or an advantage, to the overall system. The evolution of new ideas has a process that mimics the process of human evolution. Over the long haul, good and useful ideas tend to survive.

Over the long haul [...] many mistakes and competing claims will arise along the way. To continue the analogy, living species, including humans, have not been designed to be free from errors, but instead have developed the capacity, over hundreds of thousands of years, to survive and multiply despite errors. In the physical world, success in this endeavor has been greatly aided by the development and incorporation of genetically driven redundancies: multiple processes and pathways, duplicate systems and organs, over-capacities of components, and so forth. Each of our bodies contains multiple processes and pathways, duplicate systems and organs, over-capacities of components, and even a multitude of formerly important but currently unused stretches within our DNA. Earth's living organisms have developed the tools to overcome the many changes and challenges of the past, and these tools will be available to solve most of the new challenges we will face . . . but not all. A simple human example: our body is able to repair itself following cuts, falls, abrasions, etc., but it is unable to recover from many accidents that involve very rapid deceleration or acceleration—inside a speeding car that hits a cement wall, for example. As a species, we've not had any experience before, nor the evolutionary time, to develop any kind of resistance to this class of accidents.

Further Evolution of the Scientific Method

The need for a greater emphasis on, and a broader approach

in, the prediction and testing stages of hypotheses is recognized by increasing numbers of scientists and the public today. As knowledge in all fields (especially that of living organisms) increases, i.e. as research and findings move from an "anatomical" or cataloging mode into a "functional" or process-oriented mode (how systems work together), the need for predictive testing increases. We begin to encounter "If . . . then" situations with new processes and technologies that can result in technologies and products that might, in some cases, be terminally destructive to humans or the environment. Questions concerning the usage of new knowledge surface: are specific advances "good" to use, "bad" to use, [never to] be used, etc. One needs only to consider the societal timing associated with critical "advances." It has been tacitly accepted that there's always time enough to correct manmade changes resulting in detrimental effects to humans and/or the environment. At some point, however, situations will occur in which the time to recover from an error will exceed the time available to avoid the failure (non-recoverable) mode. Global warming might well prove to be one of these technological usage situations [. . .] (A few scientists once thought the first atomic detonation would be one.) As we develop more and more control over our planet's environment and more and more control over our own bodies, the frequency of advances with potentially critical consequences will also increase. It will be necessary to thoroughly pretest potential "advances" as part of the research program.

In medicine, we encounter similar situations in the study of human "homeostasis." Homeostasis may become a useful term in evaluating timing-critical scientific problems, since its meaning in medicine includes the definition of upper and lower limits for each variable under consideration, within which the body can self-correct (recover), and outside of which an outside force is necessary or death ensues (variables include: temperature regulation, pH regulation, sugar/salt/acid regulation, $O^2/CO^2/H_2O$/etc. regulation).

Current advances in the medical field (especially implantable devices and drugs) are subjected to years of pretesting prior to use. Part of the testing is driven by government regulations requiring proof of "safety and efficacy" for each advance: Does the new advance have any detrimental and/or lethal effects? Can it be demonstrated to have the power to produce the desired effects? Illustrative cases: Thalidomide, a synthetic sedative and hypnotic drug, passed the efficacy tests and initially the safety testing until it was found to be extremely detrimental to fetuses during the first three months of pregnancy. Diamox, an established drug used classically in the treatment of glaucoma, has the side effect of doubling breathing rates ([from] 14 per minute to 25–30 per minute) without affecting heart rates. In the last ten years Diamox has a new use: increasing passive oxygen uptake for hikers and climbers above 10,000 feet.

The scientific method has served humanity well, but it needs to evolve further to include the broader safety and efficacy tests and evaluations of new advances prior to their use.

Politics and Economics

Another theme that has provoked thoughtful writing is political issues. Sometimes the articles are light-hearted (though serious), as in this 1995 article by Rhoda Gilman.

Rhoda Gilman was a founding member of the Scholars. She continued her membership through the years. She worked as a researcher and writer for the Minnesota Historical Society and was the author of several history books.

A Scholar Writes

A Natural Affinity: Independent Scholars and Independent Booksellers
Rhoda Gilman, 1995

I think Isaac Asimov was the source for a description I once read of the ideal information storage and retrieval technology for the citizen-scholar of the 21st century:

- It must have a large capacity and yet be light and compact, preferably pocket size.
- It must be durable and not subject to damage from heat, cold, heavy impact, long storage, or ubiquitous electrical and magnetic currents.
- It must need no external power supply and be usable in any location.
- It must be easy to access, not requiring exceptional skills or training.
- It must be inexpensive and widely available.
- Finally, in authoritarian societies or police states, it should be easy to conceal and, when in use, not detectable by electronic eavesdropping.

The answer is, of course, a book.

So, when you stop to think about it, it seems inevitable that books, book publishers, and booksellers will be with us at least as long as independent scholars. The only questions are: Where? How many of them? What kind?

There has been a good deal of discussion in recent years about the galloping consolidation of the publishing industry. What used to be a field of many small- and medium-sized firms, judged almost as much by intellectual and artistic prestige as by monetary returns, has become in the last 25 years a fiefdom of multinational corporations and their financial empires.

Now it is the turn of retail book outlets. Not only are locally owned bookstores being crowded out by chains, the chains themselves are merging into corporate kingdoms. K-Mart now owns three major chains, including Borders Books, Waldenbooks, and Brentano's—more than a thousand stores in all. The Barnes & Noble stable includes not only its own supermarkets, but B. Dalton, Bookstop, Bookstall, Scribner's, and Doubleday—not to mention five or six hundred college bookstores across the country.

The next step is, obviously, consolidation with television networks, computers and the whole field of electronic information and entertainment. (Currently, Viacom is said to be dickering with K-Mart for purchase of Borders Books.) What does all of this mean for locally owned bookstores? The answer is only too obvious. Nor does it rest solely with competition for customers. [*Ed. note: Borders Books went out of business in 2011.*]

Last spring, the American Booksellers Association filed suit against six major publishers (including Viking-Penguin and St. Martin's Press) for collusion with book chains. Not only did the chains get better prices than the independents, they also got more liberal credit terms, faster shipment of new titles, and other advantages. The Federal Trade Commission had previously filed a similar suit. So much for the free market!

The demise of independent bookstores will unquestionably have a domino effect on small independent publishers. While computer technology facilitates production of limited-market books in small editions, their distribution will become almost impossible if left to national and international chains.

And independent scholars need not be told what that means for them.

David Unowsky, owner of the Hungry Mind and a recognized spokesman for independent book dealers nationwide, lists three reasons for supporting independent publishing and bookselling:
1. To maintain a competitive economy;
2. To prevent the stifling of artistic and intellectual diversity;
3. To prevent control over what information reaches the public.

In the Twin Cities, the battle has already commenced. Minnesota has long been a stronghold of small literary presses and an independent book trade. But since 1989, Barnes & Noble alone has opened eight new stores in the metropolitan area. There are only six or eight (depending on how you define the area) locally owned general book stores, plus 15 or 20 specialty stores (science fiction, mystery, art books, New Age, women's, etc.). Three general stores have closed in recent years: Odegard's (Minneapolis), Gringolet, and Savran's. As long as competition is fierce, the book supermarkets will go out of their way to accommodate groups like the Independent Scholars' Forum. But there are persuasive reasons why we should stick with independents. I urge our members to do so.

In the 1980s, Lee Wenzel, then working for Toro Corporation, designed alternatives to medical coverage. He is all-but-dissertation for a Ph.D. in the area of alternatives to medical coverage. He is also a registered investment advisor with his own company, Wenzel Analytics. This article appeared in *Practical Thinking*, September 2010, shortly after the Affordable Care Act was signed into law.

A Scholar Writes

Yes, But Is It Health Insurance?
Lee Wenzel, 2010

The problems of access, quality, and cost inherent in the current health care delivery system are a direct result of using the insurance framework or paradigm for a set of services that mostly do not conform to being an insurable risk. We blame insurance companies when we should blame insurance itself. There is a strategic misalignment between the inherent nature of the form of finance, that being insurance, and the inherent nature of health and, more narrowly, even most medical services. These strategic problems will not be resolved by tactical maneuvers and adaptations. Fortunately, insurance is only one of eight paradigms available in our toolbox for forms of finance governing all financial transactions. The strategic task is to open the toolbox and design a viable way to finance health care.

The purpose of this article is to make explicit the implicit abandonment of insurance implied in the recently enacted national health care legislation. When everyone can obtain coverage and premiums are not related to risk, that is no longer insurance. To the extent that the concepts of insurance guide implementation, the system might well implode for lack of outcomes and uncontrollable costs. Reform is to move into alternative forms or paradigms.

Clean Up Our Language

We need an accurate use of terms and a solid and logical conceptual base before economic science and business expertise can bring alternatives and data to design and implement a viable system. Health insurance is an oxymoron that desperately needs elucidation if we are to design an adequate system to finance medical and broader health care services.

To take the first term, the health in health insurance usually refers only and primarily to medical services under the control of physicians. Health clubs obviously provide health services, or they wouldn't be called health clubs, but most health club revenue does not come from health insurance. Nursing homes and custodial care provide health care services but have only minimal financing from what we refer to as health insurance. Instead, they are mostly financed by procurement (people buying directly), Medicaid (an entitlement, not insurance), Medicare for a short time (also an entitlement and not insurance), and increasingly long-term care insurance.

One would think that health insurance would provide financial compensation for the financial risks attendant to loss of health. In addition to paying for required medical services, this would include inability to work (disability), chronic and long-term nursing and health care services, and, of course, the ultimate loss of health which is death.

An entitlement plan that had financial liability for situations when a cure is not available, such as for ALS or Alzheimer's, would provide necessary ongoing care and have financial incentives to invest in critical research. Our insurance system has provider incentives for expensive treatments, if approved by the claims process, but no incentives for medical research. The nature of insurance makes insurance most appropriate for medical cure in contrast to health care. Health services are broader than medical services. In addition, services oriented to care, rather than cure, generally do not conform to being an insurable risk.

What makes this matter of being an insurable risk so important is that the paradigm rules. Systems built on the principals of insurance tilt towards paying for insurable services and tend to deny or limit uninsurable services. This tilt happens despite the best intentions of providers, consumers, and public policy. The good news is that most medical insurance plans and companies abandoned medical insurance long ago. They function mostly as third-party administrators (TPAs) and do not underwrite risk. The bad news is that even as we have shifted mostly from insurance to entitlements, we still call it insurance and apply many of the concepts and principles that are ill-suited to financing healthcare services.

An Insurable Risk

And what is an insurable risk? Think about insurance. Insurance is a way to have the money we need when improbable catastrophes occur. Using the laws of large numbers, a premium is charged when the policy is sold based on the probability of the undesirable event and the amount of money needed should that happen. Insurance is always for undesirable events and to compensate for a loss.

Insurance is always a conditional contract. If this happens, then that is what will be paid or provided. For insurance to work, there has to be an objective and legally definable basis for a claim and for the consequent benefits or obligations of the insurance provider.

Third-Party Transactions

To understand how this works, one must dissect the dynamics of any third-party payment design.

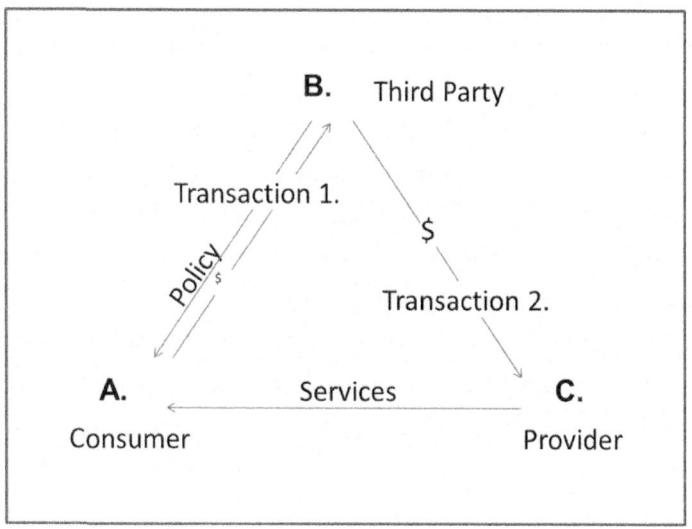

In order to fulfill its contractual obligations to A, the third party, B, buys services from C, the provider, which are delivered to A, the consumer. The consumer could submit a claim to B and receive payment which is then sent to C, although that is rarely done in practice, as it creates uncertainties for the provider and more bookkeeping and work for the consumer. The provision of services by C for A is not an economic transaction in itself but a consequence and the completion of the other two transactions.

These two transactions are in very different markets. Transaction One (A to B) is insurance. Transaction Two (B to C) is procurement.

Note that the consumer is not buying healthcare or medical services. The consumer is buying coverage for the possibility of being eligible for services. In practice, the services are purchased by the third party, who becomes the provider's customer. The incentives for the consumer are to pay as little for coverage [as possible] and get as much as possible from the provider or plan. The incentives for the third party are to collect as much in premium[s] as possible and pay out in claims as little as possible. One lucrative way to do this is to make the policy commitments to the consumer as vague or buried as possible, or deny the providers' judgment as to necessity. This is particularly easy to do in areas such as need for psychotherapy. The incentives for party C, the provider, are to provide the maximum volume of services and at the highest price that the third party will tolerate. Of course, there are other tactics in how B treats C, such as those related to claim denial, difficulties in filing claims, or timeliness of payments.

Note that a third-party payment preempts a financial transaction between the consumer and the provider. As a consumer, I'm left out of weighing cost-to-benefits and excluded from service considerations and decisions based on cost. What about deductions and copayments? Deductions and copayments are not insurance; they are exemptions from insurance. They define risk that is not covered. The result is that the consumer's health and welfare are dependent upon the negotiations between these two other parties, the third-party payer, and the provider, each with their own financial incentives.

In this tripartite arrangement, who decides medical necessity and the services I should receive under the terms of the policy? If the services are indeed medically necessary, then I shouldn't be asked about my insurance when I go to the clinic or hospital. By definition, I need necessary services and should get them regardless of who is paying or how much is paid. If the services are contingent upon who is paying and how much, then they are contingent services and not medically necessary services.

The original meaning of a professional service is that because of the nature of the services and the technical knowledge and trustworthiness of the provider, the provider decides what I need and what I will pay. The professional has a fiduciary responsibility for the economic transaction to be in my best interest. Under this meaning of professional, every bankruptcy from medical costs is prima fascia evidence of non-professional conduct.

More About Insurable Risk

Insurance pushes to take medical providers out of the diagnosis process. The consumer or a technician could feed the objective data into a computer which contains algorithms to determine the diagnosis, the course of treatment, and automatically send prescriptions to the pharmacist. Doctors are only needed for interventions requiring specialized skills, such as [surgery]. Insurance doesn't support the importance of personal relationships for most chronic health conditions. The insurance problem with chronic conditions is that they begin so gradually that it is difficult to determine eligibility for a claim. Moreover, they are often not cured.

Some naïve people argue that insurance should cover prevention as a way to avoid costly acute interventions. Such arguments fail to understand the pervasive influence of the financial paradigm, and how prevention is antithetical to insurance. Insurance pays for claims and loss, not prevention. Things that are preventable should be managed and prevented, not insured. Insurance is for events over which we do not have control.

In a similar naïve vein, some argue for outcomes-based medicine. Insurance is based on compliance and is indifferent to outcomes. Ask any life insurance company about the outcomes of the claims they have paid, and they would be hard-pressed to provide any data beyond the timeliness and accuracy of sending checks.

Professionals are paid independent of outcome. Doctors are paid whether their treatments work or not. Indeed, mortality amongst doctors' patients is 100 percent, although we still pay in hopes of postponing the event.

Any serious move towards outcomes in healthcare is paddling upstream, if insurance is the finance paradigm.

Why Insurance?

So why is our society fixated on medical insurance? The most obvious reason is that insurance provides the cash flow when services are needed. However, there are lots of other ways to accomplish the same thing. The function of insurance is for cost not to be an issue, should the catastrophe occur. Since insurance is designed precisely to remove the cost issue, why are we surprised when health insurance costs move up without apparent constraint?

Ignorance Insurance?

The arbitrariness of using the insurance paradigm to finance medical and health services can be revealed by a hypothetical proposal to use insurance to fund education. We could insure against ignorance, since learning is essential to individual career advancement, and if we don't get rid of ignorance, our economy is going down the tubes! The way it would work is that education professionals could do assessments in their private clinics, and then refer people to the institutions where they have staffing privileges (schools, as opposed to hospitals). Claims could also be based on standardized tests, such as those done for No Child Left Behind. Claims could then be submitted for each educational intervention, whether it was tutoring, web-based instruction, or classroom instruction. Defining the interventions very specifically and for brief, discrete time periods could produce more claims and more income. The insurance could be purchased by individuals, families, corporations, or any other public or private entity. The third-party administrators would love all the new business, and a lot more teachers would be making $200,000 a year. A lot of people and organizations would be relieved to have the focus shift away from outcomes and towards instruction delivered. You say it is different from health care? How and why?

Insurance claims, whether for ignorance, illness, or injury, are for what we want to get rid of, not for learning and health, which we desire. Insurance implements an avoidant rather than a goal-oriented endeavor. The shift from obsessing about illness, aches, and pains to enjoying positive health practices is a challenge for more than a small minority of hypochondriacs. Insurance puts the providers' and consumers' focus in the wrong direction.

So, What Are the Alternatives to Health Insurance?

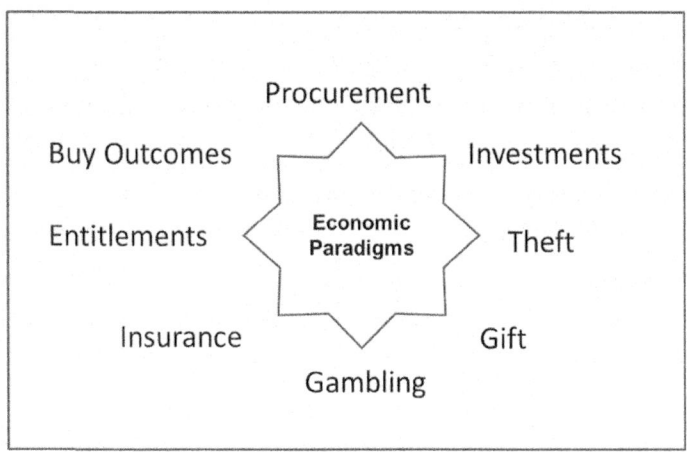

There are eight alternative paradigms that govern economic transactions. Each has its own language and dynamics and is more or less appropriate for different situations. Economists talk about rational economics as if there is only one rational way to make an economic decision. In reality, what is rational is configured and determined by the specific paradigm. I will review possible applications for healthcare financing.

1. Entitlement

The most common alternative to insurance is entitlement. If an employer offers a health plan to its employees, and all employees pay the same fee (technically not a premium), the employees have an entitlement plan and not health insurance. Insurance always has individual underwriting, where the premium is adjusted to the statistically calculated risk of benefits or claim payment. The employer may have an insurance plan to cover the cost liabilities attendant to the offered entitlement plan. We then have a significant private or employer form of socialism.

For an entitlement, in contrast to insurance, the cost to the specific individual is unrelated to the entitled benefits. Entitlements are often goal- or service-oriented, and may or may not be contingent upon a loss, such as is the function of insurance. So, we are entitled to go to the library and drive on most public roads. We buy a membership to a health club, or any other association, and are then entitled to the benefits of that membership. I buy an online subscription and pay the same whether I use the subscription or not. Our earliest and most primal economic experiences are with entitlements, as most of us are born into families, where we are provided with food, clothing, housing, and a whole host of entitlements.

There can be limits to entitlements or forms of rationing

according to rules, although entitlements work best in situations where there is a natural satiation—such as the public library. To avoid stigma, a third or so of a population must perceive a service or program as something they will or potentially might use. While entitlements provide security, as does insurance, excessive entitlements inhibit the motivation to conserve scarce entitlement resources. Since the demand for medical and health care services is highly elastic, any entitlement system needs some form of rationing just as every family rations who gets what and when. Don't be alarmed. The rationing of scarce resources is a primary function of all economic transactions. It just happens differently under different economic paradigms.

The biggest challenge in designing an entitlement plan is how to balance a rights-based system and leave room for judgment and discretion in determining access and availability of services. This dichotomy between rights and needs is sometimes referred to as the hard versus [the] soft. To illustrate the contrast, retirement benefits under Social Security are a right, while social work and children's rights activists argued successfully that caseworkers should provide services and use their discretion in determining eligibility for financial help to needy children and their families. The result some seventy-five years later is that I make a good living and collect Social Security without social stigma, while many poor, hungry children and their parents in our country collect limited benefits accompanied by considerable stigma, or receive no benefits at all.

Any entitlement program based strictly on rules or rights is going to tilt towards acute cure medicine, to the neglect of chronic healthcare, where the determination of need requires individual judgment and flexibility.

Isaac Rubinow was the brains behind Social Security, our first significant entitlement program. Rubinow was not only the pioneer in actuary science, but a pioneer in understanding the psychology and sociology of how people and peoples handle and mishandle their needs for economic security. In 1917, he was employed by the American Medical Society, speaking to large groups around the country promoting national health insurance. He wrote in a weekly magazine that we were within six months of making such insurance a reality. Of course, health insurance at that time would be more like disability insurance today, and the window of opportunity closed with World War I. Rubinow was writing books in the 1920s about the reasons why people were not financially prepared for disability or old age, and the same remains largely true today. It is interesting that while many bemoan big government and deficits, only a few people advocate dismantling Social Security or refuse, on principle, to take the checks.

There is little reason for employers to be involved in medical or health plans, apart from workplace safety and health promotion. The annual rotation in and out of plans is particularly destructive of any longer-term investment in an individual's health. The expenses detract from the employed or don't have an employer, and few employers have the expertise or motivation to design and implement state-of-the-art health plans.

2. Insurance

A second paradigm, which I would rather see, is large group health plans, perhaps with geographic boundaries like large school districts. The primary alternative to the tensions and dysfunctions of any third-party payment system as outlined above is to merge parties B and C and make it an entitlement instead of insurance. This may have been the intent of Health

Maintenance Organizations (HMOs), although for the most part they have not escaped the linguistics and baggage of the insurance paradigm. The model holds promise, if some of the insurance mentality could be monitored and removed, if incentives could be controlled by controls on things like executive compensation and what happens to profits (or fund balances in the case of nonprofits), if adverse selection and annual membership rotations were limited, and if the boundaries between medical and broader health services could be appropriately managed. One move in that direction might be financial responsibility for total outcomes, such as disability, long-term care, and death.

3. Procurement

A third paradigm is procurement, the way we go to a store and buy something because we would rather have the object than the money. Veterinary services are mostly purchased by procurement, and it seems to work. Procurement could be supplemented by a large deductible or sliding copayment for catastrophic costs. Leaving off the psychological and political realities, financially, it makes sense for anyone with financial means enough to retire or aspire to retire without a pension to buy a $10,000 or $20,000 deductible medical plan and purchase the balance of needed medical services. However, this option makes sense only if there were a fair and open market and providers were prohibited from having under-the-table preferred provider rates.

4. Purchase of Outcomes

A fourth paradigm is the purchase of outcomes, rather than the components to accomplish the outcomes, as in procurement. I can purchase the outcome of a roofing job for our house, or I can purchase the shingles and labor.

Last summer I went to a pain clinic for a pain in my hamstring that prevented me from running. After an MRI and two epidurals, the pain was still there. When I stopped taking the statin medication, the pain went away. If compensation was based on outcomes, the doctor might have told me to discontinue the statin and I could have saved myself the discomfort—and Medicare the costs of the MRI and epidurals.

5. Charity

A fifth paradigm is charity. Many of our major medical institutions still carry the legacy names from charities that were part of their founding. Many churches have nurses delivering health services that are largely charitable. Research organizations devoted to specific disorders are often funded as charitable organizations. Whether charity is adequate to provide the continuity and advances in science that we need is perhaps questionable.

6. Theft

The flip side of charity is theft, in that the recipient rather than the giver is the primary decision maker for the transaction. Medical services are frequently funded by unpaid bills, a form of theft.

7. Gambling

A large proportion of health and even medical interventions are done without a solid probability that they will be efficacious. Even where we do have the benefits of good research, many interventions are a gamble. The odds might be seventy percent that it will work, or even ten percent, but given the alternatives, we take the gamble. Insurance systems pay or provide what is specified in the policy. An entitlement program might provide services based on a ratio of probabilities to cost. For example, should a procedure costing $500,000 be supplied when the probabilities of extending life up to six months are 10 percent? Or are those resources better deployed in a children's health program that improves health status by 10 percent for a thousand children? These are gambling decisions in that they are not just about compensating for loss, but about odds to achieve goals. Honeywell pioneered an employee organ transplant benefit that selected providers on a national level for each organ transplant and then only paid based on patient survival. The provider then had to set rates based on probabilities and take the gamble.

8. Investments

The final paradigm, investments, is when we buy something not to use it or benefit directly, but to have it produce income or increase in value for a consequent sale. We often refer to health promotion as an investment in our health. Endowments and foundations can produce a significant source of revenue for healthcare services.

What's Wrong with Calling It Health Insurance?

Calling it insurance perpetrates the illusion that my health is beyond my control. I'm passive and need to be (a) patient. My health is determined by the doctor who "treats" me. My health must be a matter of fate, since the purpose of insurance is to provide financial protection for improbable and uncontrollable events. Health promotion programs are undermined by the implicit premises of the insurance paradigm.

Insurance pays what is required by contract and is not responsible for achieving specific outcomes. Outcomes are discredited. Outcome-based medicine is contrary to the financial incentives and framework of the primary funding mechanism.

Conclusion

In summary, we need more strategic thinking to lay a solid foundation for how medical and health services should be financed. Instead of blaming insurance companies for adhering to the principles of insurance, we need to examine the applicability of insurance. The paradigm of insurance has significant negative implications for providers, consumers, and payers. Yet, it is the paradigm which frames all the other choices. We need to think creatively about how to frame a system based primarily on entitlements and procurement.

While a relatively small number of individual medical insurance policies exist in the United States, most of what passes for health insurance is, in reality, a medical entitlement plan. An important step towards creating a workable delivery system is not to call insurance that which isn't insurance. This means precision in not using many insurance-related words and concepts, such as premiums, risk, claims, and underwriting. Journalists, politicians, and legislative authors need to be more precise in their use of language. When I check in at a clinic, they might ask about my medical plan and not mention the word insurance. The term insurance should not be used for what is not insurance. The term health should not be used to refer only to medical services. The use of language defines the discourse and the framework for how people think, what they expect, and how they decide.

The people designing administrative rules and mechanisms to implement healthcare reform need to be clear as to the paradigms being deployed. If it is entitlement rather than insurance, then abandon the insurance language and principles. The effectiveness of programs, to say nothing of their efficiencies, are going to be dependent upon a level of implementation below the radar of political euphemisms.

Remember, the paradigm rules.

Writing About History

Since there are many historians in the membership of MISF, we have published many good accounts of days gone by.

Dale Schwie is a longtime member of MISF. He is also a member of the Board of Directors of the Concord, Massachusetts-based Thoreau Society. Retired after a career in photography, Schwie has written a biography of photographer Herbert W. Gleason. Gleason's photographs were used extensively to illustrate the writings of Henry David Thoreau and other nineteenth-century American authors. This article appeared in *Practical Thinking* in June of 2008. Schwie's book on Gleason, *Taking Sides with the Sun* (Nodin Press, 2017), came out in July of 2017 and was a finalist for the Midwest Book Awards.

A Scholar Writes

Fame Was Not Fair to Herbert W. Gleason
Dale R. Schwie, 2008

"Fame is not just. It never finely or discriminatingly praises, but coarsely hurrahs. The truest acts of heroism never reach her ear, are never published by her trumpet." —H. D. Thoreau, journal entry, June 6, 1854

"I would not subtract anything from the praise that is due to philanthropy, but merely demand justice for all who by their lives and works are a blessing to mankind." —H.D. Thoreau, *Walden*

Today, when outstanding achievement is not a prerequisite for fame, and one can become famous merely for being famous, the lives and works of those who are truly worthy of our interest and admiration are often overlooked.

Photographer Herbert W. Gleason (1855–1937) is among those to whom justice is due. Gleason never achieved fame during his lifetime, nor posthumously in photographic history. Though fame may have been of little concern to Gleason, he probably would derive satisfaction from knowing that his contributions as a landscape photographer and environmentalist are at last earning him a rightful place in photographic history. At the core of his work are his photographs of "Thoreau Country," which were inspired by the writings of Henry David Thoreau and recorded over a period of nearly forty years.

Gleason, originally from Malden, Massachusetts, moved to Minnesota in 1883, not to pursue a career in photography, but to answer a call as a Congregational minister. He served in that capacity for two years in Pelican Rapids, and another two years in Minneapolis, where he was the pastor of the Como Avenue Congregational Church and helped to start another church in Saint Anthony Park in St. Paul. For the next twelve years in Minneapolis, Gleason served as managing editor of a regional Congregational newspaper, the *Kingdom*.

Of greater significance is that during this time, Gleason first became acquainted with portions of Thoreau's journal and began to experiment with photography. Over one hundred of Gleason's Minnesota negatives, dating from 1899, are now included in a collection of over seven thousand of his negatives in the Concord Free Public Library in Concord, Massachusetts. The catalyst for Gleason's career change from managing editor of the *Kingdom* to photographer was not ill health, as is generally believed, but a libel suit against the Kingdom Publishing Company—a suit that was lost on a technicality, despite the best efforts of attorney Clarence Darrow, who took on the case for the defense.[118]

When the *Kingdom* newspaper closed down, leaving Gleason unemployed, he and his wife, Lulie Rounds Gleason, an accomplished pianist and music teacher at the Northwestern Conservatory of Music and president of the Thursday Musical for its first eight years, moved back to Boston. At the earliest opportunity, Gleason visited Concord, Massachusetts, to search for and photograph places described by Thoreau. While on Thoreau's trail, he found a new career and a relationship with the author that he later described as "remunerative in more ways than one."[117] His Concord excursions, he wrote, ". . . were self-rewarding, entirely apart from their historical or personal interest. A breezy walk over Concord meadows or uplands far exceeds in exhilaration and inspiration any afternoon upon a golf course or any conceivable trip in a motor-car."[119]

Gleason Needed Work

When Gleason returned to Boston, his first priority was to generate an income while searching for permanent employment. He returned to his earlier profession of court reporting, where he found a demand for his services among his former stenographic associates. Gleason's willingness ". . . to take twenty-five dollars a day out of the lawyers"[121] enabled him to invest in photographic equipment and devote more time to rambling among Thoreau's "beloved haunts." Not intending to make a career of court reporting, and doubting that he could succeed as a professional photographer, Gleason continued to explore other options including returning to Minnesota.

When, however, the Houghton Mifflin Company became interested in Gleason's photographs of Thoreau country, his confidence grew and doubts about succeeding as a photographer vanished. He signed lucrative contracts with Houghton Mifflin to supply photographs for special editions of the writings of Thoreau, and eventually for the writings of Ralph Waldo Emerson, John Muir, John Burroughs, and others, as well as Gleason's own book, *Through the Year with Thoreau*, which was published in 1917.

When Gleason first began photographing in Minnesota, and using photographs to illustrate a series of "Out of Doors" articles for the *Kingdom*, he was taking the initial steps of a journey that would lead him across the North American continent some forty times. Along the way, he was appointed by Stephen Mather, the first director of the National Park Service, as an Interior Department Inspector assigned to photographing current and potential park sites. Some of Gleason's lantern slides, hand-colored by Mrs. Gleason, make up what has been considered ". . . one of the first and best national park lantern-slide collections."[122]

In addition to his work with the National Park Service, Gleason photographed other threatened landscapes and lectured extensively in support of the conservation of natural areas. Organizations such as the Appalachian Mountain Club and the Sierra Club provided Gleason with new outlets for his illustrated lectures and introduced him to leaders in the conservation movement. Foremost among these was John Muir. Gleason and Muir became close friends, who worked together in efforts to preserve the California redwoods, and on a hard-fought, but unsuccessful, battle to prevent the damming of the Hetch Hetchy Valley in Yosemite. Today, Gleason's photographs of the valley before it was flooded are being used by activists in a movement to restore the Hetch Hetchy Valley.

Although Gleason has gained some recognition since the 1970s, after the publication of two beautiful books of his photographs, *Thoreau Country* and *The Western Wilderness of North*

America, and others illustrating the writings of Thoreau, he is still relatively unknown except to photographic historians and to those familiar with his Thoreau country images.

Perhaps [one reason that Gleason did not achieve] fame as a photographer may be found in the venues he chose for displaying his images, and in his own independence. Gleason was a self-promoter; he was not dependent on the gallery scene and photographic societies; he specialized in illustrated lectures and books. Thousands of photographs taken by Gleason while he was employed by the National Park Service became NPS property. Gleason lectured to audiences throughout the US, but the ephemeral nature of illustrated lectures, and early sales of books by Henry D. Thoreau, John Muir, John Burroughs, and others containing his photographs, did not bring fame his way. However, Gleason, who found ". . . a peculiar satisfaction in being on hand at the beginning of things,"[123] might also concur with Thoreau's words: "For it matters not how small the beginning may seem to be: what is once well done is done for ever."[124] Today, many of Gleason's Concord images, along with Thoreau's botanical notes, are being studied by biologists researching the effects of global warming on plant growth. In Minnesota, examples of Gleason's work and multiple talents can be found not in photographs, but in the logo of the Thursday Musical where his laurel wreath design is still in use after 116 years, and in a pulpit that he built and hand carved in 1884 for the Pelican Rapids Congregational Church. His articles in the *Kingdom* newspaper provide valuable insight into his years in Minneapolis, as well as interesting local history.

Fame's trumpet may not have published Gleason's achievements, but his commitment to photography and the conservation of natural beauty was not dependent on coarse hurrahs. No doubt, he would find a peculiar satisfaction in knowing that the photographs he dedicated nearly forty years of his life to creating are today a source of new life for him and his works. Fame may not be just, but perhaps for Gleason it has been delayed rather than denied.

Why Genealogy
Getting to know more about fellow members...

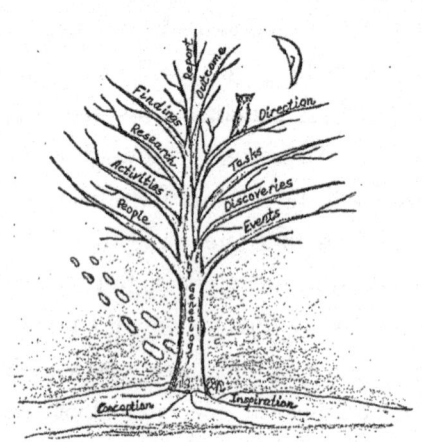

Table of Contents

Features:
2 -The Driving Force
  by Evelyn Klein

4 -Pursuing Family Roots
  by Gus Fenton

5 -Voice of the People
  by Mike Woolsey

Book Review: Lucy Brusic,
7 -*Her Honor* by Lori Sturdevant

Forum Programs:
9 -War and Russian Art,
  Carol Veldman Rudie
10 -Trip to Cuba, Gus Fenton
10 -Sad Stories of the Death of
  Kings, James Hart
11 -World without Genocide,
  Ellen Kennedy
12 -Poetry Day
  Amato, Irwin, Klein, Whiting

Tribute:
8 -To Lucy Brusic

14 -Submission Guidelines

15 -Upcoming Programs & Events

The Minnesota Scholar is published semi-annually.

In this issue, *The Minnesota Scholar* will begin featuring, a series of articles under the general heading of *Why Genealogy*. Since fields of interest and scholarship vary from the sciences to the arts, technology to sports, crafts to trades, business to industry, philosophy to psychology and everything in-between, we are calling for scholars to share with other members of the Minnesota Independent Scholars Forum the passions in their chosen areas.

In June 2016, Evelyn Klein became the editor of the *Minnesota Scholar* and inaugurated a new series of articles about members' interests. Initially the series was called *Why Genealogy?* but has now expanded to include *Why Art?* and *Why the Independent Scholars?*

Another aspect of history is personal biography as it relates to independent scholarship. In June 2017, Evelyn Klein, as the new editor of the

Minnesota Scholar, penned the following personal account of independent scholarship and offered her vision of the future.

A Scholar Writes

of Independent Scholars
Evelyn D. Klein, 2017

With today's globalization and technology, the world has become more accessible. For those of us who have traveled outside as well as inside the U.S., we have a firsthand glimpse of the diversity of our world, not only in terms of the people who populate it but also of the cultures, ideas, and perspectives that mark it.

If some of us painstakingly worked our way through undergraduate college, it was not because we followed a tradition or were expected to, but because we instinctively knew there had to be more to life. And if we went on to an advanced degree sometime after that, it was because we held out for a more in-depth view of whatever field we were in. In my case, it was the teaching of English. My thesis, "Virginia Woolf, the Creative Vision," brought me to a new concept of creative process, opening the door to my lifelong dream—writing. This, in turn, helped me climb, independently, from teaching to editing to publishing, which, in turn, led to graphic art and on to independent scholarship. And on it goes.

Emily Dickinson referred to her poetry as her "letter to the world." Writing for me is not so much a letter as it is an exploration, a discourse, or [a] conversation with the world, albeit on paper. Yet every poem, every article, every story I write is a response or processing of something already existing in the environment, something I did not see before, something that struck me as needing a response, or requiring further thought and inquiry. Drawing has become the visual version of perspectives explored in writing.

In this "swiftly moving" world of new possibilities, the greatest challenge is to catch up and keep up, perhaps even get ahead of the game a bit. We may not even have realized it until it became official, but the notion of lifelong learning, born in this age of technology, moves along faster than some of us, working on our own, can follow. Still, many of us have a hand in the changes, because they help us move forward too.

Since the world seems to have moved closer together, made more accessible through technology and media, we hear diverse voices of varying credibility, depending on which media and which voice is presenting fact or belief, myth or alternate fact, even post-truth. These do not usually come with labels attached, so the listener or reader has to decide. Someone may say "I believe my friend. Therefore, I take whatever he/she says as fact." We all love the story of Thanksgiving with the Pilgrims. But is it fact or cultural myth? And if we choose a political candidate on the basis of appeal to our fears rather than the individual's given track record, are we dealing with facts or post-truth? But all of these ideas have been around in human discourse for eons, if perhaps by different names. Yet, the issues are much more sweeping than that. With all that is going on in the world, it is important to stay informed. The trick is to sort out the different voices.

Many of us like to ponder truth; the meaning of existence; our way of life; our environment, institutions, commerce, politics, etc.; and our place in them beyond the everyday. While our culture greatly esteems the authoritative voice of academia, as far as scholarship and expertise are concerned, not every inquiring mind or scholarly individual is necessarily connected to academia, even after earning a degree. There are many reasons for it. Not every scholar chooses teaching, for instance. Some may have no connection to academia or find it too confining. Or perhaps opportunity for employment was not there when they were ready to enter the field, as was the case for me, some years ago. But some people continue their studies on their own, nevertheless, free spirits of sorts. And the voices of some of these may be as expert as any today. Growth is a state of mind, along with the need to engage in intellectual and scholarly discussions or exchanges, in person and/or on paper.

Historically, we are preceded by great scholars, who were not linked to academia in their creative output. And while the term "independent scholar" may have been coined in the late twentieth century, we find some impressive names, coming from every imaginable field of study, creativity, expertise, or innovation, who fit that category. Among them are Leonardo da Vinci, Nicolaus Copernicus, Johannes Kepler, Hildegard von Bingen, Martin Luther, William Shakespeare, René Descartes, Benjamin Franklin, Thomas Edison, Ludwig van Beethoven, Henry David Thoreau, Emily Dickinson, Henry Ford, Käthe Kollwitz, Carl Jung, Kate Millet, Jane Goodall, Pinchas Zukerman, Gloria Steinem, and Steven Jobs. They represent only a few of the luminaries on the long list of the curious, the seekers, the originators, the savants—the independent thinkers.

Of course, these thinkers have contributed to the way we live today. And knowledge and education as well as life experience have become the prerogative of the ordinary person. Fortunately, independent thinkers are still busily at work. Independent scholarship offers a parallel, a balance, and supplement to academia, arising out of a variety of needs and allowing for more flexibility and, perhaps, even a quicker surfacing of new influences, ideas, and creativity.

A case in point is the Loft Literary Center in Minneapolis. When I completed my M.S., the writing inspired by my course work found support not at the university but at the Loft. Considering my professional background, they asked me to facilitate a poetry group, which I then did for seven years. This led to my teaching at the Loft off and on, when my schedule of writing, publishing, and editing allows.

When the creative process of writing was first beginning to take hold among writers in the 1980s, I was among those writers by virtue of my master's thesis. The Loft, recently established, had already dedicated itself to creative writing at a time when academia did not pay much heed to it, because it uses the inverse approach of expository writing required for scholarly writing. Yet the Loft, sidelining the academic approach, attracted increasing numbers of students. Even academicians and people of all educational backgrounds began to attend Loft classes. Soon academia, not to be outdone, added creative writing courses of their own to their other academic offerings. Thus, while the Loft considers itself a community-based literary arts organization, it also represents independent scholarship by exploring and promoting, in-depth, the process and rendering of creative writing.

A more recent example of independent scholarship is the East Side Freedom Library in Saint Paul. Founded in 2014 by Peter Rachleff and Beth Cleary, both educators, it turned to "Producing Knowledge Outside the Walls of Academia." The library houses non-circulating research collections with appeal to general learners as well as to scholars. Here, diverse people can come and access knowledge about a diverse neighborhood and do research and develop their own ideas.

The general need and desirability of independent scholarship is evidenced, also, by organizations that capitalize on scholarly topics in their programming. In the Twin Cities, we have such groups or organizations as Conversations of the Valley and the AAUW–St. Paul with weekly and monthly programs respectively. The Minnesota Jung Association is another standalone organization with regular scholarly salons, lectures, workshops, and seminars on psychology, at times publishing an online journal, to give only a few examples.

Groups like MISF have made it easy for anyone from a stay-at-home parent to an academic, from a hobbyist to a professional and everyone in between to carry on the discourse about the world we live in.

Today, we have a number of organizations that specifically promote independent scholarship per se, offering a place to otherwise unheard voices. In the United States, we have the National Coalition of Independent Scholars, located in San Antonio, Texas, of which the Minnesota Independent Scholars' Forum is an affiliate. Formed in 1989 to support independent scholars, it boasts five affiliates in the US and one in Australia. According to their website, the coalition caters to those "who have not or never wished to enter academia" or have left its increasingly "unstable" climate. It also includes emerging scholars or those seeking a second or new career.

Our neighbors to the north, the Canadian Academy of Independent Scholars in Vancouver, British Columbia, function much as the US organization does. Further, it caters to "a network of lifelong learners" and offers grants and library support for its members.

If we observe the trend, despite the fact that academia remains the esteemed model of expertise, independent scholarship seems to be the wave of the future, along with the changing world of publishing. With increasing numbers of people who are educated, have intensive or longtime work experience, traveled extensively, found new insights, and conducted their own experiments, we may, increasingly, draw scholars of the future from this pool of independents at large. Since the prevalence of scientific method and expository writing enjoys more widespread accessibility and application than formerly, it helps open this new door.

When in 2010 Shirley Whiting suggested I join the Scholars, I was intrigued by the intellectual and scholarly discussions of its members. I soon joined the philosophy group, because I always wanted to study philosophy but never found time. Being part of a discussion group helps me see the world through others' eyes as well, which helps me expand on my own ideas and allows me to put them in a relevant frame of reference.

Sometime after I joined the philosophy group, I was asked to serve on the board, which I was happy to accept. Only then did I discover the mission, purpose, and kind of participation open to MISF members. When the board president [at the time], Mike Woolsey, asked me to be the new editor of the *Minnesota Scholar*, I felt inspired enough that I managed to carve out a space in my busy freelance schedule to make it become reality.

As writer and artist, what I appreciate most about the Minnesota Independent Scholars' Forum, aside from gregarious meetings, are the opportunities to be part of a forum of discussion, attend stimulating programs, and go on field trips to the MIA and other cultural venues, as well as presenting, on occasion, programs for which I receive instant feedback from peers. Besides, writing left to itself can easily become stale, even be forgotten, and ideas neglected or ignored in the first place can die on the vine.

Therefore, I encourage members to tell their stories, because as Brenda Ueland said, "everyone has an interesting story to tell." Essays and articles, whether based on research or experience, practical application or philosophical thought, travel or exploration, or on a lost or newly discovered way of doing something, qualify. After all, Carl Jung said that life is an experiment! The thing about independent scholarship is to keep the discourse flowing. Yes, Charlie Brown, independent scholarship, by any other name, is still independent scholarship.

Notes for Chapter 11

118 The American Book Company vs The Kingdom Publishing Company. Libel suit against the Kingdom Publishing Co. for publishing a booklet entitled "A Foe to American Schools," which accused the American Book Company of using corrupt business practices to introduce their textbooks to public schools.

119 Letter, Herbert W. Gleason to Dr. Thomas S. Roberts. 2 June 1920. University of Minnesota Archives. T.S. Roberts Natural History Correspondence.

120 Herbert W. Gleason, *Through the Year with Thoreau* (Boston and New York: Houghton Mifflin Company, 1917), xxix.

121 Letter, HWG to TSR, 12 January 1900. University of Minnesota Archives. T. S. Roberts Natural History Correspondence.

122 Robert Shankland, Steve Mather of the National Parks. 3d ed. (New York: Alfred A. Knoff, 1970), 93.

123 Herbert W. Gleason, "Early at the Lake," The Kingdom, 12 May 1898, 590.

124 Henry David Thoreau, « Resistance to Civil Government," Reform Papers, ed. Wendell Glick (Princeton Univ. Press, 1973), 75.

CHAPTER 12

WHAT IS THE FUTURE OF INDEPENDENT SCHOLARSHIP?

So, what is the future of independent scholarship and of MISF in particular? The historian in me suggests that we should first look to the past to see how the problem emerged, was defined, or was resolved in the past. I start from a *Practical Thinking* article I wrote in May 2013. I was reviewing Ronald Gross's book, *Handbook for Independent Scholars* (1982, 1993). To begin the review, I paraphrased his definition of an independent scholar and added reflections to bring the point home to *Minnesota Scholars*.

> What these reflections have in common is that the place of the independent scholar is regarded as outside the mainstream. Someone has said that if you are obsessive about something, you are probably an independent scholar. (Incidentally, as our recent marketing statement says, MISF membership is open to anyone who supports the cause of independent scholarship.)

In my time with the MISF, I have noted that our scholars have investigated many and varied topics: capital punishment, memes, Henry David Thoreau and photographer Herbert Gleason, Henry Sibley and aspects of early Minnesota history, mathematics, poetry, the authorship of Shakespeare's plays, the assassination of JFK, rural Minnesota churches and their disappearance, the relationship of music and culture—to name only those that I can quickly call to mind. Truly, our interests and obsessions have been varied and, in all these cases, handled with scholarly expertise.[125]

Our definition of what scholarship is has not changed much since 2013 (or even since our founding in 1983). Nonetheless, as David Wiggins pointed out in a recent interview, we do scholarship very differently from the way we did it in the 1980s:

What we define as scholarship is profoundly different from the late 1980s. You had to go to the library, had to pick right word to search. [You] had to be very astute in picking your search terms. Now all you have to do is put the right word in [the search form], and you find books, with good commentary and references. I can't believe the amount of research I can get done with the internet. The research side of how we do our work has expanded our world. Change like going from quill pen to word processor. I love the image on the old logo, where research is kind of like the monk in his cell . . .

These are golden years for independent scholarship whether we call them that or not, and more and more people are backing up opinions with scholarship because research is easy. Lots of independent scholarship is going on. Wiki is a whole bunch of IS [independent scholarship] that has established a sort of credibility. Exceeds credibility of academic work. It really does hold its own against academic scholarship. Wiki is a process—whole bunch of independent scholarship.[126]

Changes in MISF

As the nature of scholarship has changed, the nature of the organization has changed. MISF has become more democratic and less self-conscious.

While still offering many "academic" perks—fiscal agency and a chance to publish being two of them—MISF prides itself on its eclectic spirit as described in Steve Miller's president's message in June of 2017. Miller is a labor and employment lawyer representing management. He was elected president of MISF in June 2017.

A Scholar Writes

President's Message
Steve Miller, 2017

One of the real joys of being president is seeing how much MISF means to its members. Each brings a passion which shows up in hard work done on behalf of the organization.

Part of that hard work has been a series of popular Saturday morning programs at Washburn Library. The excellent *Minnesota Scholar* is a lively journal with articles and reviews on a multitude of topics, and, through the "What's your passion?" [series], introduces members to each other. We are the fiscal agent for a study of the Booth Memorial maternity hospital. A history of MISF will hopefully be available next year. Study groups on philosophy and history continue to meet.

My vision is to help foster the eclectic spirit of MISF, which can host events on G. K. Chesterton, cold fusion, Sicily, political polling, limits of liberalism, and poetry in its Saturday programs. Scholarship should range widely, address many divergent interests, and appeal to as many eccentric spirits as possible. If we can facilitate scholarly research that might otherwise not be done, so much the better.

Each of the components of MISF means something. Minnesota, because that's where we are. Independent, because we are hard to pigeonhole and not tied to an academic or corporate structure. Scholars, because we seek to understand the world around us and even meditate on what it's all about. Or we can just learn about some peculiar topic of personal interest. Forum, because we provide a place for likeminded and even unlikely minded individuals to commune together.

A longtime member, David Juncker, said it even more succinctly, in an interview with David Wiggins:

> I do intend to stay with independent scholarship. I derive a lot of benefit from people who are free thinkers, who have enough faith in themselves to try to tell the truth on things that they know (rather than someone else's made-up version) and who are critical about things that come up.[127]

Notes for Chapter 12

125 Brusic, *Practical Thinking*, May, 2013.

126 Megarry-Wiggins interview, July 2016.

127 Megarry-Juncker interview, August 2016.

Appendices

Essays in Chronological Order

Following is a list of all the MISF essays quoted in the book in the order in which they were written. Essays in this list are organized by the year in which they were published. Then, the page numbers following will enable the reader to find the essays in this publication. Further references to writers, titles, and topics can be found in the index.

1982:   Grant request submitted to the Northwest Area Foundation for the Recognition and Encouragement of Independent Scholarship, no specific author *(p. 25)*
1986:   "The Role of the Independent Scholars' Forum," by Curt Hillstrom *(p. 35)*
1989:   "Independent Scholarship Enters a New Era," by Susan Margot Smith *(p. 50)*

1990:   "Independent Scholarship and the Revolution in Information Technology," by David Wiggins *(p. 53)*
1991:   "Message from the President," by David Wiggins *(p. 57)*
1991:   "Science and the Independent Scholar," by Roger S. Jones *(p. 158)*
1992:   "A Charter Member Reflects on Benefits," by Ginny Hansen *(p. 62)*
1992:   "Building the Noosphere," by Curt Hillstrom *(p. 65)*
1993:   "President's Message," by Robert Thimmesh *(p. 69)*

1995: "30s, 60s, 90s: A Century of Three Revolutions," by Arthur Naftalin *(p. 197)*
1995: "A Natural Affinity: Independent Scholars and Independent Booksellers," by Rhoda Gilman *(p. 227)*
1997: "Support of Independent Scholars: An Eight-Year Journey," by David Juncker *(p. 78)*
1998: "National Scholars Coalition Conference Held Here," by Ginny Hansen *(p. 82)*
1999: "Reckoning MISF's Past with Its Present," by George Anderson *(p. 86)*
1999: "Nurturing a Flow Chart for Learning," by Ginny Hansen and Helen Watkins *(p. 90)*
1999: "A Comparative Study of Religious Architecture," by Marilyn Chiat *(p. 171)*

2000: "Broken Symmetry," by George Anderson *(p. 212)*
2001: "Making Sense—Moving Forward," David Juncker *(p. 96)*
2001: "President's Column," by Shirley Whiting *(p. 101)*
2001: "The Bat of Minerva," by Peter Shea *(p. 175)*
2002: "Everyone's a Philosopher," by Tom Abeles *(p. 104)*
2003: "All That Fiddle," by Morgan Grayce Willow *(p. 108)*
2003: "Somebody Had to Do It: The Beginnings of MISF," by Cheryl Dickson *(p. 15)*
2005: "Theories vs. Hypotheses, Ideas, and Opinions: The Role of Scientific Methodology," by David Juncker *(p. 216)*
2005: "National Coalition of Independent Scholars Meets in New York," by Rhoda Lewin *(p. 116)*
2007: "The Curious Case of the Recurring Philosophies," by Curt Hillstrom *(p. 161)*
2008: "Reflections from the Wireless Pond," by Charles Cubrimi *(p. 124)*
2008: "Celebrating Thoughtful People," by Robert Brusic *(p. 130)*
2008: "Fame Was Not Fair to Herbert Gleason," by Dale R. Schwie *(p. 245)*

2009: "The Underground Scholar," by Curt Hillstrom *(p. 132)*

2010: "Scholars Without Walls," by Mary Treacy *(p. 5)*
2010: "Yes, But Is It Health Insurance?" by Lee Wenzel *(p. 230)*
2014: "To Bear the Mark," by Kim Heikkila *(p. 182)*
2014: "Secret Writing Through the Ages," by Bill McTeer *(p. 201)*
2016: "Pursuing Family Roots," by Gus Fenton *(p. 144)*
2016: "Who Owns History?" by Mike Woolsey *(p. 148)*
2017: "Of Independent Scholars," by Evelyn Klein *(p. 251)*
2017: "President's Message," by Steve Miller *(p. 261)*

Presidents of the Scholars

1982–1983   President, John Butt;
            Vice President, Deborah Leuchovius

1983–1984   President, Rhoda Lewin

1984–1985   President, Jim Casebolt

1985–1987   President, Susan Sandell;
            Vice President, Patrice Koelsch.

1988–1990   President, Susan M. Smith;
            Vice Presidents, John Fierst and David Wiggins;
            Editors, Susan Milnor and Merryalice Jones.

1991–1993   President, David Wiggins;
            Vice President, Laura Weber;
            Editors, David Juncker and Lucy Brusic.

1993–1995   President, Robert Thimmesh;
            Vice President, Donna McGarry;
            Editors, Tom Abeles and Lisa Foote.

1995–1996   President, Ross Corson;
            Vice President, David Juncker;
            Editor, Tom Abeles.

1996–1998   President, David Juncker;
            Vice Presidents, John Bessler and Helen Watkins;
            Editors, Rhoda Gilman and David Juncker.

1998–1999   President, Pat McDonough;
            Vice President, Mary Treacy; Editor, Helen Watkins.

A History of the Minnesota Independent Scholars' Forum

1999–2001   President, George Anderson;
             Vice President, Richard Thompson;
             Editors, Helen Watkins and Rich Thompson.

2001–2004   President, Shirley Whiting;
             Vice President, Alice Schroeder;
             Editor, Lucy Brusic.

2004–2008   President, David Juncker;
             Vice President, Terry Di Novo;
             Editor, Lucy Brusic.

2008–2012   President, Curt Hillstrom;
             Editor, Lucy Brusic.

2012–2016   President, Mike Woolsey;
             Editor, Lucy Brusic.

2016–present President, Steven Miller;
             Editor, Evelyn Klein.

Bibliography

Most of the material referenced in this book is in the archives of the Minnesota Independent Scholars' Forum. These archives, which have been privately held, will be transferred to the Minnesota Historical Society Library upon completion of this book. It is our hope that funds will be made available to digitize the entire run of journals, which will then be available to any web searcher from the MNHS site.

All quotes in this manuscript have been identified as to their sources. Material that is not in MISF archives is in other archives at MNHS. The library of MNHS was a resource for this project.

Books

Gross, Ronald. *The Independent Scholar's Handbook: The Indispensable Guide for the Stubborn Intelligence.* (Berkeley: Ten Speed Press, 1982, 1993).

Kimball, Roger. *The Long March: How the Cultural Revolution of the 1960s Changed America.* (San Francisco: Encounter Books, 2000).

Sturdevant, Lori. *Her Honor: Rosalie Wahl and the Minnesota Women's Movement.* (St. Paul: Minnesota Historical Society Press, 2014).

Articles

Hertog, Judith. "Why we need the humanities now more than ever." *Dartmouth Alumni Magazine*, March April, 2017.

Orlans, Harold. "Independent Scholars: A Neglected Breed," in Society, November/December 2002.

Web articles

Gross, Ronald and Beatrice. *Independent Scholarship: Promise, Problems, and Prospects.* 1983. Report can be found at <https://files.eric.ed.gov/fulltext/ED240932.pdf>.

Other

The Independent Scholar: A Newsletter for Independent Scholars and Their Organizations. Published by the Institute for Historical Study, San Francisco. Volume1, No. 1 Winter 1987 passim through Volume 19, No. 1 (Winter 2005)

Books by MISF Scholars

Joe Amato:
 Buffalo Man: Giants of the Waters and Winds. Forthcoming Fall, 2018.
 Diagnostics, Poetics of Time. New York: Bordighera Press, 2017
 My Three Sicilies: Stories, Poems, and Histories. New York: Bordighera Press, 2016.
 Everyday Life: How the Ordinary Became Extraordinary. London: Reaktion Press, 2016.
 The Book of Twos: The Powers of Contrasts, Polarities, and Contradictions. Granite Falls, MN: Ellis Press, 2015.
 Buoyancies, A Ballast Master's Log. Granite Falls, MN: Crossings Press/Spoon River Poetry, 2014.
 Surfaces, A History. Berkeley, CA: University of California Press, 2013.

Lucy Brusic:
 A Thread Through Time (History of the Handweavers Guild of Minnesota). Minneapolis, MN: Kirk House, 2015.
 A Crackle Weave Companion. Minneapolis, MN: Kirk House: 2012.
 Weaving for Worship: Handweaving for Churches and Synagogues. With Joyce Harter. McMinnville, OR: Robin & Russ, 1998.
 The Apples of Our Eyes: Apple Growing in Connecticut. North Haven, CT:, North Haven Historical Society, 1991. Book to accompany 30-minute video, "Yes, Mr. Greeley, You Can Grow Apples in Connecticut."
 Histories of Connecticut Orchards. Glastonbury, CT: Connecticut Pomological Society, 1990.

Marilyn Chiat:
 North American Churches: From Chapels to Cathedrals. Lincolnwood, IL: Publishers International, 2004.
 The Spiritual Traveler: Chicago and Illinois. Mawhaw, NJ:

HiddenSpring, 2004.
America's Religious Architecture: Sacred Places for Every Community. New York: John W. Wylie & Sons, 1997.
The Medieval Mediterranean: Cross-Cultural Contacts. Ed. with Kathryn Ryerson. Medieval Studies of Minnesota 3, 1988.
Handbook of Synagogue Architecture, Brown Judaic Series 29. Chico, CA: ScholarsPress,1982)

Lois Glewwe:

A Brief History of South St. Paul, Minnesota. Charleston, SC: Arcadia/ The History Press, 2015.

"The Journey of the Prisoners," in *Trails of Tears: Minnesota's Dakota Indian Exile Begins.* Mary Hawker Bakeman and Antona M. Richardson, Editors. Roseville, MN: Prairie Echoes Press, 2008

Memories, by G.A. Schulte; Donald H. Madvig, Translator; Lois Glewwe, Designer and Editor. Sioux Falls, SD: North American Baptist Heritage Commission, 2006.

The Glewwe Family History. South St. Paul, MN: Globe Publishing, 1999.

Inver Grove Heights: Minnesota's Treasure. Inver Grove Heights, MN: Josten's Press, 1990.

West St. Paul Centennial, 1889–1989. West St. Paul, MN: Josten's Press, 1989

South St. Paul Centennial, 1887-1987. South St. Paul, MN: Josten's Press, 1987.

Kimberly Heikkila:

Sisterhood of War: Minnesota Women in Vietnam. St. Paul, MN: Minnesota Historical Society Press, 2011.

Evelyn D. Klein:

Seasons of Desire. St. Cloud, MN: North Star Press, 2012.
Once upon a Neighborhood. St. Cloud, MN: North Star Press, 2009.
From Here Across the Bridge. Minneapolis, MN: Nodin Press, 2006.

Stage Two: Poetic Lives. Evelyn Klein, Editor. Saint Paul, MN: Journey Editions, 1994.

Dale Schwie:

Taking Sides with the Sun: Landscape Photographer Herbert W. Gleason. Minneapolis, MN: Nodin, 2017

Barbara Sommer:

The Oral History Manual, 3rd ed. With Mary Kay Quinlan. Lanham, MD: Rowman & Littlefield, 2018.

Doing Veterans Oral History. A publication of the Oral History Association in collaboration with the Library of Congress Veterans History Project, 2015.

Practicing Oral History in Historical Organizations. New York: Routledge, 2015.

Community Oral History Toolkit, 5 volumes. With Nancy Mackay and Mary Kay Quinlan. New York: Routledge, 2013.

Quilt House: The International Quilt Study Center & Museum. Lincoln, NE: The International Quilt Study Center & Museum in association with the University of Nebraska Press, 2012.

Hard Work and a Good Deal: The Civilian Conservation Corps in Minnesota. St. Paul, MN: Minnesota Historical Society Press, 2008.

American Indian Oral History: Making Many Voices Heard. With Charles E. Trimble and Mary Kay Quinlan. New York: Routledge, 2008.

"The Bush Foundation – the First Fifty Years." Historical summary of the Bush Foundation. With Anita Pampusch. St. Paul, MN: Bush Foundation, 2007.

The People Who Made It Work: A Centennial History of the Cushman Motor Works. With Mary Kay Quinlan. Lincoln, NE: Textron, Inc., with grant support from the Nebraska Humanities Council, 2001.

Remembering Rudy: Excerpts from the Governor Rudy Perpich Oral

History Project and the Memorial Statements. Chisholm, MN: Governor Rudy Perpich Memorial Committee, Friends of the Iron Range Interpretative Center, 2000.

Through the Window: The Stories of Mary Elizabeth "Betty" Andersen Hulings. As told to Barbara Sommer. Bayport, MN: HRK Group, 1998.

Carrie Zeman

A Thrilling Narrative of Indian Captivity: Dispatches from the Dakota War of Mary Butler Renville. Edited with Kathryn Zabelle Derounian-Stodola. Lincoln, NE: University of Nebraska, 2012.

INDEX

Please note that entries in bold indicate defined terms and entries with *n* indicate notes.

A

Abeles, Tom, 71, 73*n*53, 75, 95, 104, 111
Academic privilege, 30
Academic scholarship, 68
Administrative assistant, 60
Advertising programs, 81
Affinities, 35. *see also* Humanities Scholars Newsletter (HSN)
Affordable Care Act, 229
"Afloat in the Wireless Pond" conference, 122–123, 181–182
Alexander Humboldt and the Invention of Nature (Wulf), 166
"All That Fiddle" (Willow), 108–111
Allen, Janet, 177
Amato, Joe, 209
American Book Company, The vs. The Kingdom Publishing Company, 258*n*118
American Society for State and Local History, 76
American Society of Information Science and Technology (ASIST), 180, 181
America's Religious Architecture (Chiat), 178
Anderson, George, 86, 89, 93, 210, 212
Andrew Mellon Foundation, 169
Annual meeting, 77, 85, 116, 155, 209
Antiwar movement, 193
Art, women and, 155
Art museum tours, 150
Arth, Jeanne, 177
Article. *see also* "Scholar Writes, A" section
   about internet, 72
   about members' interests, 250
   about truth-telling in exhibits, 76
   importance in journal, 211–212
Astronomy, 137
Avlon, John, 166
Awards
   in early years, 28
   grant, 140, 141, 168, 175
   journal and, 211
   Midwest Book, 245
   Scholar of the Year (*see* Scholar of the Year award)

B

Bachman, Elizabeth, 186
Bachman, Walt, 186
Bat of Minerva, The, 174–176
Bellinzone, Bernardo, 43, 120, 121
"Belonging Addiction, The" (Miller), 147
Benedictine Monastery of Saint Paul, 118–119
Benefits, 62–64, 211
Bennett, James, 27*n*2, 52, 73*n*35
Biography, 250–257
Birk, Doug, 34
Birmingham, Mary Treacy, 47*nn*32,33. *see also* Treacy, Mary
Blake, Steven, 30
Bloomington Historical Society, 137
Bly, Carol, 154
Board meetings, 120, 150–151
Book reviews, 147
"Boundaries of Knowledge" meetings, 103–107
"Broken Symmetry" (Anderson), 212–216
Brookins, Jean A., 177
Brusic, Lucy, 2, 95, 119, 136, 140
Brusic, Robert, 130, 138, 147, 152*n*101, 263*n*125
Buckingham, Cynthia, 12
Budget
   McDonough wrote first, 81
   Schroeder and, 89
   Smith and, 57
"Building the Noosphere" (Hillstrom), 65–67

Butt, John, 13, 27n12, 30, 154
Butt, Martha, 12

C

"Can the University be Saved?" (Sarles), 104
Carson, Rachel, 33
Casebolt, Jim, 33, 34
Cave and the Light, The (Herman), 160
"Celebrating Thoughtful People" (Brusic), 128, 130
Cell phones, 136
Chaos & Complexity study group, 60
Chaos study group, 56, 156, 157
"Charter Member Reflects on Benefits, A" (Hansen), 62–64
Chester, Newell, 138
Chiat, Marilyn, 44, 45, 170, 171, 177
"Children as Pawns in Public Policy" (Schapiro), 135
Children's Literature study group, 13, 154, 155
China, History, and Culture study group, 155
Chronicle of Higher Education, 111
Chutich, Margaret, 177
Civil rights movement, 93
Coffee houses, 71
"Coffee with a Scholar," 95. see also Philocafes
Cokato Museum/Historical Society, 170
Collaboration, 95
"Collecting and Archiving in a Digital Age" (Brusic), 136
College enrollments, 11
College presidents, 33
Colorado State University, 107
Coming of age
  conclusion in, 151
  marketing strategy in, 143
  media connections in, 141–142
  Minnesota Scholar in, 143–150
  mission statement in, 140, 142
  monthly programs in, 150–151
  website in, 141–142

Woolsey in, 140, 141, 143, 144, 148–150
Communications and Information Technology study group, 56, 156
Communitarianism, 76
"Comparative Study of Religious Architecture in the Old and New World, A" (Chiat), 170–174
"Complexity and the Pragmatism of Time" (Eoyang), 135
"Computer Tools for Independent Scholars" program, 55
Computers, 55–56, 72, 167n114, 201
Conference
  "Afloat in the Wireless Pond," 122–123, 181–182
  "Henry David Thoreau," 122
  historical theme at, 76
  NCIS, 81–82, 116–118
  Nobel, 96
  Spring Hill, 12, 13, 30
  symbol, 123
Consequences of Pragmatism, The (Rorty), 154
Control Data, 73n39
Corson, Ross, 75, 76, 77
Cubrimi, Charles, 123, 124, 182
"Curious Case of Recurring Philosophies, The" (Hillstrom), 161–166
Curry, Jane, 33

D

Dahlen, Phil, 209, 210
Dakota people, 186–187
Davis, Lionel, 107
Davis, Marsha, 12
"Dear Independent Scholar" (Thimmesh), 160
"Defend our Archives" (Treacy), 136
"Democracy in Contemporary Society" seminar, 107
Dickson, Cheryl, 12, 13, 14, 15, 27n15, 30, 107
Digital justice agenda, 181–182
Discussion groups, 154. see also Study groups

Discussion of Physics as Metaphor study group, 13
Discussion of the Consequences of Pragmatism study group, 13
Diversity study group, 56
"Does the Forum Have a Future?" (Smith), 34, 35
Down to Earth History (White), 34
Draft, for war, 11
Dues, 122
Dukich, Tom, 129, 135

E

Early years of MISF
  501(c)(3) status in, 41
  independent scholarship continues in, 42–45
  introduction to, 28–33
  Scholar of the Year Awards in, 33–41
Earth Day, 210
Economics, 226–244
Editor
  Brusic as, 95, 119, 140
  list, 267–268
Editorial
  by Brusic on predicting ideas, 136
  by Smith on Scholars' progress, 56–57
  by Smith on scholarship in new era, 50–53
  Thimmesh's presidential, 68
  by Wiggins on five-year plan, 60–61
Education, **67**
Eighteenth Century study group, 50, 56, 60, 154
E.L. & E.J. Andersen Foundation, 168, 176
Eland, Tom, 139n81
Electronic communication, 72
English, trends in, 11
Eoyang, Glenda, 135
Ervin, Jean, 12
Ervin, John, 12
Essays, 176–177. *see also* "Scholar Writes, A" section
Evans, Sarah, 12

"Everyone's a Philosopher" (Abeles), 104–107
Exxon Education Foundation, 12

F

Facebook, 143
"Fame Was Not Fair to Herbert W. Gleason" (Schwie), 245–250
Farm Bill, 209
Fenton, Gus, 8, 144
Ferlauto, Ed, 137
Fessler, Ann, 195n116
Fink, Gertrude, 177
First Unitarian Society, 103
Fiscal agency, 60, 71–72, 77, 140–141, 142, 151, 168, 261. *see also* Grants
  501(c)(3) status, 57–60, 72
Foner, Eric, 148
Forum, The
  articles about internet in, 72
  continues, 52
  controversies, 75–77
  defined, **68**
  first issue of, 49, 50
  grants and, 171, 180
  library access in, 111
  on meaning of the scholars, 64
  meetings and, 197
  name changes of, 211
  NCIS in, 116
  Practical Thinking replacing, 118
  study groups and, 158
  technology revolution and, 53
Freeman, Jean, 177
Freenet, 93, 95
Fuller, Richard, 135

G

Gender Roles and Culture study group, 34, 155
German Literature and History study group, 155
German Literature study group, 155
Gilman, Carolyn, 76
Gilman, Rhoda, 157, 167n111, 226, 227
Gingrich, Newt, 76

GiveMN.org, 143
Gleason, Herbert, 139*n*97, 245, 258*nn*119, 120, 123
Glenn, David, 113*n*75
Glick, Wendell, 258*n*124
Glines, Timothy, 12
Grant awards, 140, 141, 168, 175
"Grant Request Submitted in 1982," 25–26
Grants
  for *Bat of Minerva*, 174–176
  to begin MISF, 24–26
  for *Comparative Study of Religious Architecture*, 170–174
  for development of psychiatric nosology, 178–179
  for digital justice agenda, 181–182
  introduction to, 168
  Juncker and, 77
  legacy, 141, 152*n*99
  Lewin and, 116
  for *Minnesota Women in Sports*, 176–177
  network, 85–86
  Nuer Journeys, 169
  NWAF and, 14, 68
  for oral history project, 192–194
  for project regarding refugees, 190–192
  regarding Dakota people, 186–187
  for revitalizing infrastructure of MISF, 180
  for Salvation Army Booth Memorial Hospital, 182–186, 187–189
  for *Scholars Without Walls*, 189
  sixteen, 168
  Songs, Heroes, and Legends, 169–170
  for *Spiritual Traveler*, 177–178
  success with, 2
  for TIPR, 180, 181
  for twentieth anniversary celebration, 107
  Wiggins and, 60
  Woolsey and, 140–141
Great Depression, 170
Great Northern Railroad, 14

Gross, Beatrice, 12, 27*nn*5,8, 46*n*18
Gross, Ronald, 12, 27*nn*5,8, 46*n*18, 259
Group on International Feminism, 155
Growing pains of MISF
  "back to basics" as, 75
  controversies in *Forum* as, 75–77
  NCIS meets as, 81–86
  new position on board as, 89–92
  newsletter redefined as, 80–81
  Thompson becomes editor of journal as, 92–93
  trying to increase membership as, 86–89
  works-in-progress programs as, 77–80
Guidestar.com, 143
Gulf War, 60
Gustavus College, 135

H

Hamline University, 103, 113*n*71
Handbook for Independent Scholars (Gross), 259
Hansen, Virginia
  "Charter Member Reflects on Benefits" by, 61, 62, 64
  "How to Use an Editor" by, 136
  League of Women Voters and, 210
  letter to Hillstrom, 139*n*83
  "National Scholars Coalition Conference Held Here" by, 81, 82
  "On Nurturing a Flow Chart for Learning" by, 89, 90
  poetry meeting and, 150
Heikkila, Kim, 182, 187
"Henry David Thoreau" mini-conference, 122
Herman, Arthur, 160
Hess, Jeffrey, 42, 43
Hillstrom, Curt
  "Building the Noosphere" by, 65
  "Curious Case of Recurring Philosophies" by, 161
  letter from Hansen to, 139*n*83
  logo and, 120
  on meeting schedule, 122, 132, 135,

196, 210
on MISF board, 8
presidency of, 136, 150, 152n102
president's column by, 135
"Role of the Independent Scholars' Forum" by, 35
Smith and, 35, 48
study groups and, 72, 77, 160, 166
on trends in membership and expenses, 87
"Underground Scholar" by, 132
Hillstrom, Molly, 120, 121
Historiography study group, 13, 154, 155
History
  in journal, 212, 245–257
  trends in, 11
"History for Hire" (Hess), 42, 43
"History of Astronomy, A" (Ferlauto), 137
"History of Rasselas, Prince of Abissinia" (Johnson), 139n82
History study group, 135, 166
Holtzman, Jon, 169
Hosmer library, 135
"How to Use a Research Library" (Johnson), 136
"How to Use an Editor" (Hansen), 136
Hubert Humphrey Institute, 113n71
Human Systems Dynamics Institute, 135
Humanism, 212
Humanities Scholars Newsletter (HSN), 27n9, 28, 29, 31, 32, 34, 35, 155–156
Humanities Science News (HSN), 128
Hunger Solutions, 209
Hypercard, 56

I

Ideas, meetings vs., 132
Imbo, Sam, 104, 113n71
Immigrants, 169, 170
Independent scholar movement, 11
Independent scholarship
  attractions of, 212
  beginnings of, 11–26

defined, **68, 259–260**
essays for, 14–26
future of, 14
grant request for, 25–26
national perspective on, 116–118
as purpose of book, 10
setting stage for, 10–11
Independent Scholarship: Promise, Problems, and Prospects (Gross and Gross), 12
"Independent Scholarship and the Revolution in Information Technology" (Wiggins), 53–55
"Independent Scholarship Enters A New Era" (Smith), 50–52
Individualism, 76
Initiatives in journal
  "Afloat in the Wireless Pond" in, 122–128
  institution of regular meetings as, 132–137
  introduction to, 115
  Jucker in, 115–116
  logo to increase membership, 120–122
  national perspective on scholarship in, 116–118
  "Philosophy Camp" in, 130–132
  Practical Thinking in, 118–120
  Thoreau Society in, 122, 137–138
  twenty-fifth anniversary in, 128–130
Institute for Minnesota Archeology, 34
Insurance, 135–136, 230–244
Intercultural Diversity study group, 60, 156
Interdisciplinary scholarship, 212–226
Internal Revenue Service (IRS), 41, 60
International Migration Program, 169
Internet, 72, 73n53, 75–76, 122–128, 141, 150, 156
"Internet Marginalia," 72
Interview
  regarding Salvation Army Booth Memorial Hospital, 188–189
  regarding Science and Humanities study group, 157
  regarding Selective Service Act,

193–194
regarding Smith presidency, 48
regarding study groups, 157–158
scholarship defined in, 260, 262
Islam, 136

J

Jaeger, Eloise M., 177
Jerome Foundation, 107
Johansen, Bruce, 190
Johnson, Marion Bemis, 177
Johnson, Samuel, 120, 139n82
Johnson, Virgil, 196
Joint Media Committee, 181
Jonathan Paddleford, 137, 138
Jones, Judy Yeager, 107
Jones, Merryalice, 52
Jones, Roger, 154, 155, 157, 158
Journal
  Abeles and, 72
  biography in, 250–257
  book reviews and, 147
  under Brusic, 95
  business editor for, 89
  changing name of, 143
  in coming of age, 151
  Corson and, 75
  economics in, 226–244
  editors of, 211
  first, 50
  Hillstrom on, 48, 50
  interdisciplinary scholarship for, 212–226
  introduction to, 211–212
  Minnesota Scholar, 143–150
  new initiatives and new (*see* Initiatives)
  newsletter redefined as, 81
  occasional and irregular, 139n94
  politics in, 226–244
  Practical Thinking, 118–120, 135, 140, 143
  purposes of, 211
  Smith on, 48, 50
  subscriptions to, 52
  Thimmesh and, 71, 72
  Thompson becomes editor of, 92–93

in 2011, 136
writing about history in, 212, 245–257
Juncker, David
  background of, 216
  grants and, 168
  in interview with Wiggins, 262, 263n126
  League of Women Voters and, 210
  logo and, 120
  "Making Sense-Moving Forward" by, 96
  McDonough president after, 80
  on 9/11, 95–101
  presidency of, 3, 115–116, 122, 128, 129
  public image and, 122
  "Side Effects of a Communication Revolution" by, 136–137
  "Support of Independent Scholars" by, 78
  "Theories vs. Hypotheses, Ideas, and Opinions" by, 216
  twenty-fifth anniversary and, 128
  Whiting to, 113n74
  on Works-in-Progress Program, 77–80

K

Kathman, Michael, 12
Kaufman, Ben, 195n117
Keillor, Steven, 44
Keller, Ken, 104
Klein, Evelyn, 147, 210, 250, 251
Klimoski, Vic, 118, 120
"Knowledge and Information in a Media-Saturated World" (Eland), 120, 139n81
"Knowledges: Production, Distribution, and Revision" conference, 89
Kulischek, Patricia, 154
Kunzel, Regina, 195n116

L

Land, Clean Water, and Legacy Amendment, 2

Late Eighteenth Century study group, 13, 154, 156
Laurila, Kathleen, 150
League of Women Voters, 210
Learning society, 12
Lecture
  Hess, 43
  on humanities, 93, 156
  by McTeer, 201
  Rhoda Lewin, 116, 143, 209
  "Voices of Concern," 104
  on women's rights by Curry, 33
Legacy Fund, 2, 140, 141, 182, 187, 189, 190, 192
Legacy grants, 141, 152n99
Letter
  on scholarship, 68–71
  on study groups, 72
Leuchovius, Deborah, 13, 27n13, 30, 47n33
Lewin, Rhoda, 30, 33, 116, 143, 209
Libraries, 12–13, 30, 44, 50, 52, 111–112, 150, 196
Library Cooperation Specialist, 52
Library privileges, 57, 111–112
"Life After the Bailout" (Dukich), 135
LincolnArchives.org, 187
Lloyd, Seth, 167n114
Logo, 120–122
"Lonely Scholar, The" (Bellinzone), 120, 121
Loose, Patricia, 12
Luther Seminary, 181
Lutter, Judy Mahle, 177

M

Macalester College, 60
"Making Sense-Moving Forward" (Juncker), 96–101
Makled, Maged, 209
Maria's Cuban Restaurant, 128
Marketing strategy, 143
Massachusetts Institute of Technology (MIT), 216
Mather, Steve, 258n122

Matthews, Will, 190
McDonough, Pat, 80–81, 85
McGrath, Peter, 33, 46n24
McInerney, Claire, 55, 73n39
McIntyre, Dorothy, 177
McKnight Foundation, 107
McTeer, William, 137, 143, 152n102, 201
Media connections, 141–142
"Media Grant Production for *The Bat of Minerva*" (Shea), 174–176
Medtronic Corporation, 216
Meeting places, 81
Meetings
  after Spring Hill conference, 30
  annual, 77, 85, 116, 155, 209
  board, 120, 150–151
  book discussions at, 166
  "Boundaries of Knowledge," 103–107
  ideas vs., 132
  institution of regular, 132–137
  introduction to, 196–200
  journal and, 50, 211
  location of, 150–151
  promoting regular, 34–35, 77, 81, 103, 122, 132, 135–137
  regarding new logo, 120
  regular, 200–210
  before Spring Hill conference, 13
meetup.com, 137, 160
Megarry, David, 2, 48, 140, 157, 167n112, 263nn126,127
Membership
  Anderson on increasing, 86–89
  benefits of, 141
  graph on trends in, 87
  Hillstrom on increasing, 135
  journal and, 50, 211
  logo to increase, 120–122
  McTeer on increasing, 137
  meetings increasing, 35
  meetup.com, 141
  of MISF, 141
  MISF *vs.* NCIS requirements for, 94n64
  in 1990, 57

paid, 141
Smith on building, 57
Whiting on, 95
Wiggins on increasing, 60
Woolsey on, 141–142
Membership application form, 50
Membership benefit, 72
Membership directory, 33, 41, 46n29
Membership perk, 57
Men/males
  in membership directory, 46n29
  scholar movement and, 11
  women and, 12
Mental disorders, 178–179
Mentors, 60, 177
"Message from the President" (Wiggins), 57–60
Metanet, 71, 73n53
"MetaNet Connection, The," 72
Metro Cable Network, 175
Metronet, 44, 75
Midwest Book Awards, 245
Miller, Leo, 33
Miller, Steve, 8, 147, 210, 261
Milnor, Susan, 49, 50, 52
Minneapolis Athenaeum, 122
Minneapolis Foundation, 141, 168, 180, 181, 186
Minneapolis Institute of Art, 42
Minneapolis Public Library, 13, 30, 180
Minneapolis Scholars' Forum, 13
Minneapolis Walker Library, 169, 170
Minnesota Association for Continuing Adult Education (MACAE), 118–120, 160, 211
Minnesota Association for Non-Smokers, 34
Minnesota Bioethics Center, 179
Minnesota Center for the Book, 75
Minnesota Coalition for Freedom of Information, 181
Minnesota Coalition on Government Information (MNCOGI), 122, 180, 181
Minnesota Historical Society
  grant awards from, 168

grants and, 169, 182, 186–190, 192, 194
journal and, 226
Legacy grants and, 141, 152n99
meetings and, 196
Naftalin and, 76
White worked for, 34
Wiggins presidency and, 60
Minnesota History Center, 151
Minnesota Humanities Commission
  Dickson as head of, 13, 15–24
  grants and, 81, 85, 168–170, 174–175, 177–178, 180
  Hess and, 42
  increasing hiring of professors, 44
  meetings and, 196
  membership directory by, 41
  twentieth anniversary celebration and, 107
Minnesota Humanities Council, 28
Minnesota Independent Scholars' Forum (MISF) future
  changes in, 260–262
  introduction to, 259–260
Minnesota Independent Scholars' Forum (MISF) past
  beginnings of, 11–26, 154–156
  bibliography for, 269–270
  board members of, 8
  books by scholars from, 271–274
  change and, 3, 115
  coming of age for (see Coming of age)
  description of, 115–116
  Dickson and, 107
  early years of (see Early years of MISF)
  first plan for, 28
  formal incorporation of, 30
  growing pains of (see Growing pains of MISF)
  independent scholarship and (see Independent scholarship)
  model emerges for (see Model for MISF)
  NCIS and, 94n64

new millennium of (*see* New millennium of MISF)
other terms for, 9
purpose of, 46*n*23
setting stage for, 10–11
starting date for, 30
statement of purpose for, 67–68
symbol of, 123
timeline of, 265–266
Minnesota Independent Scholars' Forum (MISF) today
fiscal agency for, 168–194
grants for, 168–194
journal for, 211–257
meetings for, 196–210
study and discussion groups for, 154–166
Minnesota Legacy Fund, 140
Minnesota Scholar, 143–150, 210, 211, 250, 251, 259
Minnesota Sesquicentennial Commission, 122
Minnesota state hospitals, 178–179
Minnesota Women in Sports, 176–177
Mission statement, 140, 142
Missouri Historical Society, 76
MIT. *see* Massachusetts Institute of Technology (MIT)
mnindependentscholars.org, 81, 140
Model for MISF
computers arrive in, 55–56
501(c)(3) status in, 57–60
Forum in, 48–52
introduction to, 48–52
study groups in, 56–57
technology revolution in, 53–55
Thimmesh becomes president in, 67–71
Thimmesh establishes fiscal agency in, 71–72
why scholars in, 64–67
Wiggins writes five-year plan in, 60–64
Modern life, 212
Monthly programs, 150–151

Moriarty, Colleen, 209
Morris-Grothe, Gloria, 169, 170
Mulhern, Brian, 68, 129
Museum exhibits, 76
Museum of Russian Art, 150

N

Naftalin, Arthur, 76, 196, 197
National Archives (NARA), 186, 187
National City Bank, 72, 168
National Coalition of Independent Scholars (NCIS), 68, 81–86, 94*n*64, 116–118, 151
"National Scholars Coalition Conference Held Here" (Hansen), 82–85
"Natural Affinity, A" (Gilman), 227–229
"Never Again-Genocide Prevention in the 21st Century" (Laurila), 150
New millennium of MISF
boundaries of knowledge in, 103–107
collaboration in, 95
library privileges in, 111–112
9/11 in, 95–103
twentieth anniversary celebration in, 107–111
Newberry Library, 33
"News and Views" update, 31, 32, 34, 35
Newsletter
Corson's opinion of, 75
early issues of, 52
first issue of, 49, 50
as goal of Forum, 40
Hansen's opinion on, 61
Hillstrom on publishing, 48
Humanities Scholars, 28–35, 155–156
Juncker and, 77
McDonough redefines, 80–81
redefined as journal, 81
technology changes and, 72
Thimmesh's goals on, 75
9/11, 95–103
Nineteenth Century study group, 56, 60
Nobel Conference, 96
Nonviolent Peaceforce, 150

Northwest Area Foundation (NWAF), 14, 24, 25–26, 45
Nosology, 178–179
Nuer Journeys, Nuer Lives (Holtzman), 169

O

"Of Independent Scholars" (Klein), 251–257
Office space, 60
"On Nurturing a Flow Chart for Learning" (Hansen and Watkins), 89, 90–92
Online universities, 93
"Oral Traditions" (Imbo), 104
Orlans, Harold, 27n3, 68, 94n64

P

Patterns in Women's Spirituality study group, 56, 60, 156
Peterson, Hjalmar, 44
Peterson, Sandra, 177
Pflaum, Ann, 93
Ph.D's, 11, 33, 68, 128
Philocafes, 95, 104
Philosophy and Children's Literature group, 155
Philosophy of Science, 179
Philosophy study group, 72, 135, 155, 160–166
Physics as Metaphor (Jones), 154, 158
"Physics Encounters Consciousness" (Fuller), 135
Picnic, 150
Plebiscitarianism, 76
"Poking Around with Mary" (Treacy), 5
Politics, 212, 226–244
Politics and Aesthetics study group, 34, 155
Politics of Provincial Independence, The (Keillor), 44
Pollack, Emily, 8, 132, 166
Poverty reduction, 14
Practical Thinking (PT)
 beginning of, 118–120
 changing name of, 140, 143, 259

Heikkila in, 182
Hillstrom in, 160
Juncker in, 216
McTeer in, 201
name changes of, 211
Schwie in, 245
Wenzel in, 135, 229
President
 Anderson as, 86, 93, 212
 Butt as, 30, 154
 Casebolt as, 34
 Corson as, 75
 Hillstrom as, 35, 132, 135, 136, 150
 Juncker as, 77, 115–116, 129, 168, 216
 Lewin as, 30, 116, 209
 list of, 267–268
 McDonough as, 80
 McGrath as, 30
 Miller as, 261
 Sandell as, 34
 Smith as, 48, 52, 56
 Taylor as, 14, 20
 Thimmesh as, 67–72, 160
 Whiting as, 95, 107, 112
 Wiggins as, 57, 60
 Woolsey as, 140, 142, 209
"President's Column" (Whiting), 101–103
"President's Message" (Miller), 261–262
"President's Message" (Thimmesh), 69–71
Professorships, 14, 28, 41
Programming the Universe (Lloyd), 167n114
Programs, monthly, 150–151
Public image, 122
Public schools, 11, 169, 170, 258n118
"Pursuing Family Roots" (Woolsey), 144

R

Ramsay, Alexander, 138
"Reckoning MISF's Past With Its Present" (Anderson), 86–89
Reda, Fatma, 209
"Reflections from the Wireless Pond"

(Cubrimi), 123, 124–128
Religion and Culture study group, 72, 160
Religious architecture, 170–174
Report
  by Cubrimi, 123–128
  by Hansen, 81–85
  by Heikkila, 182–186
  on increase in hiring professors, 44
  by Juncker, 77–80
  on NCIS Conference, 116–118
  by Woolsey, 209
"Report on the NCIS Conference, A" (Lewin), 116–118
Research
  on Dakota people, 186, 187
  grants for, 140–141
  interdisciplinary scholarship and, 212
  on mental disorders, 179
  MISF focus on, 119
"Resourcefulness" workshop, 44
Resumes, 41, 46n29
"Rethinking Adult Education in a Pancake World" (Turner), 120, 139n81
"Review of *Who Owns History*" (Woolsey), 144–147
Rhoda Lewin lecture, 116, 143, 209
Ridder, Kathleen, 176, 177
Roberts, Thomas S., 258nn119, 121
"Role of the Independent Scholars' Forum, The" (Hillstrom), 35–41
Rorty, Richard, 154, 155
Ross, Patricia A., 178
Rudie, Carol, 150

S

Saint Olaf College, 44
Salvation Army Booth Memorial Hospital, 182–189, 195n117
Sandell, Sandra, 34, 41, 46n28, 154
Sarles, Harvey, 104, 113n71
Schapiro, Dennis, 135, 151
Scholar of the Year Award
  Birk as recipient of, 34
  Chiat as recipient of, 44, 171
  Curry as recipient of, 33

Hess as recipient of, 42
history of, 33–41
NWAF and, 14
White as recipient of, 34
Wiggins reestablishing, 60
"Scholar Writes, A" section. *see also* Article; Essays
  "All That Fiddle," 108–111
  "Broken Symmetry," 212–216
  "Building the Noosphere," 65–67
  "Celebrating Thoughtful People," 130–132
  "Charter Member Reflects on Benefits," 62–64
  "Comparative Study of Religious Architecture in the Old and New World," 170–174
  "Everyone's a Philosopher," 104–107
  "Fame Was Not Fair to Herbert W. Gleason," 245–250
  "Grant Request Submitted in 1982," 25–26
  "Independent Scholarship and the Revolution in Information Technology," 53–55
  "Independent Scholarship Enters A New Era," 50–52
  "Making Sense-Moving Forward," 96–101
  "Media Grant Production for *The Bat of Minerva*", 174–176
  "Message from the President," 57–60
  "National Scholars Coalition Conference Held Here," 82–85
  "Natural Affinity," 227–229
  "Of Independent Scholars," 251–257
  "On Nurturing a Flow Chart for Learning," 90–92
  "President's Column," 101–103
  "President's Message," 69–71, 261–262
  "Pursuing Family Roots," 144–147
  "Reckoning MISF's Past With Its Present," 86–89
  "Reflections from the Wireless Pond," 124–128

"Report on the NCIS Conference," 116–118
"Role of the Independent Scholars' Forum," 35–41
"Science and the Independent Scholar," 158–160
"Secret Writing," 201–208
"Somebody Had to Do It," 15–24
"Support of Independent Scholars," 78–80
"Theories vs. Hypotheses, Ideas, and Opinions," 216–226
"30s, 60s, 90s," 197–200
"To Bear the Mark," 182–186
"Underground Scholar," 132–134
"Who Owns History," 148–150
"Yes, But Is it Health Insurance?", 230–244
"Scholarly Publishing Struggles with Shrinking Audience" (Glenn), 111, 113n75
Scholars Without Walls (Brusic, Klein, and Woolsey), 189
Scholarship
   articles on traditional, 136
   defined, **137, 259–260**
   Grabitske on, 2–4
   independent (*see* Independent scholarship)
   interdisciplinary, 212–226
   MISF focus on, 119
Scholarship Standards, 140
Schroeder, Alice, 89, 95, 107, 112
Schwie, Dale, 122, 137, 139n97, 245
Science, 212
"Science and Humanism" (Tapp), 104
Science and Humanities study group (Sci/Hum group), 55, 56, 60, 155, 156, 157–158
"Science and the Independent Scholar" (Jones), 158–160
"Secret Writing" (McTeer), 201–208
Selective Service Act, 193
"Shadows in the Wilderness" (Birk), 34
Shakespeare, William, 86, 196, 210, 212
Shankland, Robert, 258n122
Shea, Peter

Bat of Minerva and, 174, 175
   as editor of *HSN*, 27n9, 28, 29, 30, 35, 128, 155–156
   twenty-fifth anniversary and, 128
Sheffield, Alden, 195n117
Shupe, David, 55, 56, 73n39
"Side Effects of a Communication Revolution" (Juncker), 136–137
Smith, Eldred, 12
Smith, James, 12
Smith, Richard, 138
Smith, Susan Margot
   "Does the Forum Have a Future?" by, 34–35
   501(c)(3) status and, 57
   Forum and, 50
   "Independent Scholarship Enters a New Era" by, 50, 73nn34,37
   presidency of, 48, 52, 56–57
   study groups and, 72, 160
Social Change study group, 34, 155
Social history, 155
Social Science Research Council, 169
Social Welfare History Archives, 189
Solinger, Rickie, 195n116
"Somebody Had To Do It" (Dickson), 15–24
Sommer, Barbara W., 2, 8, 141
Songs, Heroes, and Legends grant, 169–170
Speaking engagements, 41
Speech
   by Dickson on ethos of MISF, 14
   by Naftalin on revolutions, 76
   on truth-telling in museum exhibits, 75
Spiritual Traveler, The, 177–178
Sports, 176–177
Spring Hill conference, 12, 13, 30
St. Kate's, 73n39
Stringer, Patricia A., 177
Study groups
   active 1982-1988, 13, 28, 30, 33, 34, 35
   active 1988-1995, 50, 52, 56–57, 60, 72, 156
   Chaos, 56, 156, 157

Chaos & Complexity, 60
Children's Literature, 13, 154, 155
China, History, and Culture, 155
   in coming of age, 143, 151
Communications and Information Technology, 56, 156
   during controversies in *Forum*, 77
   discussion, 154
   Discussion of Physics as Metaphor, 13
   Discussion of the Consequences of Pragmatism, 13
   Diversity, 56
   editorial on, 56–57, 62–63
   Eighteenth Century, 50, 56, 60, 154
   Gender Roles and Culture, 34, 155
   German Literature, 155
   German Literature and History, 155
   Group on International Feminism as, 155
   Hansen on, 62–63
   Hillstrom on, 77, 135
   Historiography, 13, 154, 155
   History, 135, 166
   Intercultural Diversity, 60, 156
   on International Feminism, 155
   interview on, 157–158
   introduction to, 154–156
   Jones regarding, 154, 155, 157, 158–160
   Late Eighteenth Century, 13, 154, 156
   membership and, 143, 155
   Nineteenth Century, 56, 60
   other, 160
   Patterns in Women's Spirituality, 56, 60, 156
   Philosophy, 72, 135, 155, 160–166
   Philosophy and Children's Literature, 155
   Politics and Aesthetics, 34, 155
   Religion and Culture, 72, 160
   Sci/Hum, 55, 56, 60, 155, 156, 157–158
   Social Change, 34, 155
   Twentieth Century German Literature, 13, 154
   as vital to young MISF, 155
Stuhler, Barbara, 177
"Support of Independent Scholars" (Juncker), 78–80
"Surfing the Internet," 72
Sween, Roger, 52, 73*n*36, 111–112

T

Taking Sides with the Sun (Schwie), 245
Tapp, Robert, 104, 113*n*71
Taylor, John, 12, 13, 14
Teaching jobs, 11, 33
"Technology and Human Values" (Keller), 104
Technology revolution, 53–55, 72
Telecommunications and Information Policy Roundtable (TIPR), 180, 181
Terminal amnesia, **76**
"Theories *vs.* Hypotheses, Ideas, and Opinions" (Juncker), 216–226
Thimmesh, Robert, 67, 71–72, 73*n*54, 94*n*64, 160, 167*n*113
"'30s, '60s, '90s: A Century of Three Revolutions" (Naftalin), 76, 196–200
Thompson, Rich, 92–93
Thoreau, Henry David, 137, 138, 245, 258*n*124
Thoreau Society, 122, 137–138, 245
3M, 140
Timeline of MISF scholarship, 265–266
"To Bear the Mark" (Heikkila), 182–186
Toro Corporation, 229
Treacy, Mary, 5, 6, 44, 47*nn*32,33, 136, 180, 181
Treaty of 1858, 187
Truth-telling, 76
Tuchman, Barbara, 33
Turner, Terilyn C., 139*n*81
Twentieth anniversary celebration, 107–111
Twentieth Century German Literature study group, 13, 154
Twenty-fifth anniversary celebration, 128–130
Twin Cities Freenet, 93

U

"Underground Scholar, The" (Hillstrom), 132–134
Universal insurance, 136
University of Minnesota
  Blake and, 30
  "Boundaries of Knowledge" meetings and, 103
  Chiat and, 171
  grants and, 170, 171, 182, 193
  Heikkila and, 182
  hiring independent scholars as professors at, 44
  Humanities Department at, 93
  Juncker and, 216
  Keller as president of, 113n71
  "Knowledges" conference at, 89
  libraries and, 50, 57, 111
  McGrath as president of, 33
  membership fees and, 122
  Salvation Army Booth Memorial Hospital and, 189
  Sarles at, 113n71
  study groups and, 157, 158
  Tapp at, 113n71
University of Minnesota 1945-2000, The (Pflaum), 93
University of Minnesota at Duluth, 44

V

Vanstrom, Beverly, 177
Vice president
  Juncker as, 77
  Leuchovius as, 13, 30
  list of, 267–268
  Schroeder as, 107
Vietnam, 11
Vietnam War, 193
Virtual degrees, 93
Virtual university, 71
Voelz, Chris, 177
"Voices of Concern" seminars, 104, 107

W

Walden University, 122
Walker, Dorothy, 33
Wallace, John, 12
"War and Art" (Rudie), 150
Washington's Farewell (Avlon), 166
Waterhouse, Jill, 73n43
Watkins, Helen, 81, 89, 90
Website
  Anderson revising, 93
  Freenet as host of, 93, 95
  grants and, 180
  marketing strategy and, 143
  McTeer revising, 143
  media connections and, 141–142
  meetings and, 201
  mission statement and, 142
  Scholars setting up, 81
  updating, 140
  Woolsey revising, 143
Weiland, Steven, 12
Wenzel, Lee, 135, 229, 230
Wenzel Analytics, 229
Wesley, David, 196
White, Helen McCann, 34
Whiting, Shirley
  efforts coordinate with others, 118
  to Juncker, 113n74
  as MISF board member, 8
  9/11 and, 95, 101
  political discourse discussion and, 210
  presidency of, 95, 107, 112
  "President's Column" by, 101
  twentieth anniversary celebration and, 107, 111
Who Owns History? (Foner), 148–150
"Who Owns History?" (Woolsey), 148–150
Why Art?, 250
"Why Art?" (Brusic), 147
Why Genealogy?, 250
Why the Independent Scholars?, 250
Wickre, John, 55, 73n39
Wiggins, David
  on definition of scholarship, 260, 262
  end of presidency, 67–71
  501(c)(3) status and, 57

five-year plan of, 60–61, 73n44
"Independent Scholarship" by, 53
interview with Megarry, 48, 157, 167n112, 260, 263nn126,127
"Message from the President" by, 57
presidency of, 57
Williams, Stanley, 12
Willow, Morgan Grayce, 107, 108
Women
  in leadership roles, 72
  in male fields, 12
  in membership directory, 46n29
  Salvation Army's Booth Memorial Hospital and, 182–186, 187–189
  scholar movement and, 11
  sports and, 176–177
  study groups and, 155
Women Historians of the Midwest, 60
Woodcut (Bellinzone), 43
Woolsey, Michael
  annual report of, 209
  to Brusic, 152n101
  on grants and fiscal agency, 2, 168
  journal name changes and, 143
  on online presence, 142
  on paid membership, 141
  presidency of, 140, 142
  revamping Scholars' website, 143
  Who Owns History by, 144, 148
Works-in-Progress programs, 77–80, 196
Works-in-Progress talks, 75
World War I, 170
World War II, 93
Wulf, Andrea, 166

X
XYwrite, 56

Y
"Yes, But Is It Health Insurance?" (Wenzel), 135, 230–244

Z
Zeman, Carrie, 186, 187

About the Editors

Lucy Brusic is a writer, editor, researcher, and book designer. She is also a weaver. She has a B.A. and an M.A.T. from Oberlin College. She has taken editing courses at the University of Minnesota. She has been editing newsletters since she was 12 years old and recently retired from editing the Scholars' newsletter, the *Minnesota Scholar*, for the past 12 years. Previously she edited monthly newsletters for the *Minnesota Horticultural Society*. She is the author of the following books: *Amidst Pleasant and Cultivated Fields: A Bicentennial History of North Haven, Connecticut*; *The Apples of Our Eyes: Apple Growing in Connecticut*; *Weaving for Worship: Handweaving for Churches* and *Synagogues* (with Joyce Harter); *A Crackle Weave Companion*; and *A Thread Through Time: History of the Handweavers Guild of Minnesota*. She has also designed a number of weaving books.

Evelyn Klein earned a B.S. in Secondary Education and an M.S. in the Teaching of English. She taught in the public schools and at Century College, and is currently a Loft teaching artist, writing consultant, visual artist, writer, and editor of the *Minnesota Scholar*. A prize-winning poet, her articles and poems have been published in newspapers, journals, and anthologies. Her books of poetry, prose, and art are *From Here Across the Bridge* (with woodcuts by her father, Wolfgang Klein; winner of a cover award), *Once upon a Neighborhood*, and *Seasons of Desire*; the latter two are placed in the Minnesota Historical Society's permanent library collection.

Michael Woolsey was a lead analyst in Information Technology at 3M, retiring in 2004. He has a B.A. degree in Liberal Arts from St. John's College in Annapolis, MD; an M.A.T. from the University of St. Thomas in St. Paul, MN; and an M.A. in Liberal Studies from the University of Minnesota. He is an enthusiast of adult, life-long education, particularly that of an interdisciplinary nature.

Images on cover (clockwise from upper left): "Thoreau Trip on board the S.S. Paddleford, June 2011; "Colleen Moriarty of Hunger Solutions," February 2013; "Richard Fuller on the Bohr-Einstein debates," January 2011; "Annual picnic," August 2011. Photos by Phil Dahlen and Curt Hillstrom.